COUNTER-MODERNISM IN CURRENT CRITICAL THEORY

COUNTER-MODERNISM IN CURRENT CRITICAL THEORY

Geoffrey Thurley

St. Martin's Press   New York

Library of Congress Cataloging in Publication Data

Thurley, Geoffrey.
Counter-modernism in current critical theory

Includes index.
1. Criticism. I. Title.
PN81.T48 1983   801'.95   82-23107
ISBN 0-312-17020-3

In memory of Peter Newnham

'to those not literate in it, painting is as
meaningless as any other foreign language,
though perhaps more tantalising'

George Keyt, 'Aphorisms'

Contents

1 A Criticism for a Literature without Contents

Western criticism, in England and America especially, has excelled in the thorough yet judicious description of literary texts. Yet a completely descriptive criticism remains blind, opaque to its own workings. A proper criticism must take into account the structure of critical propositions in their relation to the artefacts they describe. Only by providing such an account can description transcend itself. For the propositions of criticism are empty, and only the fact of an agreed context confers meaning upon them. A critical proposition is a struggle between factual reference and transcendence; between contingency and necessity; between the prior formal recognition and the suspectly subjective sense of value. It is, that is to say, a contradiction between truth and representation, statement and evocation, reality and fantasy, fact and illusion, grammar and rhetoric. This contradiction has always been present in critical discourse; but it is only with modern criticism that it has begun to seem imperative to resolve it.

(i) THE CONTENTION OF MODERNISM: STYLISM AND SYMBOLOGY

Broadly speaking, literary criticism and philosophy of art in the twentieth century have divided easily enough into traditionalist and modernist approaches to these questions. Traditionalism has, generally speaking, respected a certain dichotomy of form and content, and assumed that the 'purpose' of the work of art is, if not to improve or reform, at least to express emotion. It has by and large accepted certain correlations between 'seriousness' of content and the status of the artefact. Modernism, in its various

1

forms, has assumed the opposite – that there is a clear difference between 'discursive' symbolisms, which say, express or reflect something else, and 'non-discursive' art-symbolisms, which are what they say, and express nothing but themselves. The modernist position plainly corresponds to something profoundly important in the modern world, and I should say right away that I am in basic sympathy with it. Yet a great deal of modernist criticism fails to provide a critical discourse adequate to our experience of literature. When Aristotle says that a poetic figure should represent the 'native redness of the blood', and make the meaning 'flow from the heart of a genuine passion', we find no difficulty in connecting what the critic says with what the poet makes us experience. To this extent, criticism should, I believe, maintain a common stance with the discourse of 'ordinary readers'; the critic is, *vis-à-vis* the art-work, a member of the laity. (From this point of view, Aristotle is T. S. Eliot's 'perfect critic'.) It is perhaps the neglect of this fact that has led so much modernist criticism to claim its godlike status, and sever the experience of the work of art from the experience of ordinary men. Such a disseverance is unpardonable and theoretically self-contradictory. Neither is the situation different with the 'special' artefacts of the modern artist: on the contrary, they are in even greater need of being rescued from the critical sacerdotality.

What we might call the symbological school of modern criticism has applied itself as often to the art of the past as to that of the present, but it stems fundamentally from the modernist position. Robert Scholes includes the work of Susanne Langer in his general survey of structuralism,[1] and rightly so. For there is much in common between Langer's symbolic criticism and structuralism proper, and between both and modernism. In each case there is a common tacit assumption about what art is, and what goes into it. What it isn't is self-expression, what doesn't go into it is emotion.

Langer evidently felt puzzled as to how, for instance, poetic images might set up tensions and be significant if they existed only as significant in the poet's consciousness (or experience). She is driven to make a statement for which there is no reasonable explanation: 'Art that contains purely personal symbols as structural elements is impure.'[2] Now this is a rationale of Eliot's earlier criticism in general and the idea that 'the poem that is absolutely original is absolutely bad' in particular. But it is unclear from her words what distinguishes a 'purely personal' symbol from a real, external, valid one, or how it forms itself. Langer further observes that in the literary work, 'Everything must be transformed by imagination'. But what is 'imagination' here? How does it differ from the conceptual faculty? She further observes that 'a good poet can and certainly may handle even the most treacherous material; the only law that binds him – and indeed binds all other artists – is that every bit of the subject matter must be used for artistic effect. Everything', she concludes triumphantly, 'must be virtual experience.'[3] This idea derives from I. A. Richards's distinction between ordinary language and the pseudo-statements of art. Both critics derive from Bergson, with his characteristic distinction between discursive and non-discursive discourse or, as he put it, extensional and intensional manifolds.

There is much to be gained from adopting such a terminology, and I shall in part do so myself. Yet it is strikingly obvious from the quotations above that Langer does not avoid the circularity attendant upon most attempts to provide philosophical criteria for aesthetic experience. If something in an art-work is bad, the philosopher-critic says that it has not been turned into 'virtual experience'. Asked what 'virtual experience' is, she replies, 'Ordinary experience turned into artistic effect': the criterion for artistic excellence is – artistic excellence. Any experience expressed in an art-work that is granted to be artistically excellent will, in other words, be by definition 'virtual' experience – no matter how powerfully personal it may to the layman appear. (This is a prime example of the critical pseudo-criterion: see Chapter 4.) Conversely, anything that offends the philosopher-critic will be designated material the artist has failed to convert into 'virtual experience'. The circularity of the argument is plain, but no more so than the offence it offers to common sense: a great deal of poetry, for instance, that would appear to be atrocious has no tinge of feeling at all, and is bad because it peddles worn-out counters instead of emotion. How do we describe this, on Langer's model?

Certainly the modes of art are symbolic; that is, they are not the thing they suggest nor yet a copy of it. But this does not take us far enough, as we shall also see in relation to other critics. The really important omission in Langer is a proper consideration of what we can call simply 'sincerity'. Of course we shall all agree to call the good poem 'sincere'. But this is only to admit that *in*sincerity is incompatible with real art. In what way do poets become 'sincere' – creatively sincere, as it were? What is creative sincerity? How, without some such question answered, are we to account for works like Milton's sonnet 'How soon hath time, the subtle thief of youth', or John Clare's 'I am, but what I am who cares or knows?', or Hopkins's 'Terrible' sonnets? To describe such poetry, the 'virtual experience' talk seems simply inadequate, because it fails to differentiate it sufficiently from other work which is equally good technically, or as symbolised or 'virtual' experience. In the Milton sonnet, rhythm and rhyme jar and crowd each other –

> Yet be it less or more, or soon or slow,
> It shall be still in strictest measure ev'n,
> To that same lot, however mean or high . . .

Yet some great spiritual power or earnestness (sincerity) binds these infelicitous fragments together, and Langer's criteria offer no help in distinguishing such poetry from the 'purely personal symbols' of bad, self-expressive verse. For Milton's sonnet, like Hopkins's 'Terrible' sonnet 'No worst there is none . . .', is nothing if not 'personal', and it does not help us in the least to be told that the difference between such poetry and the 'Woe is me' self-pity of bad nineteenth-century poetry is that Milton and Hopkins more successfully convert their experience into virtual experience. This is to say no more than that they are better poets, which we knew already. The point is, how are they better? What is the nature of the process by which they convert evidently personal experience into great poetry? Are we talking about the technique of the artist, the qualities of the men, or both?

To these questions, Langer has no answers. Neither could she: such things are simply mysterious. What matters here is the kind of wrong answer she gives. For we are not confronted simply with a heroic effort to do the impossible, but a particular kind of effort – one that is consistent with the entire drift of modernist criticism. The effect of this criticism is, I believe, to symbolise the real pressure out of art altogether: poetry has a pressure and power that is not adequately reflected in criticism of Langer's sort. Poetry simply *does* something that her talk about symbolic conversion fails to describe.

What is at stake is the nature of literature itself: does it seriously make contact with the rest of our lives, or must it confine itself to a realm of language and codes with no claim to 'being about' our deepest emotions and thoughts? This is the issue. Langer's resolution of certain theoretical difficulties and anomalies (that, notably, of the unique but impure nature of art-statements) has been purchased at the price of a really serious and important role for literature: art has become well-mannered, vacuous, sterile and impotent. She presents an excellent account of poetry as good sense, but not as urgent life-important experience. My assumption of course is that poetry is, or should be, urgent and important in one's life, that it should not be a mere 'virtual imitation' of life processes, as it is in *Feeling and Form*.

Some such theory of what poetry or art in general ought to be must inform our criticism: real critical disagreements are never simply theoretic. The theoretics are ways of making sense of our convictions about literature itself. The image or model of poetry Langer offers fails to match up to my experience of reading and of writing poetry myself, and it is this kind of discrepancy that is at the heart of the fundamental schism that exists in modern criticism.

As much is true of the stylist modernism that descends through critics like Ortega y Gasset. Ortega consciously wishes to symbolise the pressures of art. He begins with the fully-clothed, over-fleshed realism of the nineteenth century, which he describes as 'a maximum aberration in the history of art', and asserts, fully in harmony with Langer's symbology, 'All great periods of art have been careful not to let the work revolve about the human content.'[4] Modern art-spectators are castigated: 'instead of delighting in the artistic object, people delight in their own emotions, the work being only the cause and the alcohol of their pleasure.'[5] This is directly in tune with Richards, Eliot and Susanne Langer; and also, from a certain point of view, with the use by artists themselves of various alienation-effects designed to check the spectator's rampant habits of empathy. But is it true that 'All great periods of art have been careful not to let the work revolve about the human content'? The evidence suggests the contrary: that the contemporaries of Raphael and Giotto, for instance, empathised into their works much as Dickens's readers into his. I cannot, either, make any serious discrimination in my own aesthetic experience between the emotions 'aroused' by such works as Rembrandt's 'Return of the Prodigal', Velazquez's 'Surrender of Breda' or Guillaume de Machaut's *Messe de Nostre Dame*, and those aroused by the greatest works of Wagner, Delacroix or Dickens. I am not saying that they arouse the *same* emotions – no two works do that – but there is no serious difference in kind. If Byrd's Mass in Five Parts, Dowland's 'In Darkness let me dwell', Monteverdi's 'Lasciate mi morire', Bellini's 'St Francis in Ecstasy' – if such works do not 'revolve about their human contents', then I cannot imagine what these words mean. Only a man who has never responded deeply to the languages of these artists could make any real distinction between the 'confessions' of which Ortega accuses Beethoven and Wagner, and those of Bach, Mozart or Gibbons. Think of the Sarabande of Bach's B Minor Clavier Partita, of the Adagio of Mozart's E Major Sinfonia Concertante, of Monteverdi's madrigal 'Qui rise tirsi'. Only a pedant who has not come to empirical grips with the language of these composers could set such utterances apart from those of Wagner or Schubert.

Why does Ortega pretend that he cannot tell the difference between emotion and sentimentality? Presumably because he identifies the fact of *catharsis* with some general 'art-experience', which was indifferent to 'human emotion'. In fact, catharsis only happens because human beings can feel, and feel *for* and *with* each other. The idea of catharsis in which the experience is purified of any given human experience is as absurd as the idea of 'sight' without any given thing being seen. Just as vision does not exist apart from individual acts of perception, so catharsis – the art-experience – necessarily involves 'human emotions', however these have been transmitted through the medium of the artist's skill. It is intrinsically impure.

Modernist critical modes like Langer's and Ortega's are shaped by the need for something 'pure', a dislike of this impurity which is, in fact, inseparable from art and the art-experience. Driven by such a need, Susan Sontag, one of Ortega's acolytes, hypostatises 'Style'. 'In the final analysis', she writes,[6] ' "Style" is art'. Now if such an observation is to be other than circular (reducing to 'art is art'), it must surely depend upon the rejection of a counter-position. This counter-position is that art has a content, and it is to this question, of the competing claims of form and content, that we finally arrive in this matter. Miss Sontag's master had observed: 'The content never redeems a work of art. A work of art survives by its form, not by its content.'[7] But what, we may ask, *is* the form of the work? What is the content? Where does the form end, the content begin? If the work of art is the sum of all the things we can say about it, plus their ineffable coherence together in space-time, where do the things we could say about the form end, and the things we could say about the content begin?

(ii) HARD-CORE MODERNISM AND SOFT-CORE MODERNISM

The most extreme or extremist statements of the position represented in Ortega and Langer occur in structuralism, which in effect constitutes a linguistic modernism. Generally speaking, structuralism, from Lévi-Strauss to de-constructionism, has declared the notion of content in literature to be either an absurdity or a sign of bad writing. These two distinct views often go together, unguessed-at, and it will be important to remember that they represent different possibilities, one hard-core, one soft-core. The hard-core view is that content is a theoretical anomaly. The soft-core view, best illustrated in Ortega's *Dehumanisation of Art*, asserts that, although bad literature concerns itself with its 'human' contents, good literature, in the modern age, is concerned with something else – the creation of a 'style', or just with being 'writing'.

Hard-core modernism is best illustrated by Roland Barthes, who suggested a counter-model for the 'usual' form-and-content model: 'if until now we have regarded the text as a species of fruit with a kernel (an apricot, for example) the flesh being the form and the stone the content, it would be better to see it as an onion, a construction of layers (or levels, or systems) whose body contains finally no heart, no kernel, no secret, no irreducible principle, nothing except the infinity of its own envelopes – which envelop nothing other than the unity of its own surfaces'.[8] Barthes, it is clear, took the myth of literary content so seriously as to pursue it down itself until the whole work disappeared. 'Subject', Barthes went on, is 'an illusory notion', a 'level in the hierarchy of interpretation'.[9] Seymour Chatman protested against this apparently radical disintegration of the literary text: 'There must remain some pre-existent material which is irreducibly content or subject-matter.'[10] Now this would seem to be a head-on collision. Yet in fact there is only an illusion of plurality here: both views represent the same model of the literary text. The reason why Barthes is wrong here is not that there *is* a content in literary works if only you dig long enough, but that his description of literature makes no real difference to the way we conceive it. As much is conceded in that characteristically evasive use of the conditional: 'if hitherto'. Admittedly this is so common in French as to have lost its real hypothetical quality. But Barthes's use of this classic Aunt Sally mechanism is illuminating: the proper come-back to it should have been, 'But nobody *does* conceive of works of art as apricots.'

There is something in this debate reminiscent of eighteenth-century discussions of the contents of perception, and their relations to matter. Locke assumed – along with Galileo – that there were primary and secondary properties of matter: the primary sort could not be perceived by the senses and constituted an 'underlying somewhat' within the things we perceived. These things we perceived through the 'secondary' properties of matter. Berkeley showed that Locke's view was based upon a logical fallacy: there could be no underlying somewhat, so that there was nothing 'in' matter which could not be perceived. So far our analogy with the literary critics seems clear: Chatman is the Lockean with his pre-existent material which is 'irreducibly content', Barthes the enlightened Berkeleyan with his onion skins of structure. But in fact Berkeley did not deny the materiality of matter, as Barthes denies the 'content' of literature. In England at least, Berkeley was taken to have shown up the erroneousness of Locke's analysis of matter, and to have healed the breach between what we see and what is actually there. Only a deluded idealism acclaimed the good bishop as the apostle of immaterialism. It is just such an immaterialist idealism that Barthes in fact represents.

The real egress from the theoretical difficulty about content was not, like Bathes, to throw out the baby with the bath-water and say there was nothing 'in' literature; nor, like Chatman, to affirm a blind faith in a *res materialis* which can never be perceived, but by God is *there*. The way out was to see that Barthes, like many structuralists and modernists, was simply choosing to describe 'content' in his own way, so that the literary work is concerned with nothing but its 'codes'. This is an option open to the critic, but it has no real effect upon the way we conceive literature. It is merely a methodological assertion to the effect that where the traditionalist critic speaks of meaning or content, the *nouveau critique* will speak of its codes or mythologies. For content read code, and for meaning signification, and we are none the wiser.

To take this view of the matter is by no means to describe intellectual filigrees around a methodological pinhead. It is, on the contrary, to take issue on the most fundamental matter confronting the literary critic – the status and seriousness of literary texts. Structuralism, like the other forms of criticism influenced by it, has taken the symbological or stylist philosophy adumbrated earlier in the century by critics like Rémy de Gourmont and Ortega y Gasset and developed it into a polemical system which effectively separates literature from the realm of human activity it was traditionally supposed to have served and expressed. It has done so often by sliding from the soft-core to the hard-core version of its fundamental position. Essentially, it is based upon the theory and practice of certain writers – Mallarmé and Flaubert, in particular – who emphasised a certain separation between the means of expression and any exterior meanings or terms of reference. This theorising is in substance an adaptation by creative writers to cultural circumstance: what we see in Flaubert and Mallarmé, as in T. S. Eliot and James Joyce, is a considered retrenchment within the artist's means, a development of a new subject-matter and new ways of expressing it. Modernist criticism has turned this creative evolution into a theory of language which denies the possibility of expression and therefore places the creative principle itself inside parentheses. We begin with what is, in fact, an alienation-theory derived from the work of the Romantics and their successors, the symbolists: this turns into a theory of articulation which converts the so-called contents of creative work into mere forms. The heroes of this revolution in critical theory (I speak now of the criticism that goes nowadays under the name of structuralist or post-structuralist) are certain writers – Nietzsche, Mallarmé, Joyce, Borges, Proust – who are supposed to have produced a literature which manifests the properties lauded in the criticism: they are supposed, that is, to have eschewed representation, the creation of illusion, description, realism, message – content, in other words, as traditionally understood – in order to produce discourse, *écriture*, writing, a linkage of signs owing no allegiance to anything outside themselves. Such writing has been called 'scriptible'[11] – something difficult to define except negatively, that it forbids us to empathise into it and to shelter within an imaginary world, and insists that we accept it as writing. This is the literature without contents modernist criticism has been designed to describe.

Such a theory, it is plain, makes it extremely difficult to describe what it was that enabled works like the Milton sonnet and the John Clare lyric to revolve, apparently, about their human contents. Was it that we were fooled – along with Vasari, Tolstoy and most other men who expressed their sense of the meaningfulness of art in terms of its emotional effect upon them? Or is it that modern writers cannot, and do not want, to affect us in this way? What kind of philosophy do we have before us, therefore – the hard-core one which suggests that the emotional empathising with literature was always the response of simpletons, or the soft-core one asserting that writing after a certain point in time (1660, 1789, 1848, 1914 – the dates can vary) ceases to be able to produce the kind of work which had always been held up as the triumph of the human imagination?

It is this question which underlies the present enquiry, and it is no idle one. More is at stake than methodological tidiness: it is the future of literature itself. With this in mind, common sense might be tempted at this point to assume its own rightness without more ado: 'Of course literature has "content", of course it is serious and "about" the things that concern us as human beings. Why not simply ignore these intellectual fads and aberrations, and go on as before?.'

Unfortunately, the matter is not so simple as this. Neither structuralism nor modernism in its broadest sense is the fantasy of simpletons. No amount of reasoning can spirit away the huge differences that exist between, say, the realist fiction of the nineteenth century and the works of Joyce and Beckett, Borges and Woolf, or the landscapes of the Impressionists and the work of the Cubists or of Kandinsky. However we address these questions, there will remain a residue of change that resists explanation. Unless we are inclined to dismiss it all – the whole *avant garde* tradition, Joyce, Eliot, Picasso, Schönberg – we must admit that there is a problem about the language of art and its interpretation.

What we must do is first describe the nature of this problem, and then decide whether there is something intrinsic to all art which really makes it impossible for us to talk reasonably of its 'having' content and 'expressing' emotion, or whether, on the other hand, there is simply something specific to the art produced after a certain historical moment which forbids us to look for 'human' content in it and which therefore forbids us to consider it as anything but mere assemblages of signs. To put it briefly, we have to decide whether the hard- or the soft-core variety of modernist theory is the appropriate one – or whether neither is. We must begin with the problem of art-languages itself.

2 The Problem of Art-Languages

(i) SYMBOLS OF UNIQUE REPRESENTATION

The problem is this. Art seems to insist on being analysed in symbolic terms, that is, as a kind of semantic, as a sign language articulating meanings. Yet there seems to be no way of effecting a successful analysis. We speak of the 'symbols' of art-works or literary texts, but there is something odd in so speaking. For we cannot strictly say what they symbolise in the way that we can explicate (up to a point, anyway) the symbols of mathematics. Any discursive symbol is explicable in terms of equivalent symbols (4 = 2 + 2 in the simplest type of case). In the same way, although without this degree of exactitude, we can also explicate the symbols of ordinary language. We can always use sense-data to elucidate the symbols of any rational discourse. Without some such elucidation, indeed, these symbols are likely to be condemned as meaningless. We can 'say what we mean' without just repeating our words.

It is axiomatic, in other words, that anything that can be expressed can be expressed differently. 'We must never forget', Frege observed, 'that different sentences may express the same thought.'[1] This axiom certainly holds good of all so-called discursive symbolisms, and indeed we are committed to such a course by using the verb 'express'. The formula '*X* expresses *Y*' involves two terms and a relation of expression. The concept of expression, in other words, is essentially and by definition dyadic.

Now the verb 'express' in the sentence 'This poem expresses such-and-such' is strictly non-dyadic. There are no meanings *in* works of art in this sense: and we can never properly say (though we often do say) that a work of art or literary text 'means' something, that is, something different from itself. The work of art means itself. There are no sets of meanings articulable in any other way than the form of the work itself. We cannot strictly say

12

what art-works symbolise in the way that we can explicate the mathematical symbol. In relation to works of art, the formula '*X* expresses *Y*' is strictly incorrect, and if it is taken – as it often is – as referring to the same state of affairs as obtains in mathematics or ordinary language, it is totally misleading. Yet '*X* expresses *X*' – which is the logical equivalent of saying that a work of art 'means' itself – does not make sense: *X* does not mean *X*, *X* is *X*. In this sense, we can say that 'literature' has no 'content'.

This paradox is the first peculiarity of the so-called languages of literature: they express, but express nothing but themselves. We associate this way of putting the matter specifically with symbolist or generally with post-Romantic art and literature and the accompanying criticism. The so-called 'literature without contents' seemed to fit a critical ideology based upon the self-expressive nature of the art-work. Yet although the idioms of modern art are different from those of earlier ages, they are also at one with them in certain important respects. I shall argue, in fact, that the differences are differences in world-view and societal alienation, not of creative principle, and that therefore there is no essential difference between the art-works of the post-Romantic era and those of classical times. Theoretically, it is no less true of the plays of Sophocles and the poems of Dante that they express 'themselves': everything I have written above of art-form applies as well to Pope and Rembrandt as to Mallarmé and Braque. This will emerge as important later: it is simply not true – as Wolfgang Iser asserts – that classical or traditional art can be comfortably analysed in terms of its 'representation of the whole truth' or a 'hidden meaning' that can be described as if an effective interpretation had taken place.[2] Whatever ideas, schemata or world-views are isolably present in the classical work, the formal or artistic totality which they make up must always itself need interpreting: it is a mistake to assume that classical or pre-modern art-works offer easy interpretative models. They do not: the classical artist's 'use' of his materials – world-views, subjects, religious and philosophical ideas – is really the same as the modern artist's use of his. The difference is in the nature of these materials. Essentially, it is as true of the Attic tragedy of the Augustan Epistle as it is of the symbolist lyric that it expresses, yet expresses nothing but itself.

Out of this quality of art grows a further pecularity. We find that we cannot take any element of a painting, say, and treat it as a 'symbol'. No matter how clearly defined it is – it may be an arrow in Paul Klee for example or a demon in Bosch – it cannot properly be isolated from the rest of the picture and analysed as if it were the product of a dream or a free-association test, for example, or a social survey. This is true as well of the imagery of poetry. Much has been done by way of the analysis of poetic imagery in this century: one thinks of the Shakespeare critics, Spurgeon and Clemen, of Maud Bodkin and G. Wilson Knight, and of all the sub-Freudians, as well as of Freud himself. Yet unless the images of the poet are treated as recurrent features of the poet's style or as contributing to a total picture of his entire *oeuvre*, such analyses are based upon error, the error of isolable symbols. It is plain that Clemen and Spurgeon did respect the autonomy of the imagery in this way. But faced with Freud's so-called analyses of Leonardo's imagery and Ernest Jones's attempts to analyse *Hamlet*, we are forced to conclude that these critics are operating upon the text as a body of evidence for something outside itself, and thus are destroying or rather simply *missing* the real force of the imagery they pick out. The 'secrets' of the man may well be irrelevent to the meanings of the text. For images in literary texts must be treated as creating a context and as being created by a context. This two-way pull exists in every part of the art-surface. This means that we cannot consider an image or a symbol apart from its setting or its context.

It often happens, for instance, that symbols which appear to be identical are used by different astists to totally different effect. On one canvas a symbol may appear as an integral part of a masterpiece, on another as a mere arbitrariness in a worthless scraping of pigment on canvas. In such cases we would be wrong to equate the two occurrences as the same symbol, now used well, now badly. Another kind of example might be a particular verse-form created by a master and copied by a poetaster; or a chord-sequence or instrumental effect in music. In a great work, even conventions are essential parts: for example the conventional key-sequences of late eighteenth-century music in a Mozart symphony are necessary and beautiful parts of the whole. Thus, while it is true that the artist's armoury or repertoire (chord-sequences, instrumental possibilities, 'attitudes' – what has been called his 'aesthetic ideology') exists in the culture into which he is born, so that it is impossible to speak of any

work as being wholly original in the sense of coming into exis-
tense *ex nihilo*, it is no less true that these effects and instruments,
in contributing their life to the surface of the work, at the same
time sacrifice that life and independent existence, as the elements of ordinary language do not forsake theirs in being
adapted for the millionth time to the needs of discursive communication. To believe the opposite, like Pierre Macherey,[3] is to
accept some myth of objectivity, or the means of production or
'culture' or ideology – call it what you will – which enables us to
dispense not only with the artist-as-creator but with that unique
untranslatability which is the identifying mark of the literary
text. To equate the old money-lender in *Crime and Punishment*, for
instance, and Miss Havisham of *Great Expectations* as instances of
the Terrible Mother syndrome is to say nothing about the roles
they play in the actual texts. This does not mean that we can
forget our own experiences of mothers and old women when we
read the novel, or that we can deny the 'characters' what iconographic significance they possess. It does mean, however, that as
literary critics we are obliged to acknowledge that we are doing
two different things, where (a) we identify an archetype, and (b)
subject to relevant formal analysis that surface which both
determines and is determined by them.

This means further that the literary critic cannot afford to
concern himself too much with associations. The associations
theory runs that the forms of the literary text are valuable
because of the associations they have for the reader. From this it
is inferred that the proper object of literary study is these associations, whether it be in psychoanalysis, sociology or semiology.
Admittedly, the 'associations' play an important part in the
appreciation of works of art, just as I cannot read a newspaper if
I don't know the language it is written in. But although there are
important differences between discursively and non-discursively
used symbols, there is this much similarity, that the relations
between the symbols (and a governing syntax and grammar) are
what give the whole symbol its 'meaning' and that the associations are only supplementary to this coherence and meaningfulness. I mean that just as I should not expect even a very
intelligent Chinese to understand a *Times* leader if he knew no
English, so I should not expect a Martian, though literate and
cultured, to derive anything from seeing an El Greco. Works
of art are embedded in society in this way.

Roland Barthes certainly underestimated the importance of this societal embedding. He distinguished between connotation and what he called (contemptuously) 'association of ideas'.[4] Connotation, as he defines it, mixes 'meanings which proliferate by layering because of the successivity of sentences' (that is, formal interrelationships that build up as we read on and through the text), and a so-called 'agglomerative' sense (that is, the tendency of elements in the text to 'correlate' with other meanings outside the material text to form 'nebulae of signifieds'.) Thus, the elements of a text combine together in 'successivity' what meanings they have outside the material text. But are these meanings, in virtue of which no combining can take place at all, 'outside the material text'? Surely they *are* the material text? It is the function of the poem's hidden grammar (its so-called formal logic) to create the two-way pull of the art-surface – that tension created by the exclusion of some associations, and the foregrounding of others. The directions of the pull are precisely those of the extra-textual associations of the elements by which they are combinable in the first place, and of the linear-successive (or simultaneous) interdependence they gather as we read. Barthes's arbitrary definitions obscure the dependence of that accumulation of meaning upon those associations he airily consigns to the realm of inessential nebulae, thus foisting upon him a fanciful definition of meaning as a kind of gold-dust sprinkled upon an alien, inert denotation.[5]

Certainly it is the materials of the art-work that we must observe for its secret and meaning, not the pre-existent meanings of its symbols or the life of its creator. Certainly the art-object is a unique phenomenon whose meaning is itself, and apart from the material (words, wire, stones, notes) there is nothing. But this only makes sense when the proper conception of form has been digested: I do not draw attention to the stuff on the canvas *qua* pigment, but *qua* the language of the artist. If literary works have value – the evidence suggests that they have – it must lie in the forms of the works themselves. But it is at this point that the difficulties arise. One misunderstanding consists in taking exception to the phrase 'forms of the work' and insisting on the primacy of something else in the work – 'meaning', 'story', 'emotion' or 'message', much as Seymour Chatman insisted on an irreducible somewhatness inside the forms of literature in his debate with Barthes. Alternatively, various 'essentialist' schools assert that there must be a kind of ideal work of art floating above the mere physical reality, and that it is this ghostly ideal that is the 'real' work, not the merely physical phenomenon. Does the aboriginal who has never before left the Simpson Desert really *see* Picasso's 'Guernica', essentialists ask? This invidious essentialism is surely avoided if we point out simply that the same question applies to the map of the London Underground. We do not wonder whether the aboriginal suddenly placed in front of the diagram 'really sees' the diagram or only its physical manifestation. We say quite simply that he does not understand it. In this respect, art-objects are like other kinds of symbolic object – maps and diagrams and directories: they require to be understood. There is no need either, then, of the opposite fallacy: that the work of art is just paint on a canvas, with no nonsense about unseen realities which involve us in a discredited pursuit of something somewhere which is also nothing nowhere. The Significant Form theory of Clive Bell – an early modernist account, equivalent to Ortega's stylism – had the virtue of insisting that it was the forms of art we must study; but its 'significance' was empty. It is matched in neo-modernism by the theory of Barthes and others that literature is nothing but language or discourse.

Such anomalies are bound to occur, as we shall see, in any account which, fleeing in bewilderment from the work itself, entrenches itself in the human mind amid a welter of impressions, experiences, re-creations, re-constructions. They would be avoided by reflecting that such objections apply to all other kinds of symbolism. So too would the errors of de-constructionism, in which also the real public nature of the art-work is held in question, so that the critical act is dissolved in a kind of bath of pre-criticism; here the particular problems raised by the very nature of literary texts are never addressed because they are drowned in a kind of methodological lather. This may have its place, but it is not the place previously occupied by criticism whose object is literature: the methodological hesitancies of de-constructionism apply to all texts, all utterance, and I should argue that any such approach is simply too general to make contact with literature. The area in which the 'objections' of de-construction can be discussed is not that of the art-experience; they are not so much unhelpful in the domain of criticism as absent from it.

Phenomenology, on the other hand, has tried to give a complete account of the act of reading, on the understanding that a literary work is what it is because of what it does when it is understood. It is, said Sartre, like a top that only exists in motion, and what sets it in motion is a concrete act called reading.[6] A little less paradoxical, but as intransigent, Wolfgang Iser states that it is 'an integral quality of literary texts that they produce something which they themselves are not'.[7] In Iser's view, the proper study of literary texts must include the reader's 'aesthetic response': we can't really talk intelligibly about the text unless we talk about the way it is received, because the text is really a set of instructions for the making of a different thing – the work-as-experienced. He cites Northrop Frye on a notoriously enigmatic writer: 'It has been said of Boehme that his books are like a picnic to which the author brings the words and the reader the meaning. The remark may have been intended as a sneer, but it is an exact description of all works of literary art without exception.'[8] We shall come to further implications of this observation later in respect of the nature of interpretation generally.[9] For the moment, let us observe again that what Frye says of Boehme applies as well to the map of the London Underground: to describe the use or effectiveness of the map, it is not necessary to give an exact (or any) account of the way the longer line between Hammersmith and Acton Town is interpreted by the observer in order to make an imaginary world equivalent to the reality designated by the map. The fact that maps, like literary texts, are meant to be understood does not mean that we cannot describe them as objects, but must always be labouring to describe the way they are received. It just means that the descriptions must constantly take account of the fact that the signs that make up the larger sign *mean*. 'To mean' means to relate a beholder and a beheld. In the case of the map of the Underground, the description will make no sense unless the recipient latches on to the fact that the notches on the longer lines indicate stations, and that the stations are geographically related much as they are physically related on the map: Acton Town is farther away from Hammersmith than either is from Brook Green, and to get from Acton Town to Hammersmith without using the Underground will probably take you through a place called Brook Green. And so on. This can be made to sound a more or less complicated business, and no doubt on some levels it is very complicated; neurologically indeed, indefinitely so. But the fact of this complexity should not drive us to assume that we cannot describe the map of the London Underground without describing one ideal reader's response to it. Frye is mischievous, moreover, in suggesting that the reader habitually 'brings the meaning' to the text as if all meanings were of equivalent value and all related to the text arbitrarily and equivalently. The fact that the literary work needs to be understood, like the map of the London Underground, doesn't mean that it has no objective force or identity. Iser, to be sure, is the essence of responsible discipline: it is a cornerstone of his phenomenology that the structure of the text pre-structures the reading. There is to be no subjectivised lather here. In this both Roman Ingarden[10] and Iser deserve the highest respect. Yet doesn't this very responsibility undercut itself? For what is the point of transferring attention from text to recipient if all that we get is a mirror of the text's (undenied) structural characteristics?

In a curious way, phenomenology parallels the ontological trap of the old essentialist aesthetics, which confused the art-object with people's apprehensions of it: again, the situation is the same with non-literary symbolic objects. It is no part of the map of the London Underground that there are millions of impressions of it in Londoners' minds, and millions of printed tokens of the type. What does the appreciation of the diagram mean apart from the mental act of understanding? And in what way do the varying degrees of understanding among different people alter the 'existence' of the diagram? If these questions are more obviously pretentious and silly in respect of the Underground map they are no more emphatically so than in the case of art-works. It is difficult to see how any theory basing itself upon the 'aesthetic' experience or the act of reading can be of assistance in elucidating the status or kinds of art-works. The popularity of theories based upon the aesthetic experience results from the jealous way we guard our own sensitivity and balance our own impressions against those of others. Since, it is clear, this activity of understanding is of the same kind as understanding a timetable, the ontological status of the text is not involved in the appreciation of it.

We learn to use things in the same way we learn to use words, and this includes symbolic things such as maps, diagrams, effigies, sketches and paintings. Any visual symbol must refer to our experience in some way, however complex or however schematically ideational. Contrary to received opinion in many artistic circles, there is no essential difference between paintings and such 'idea' symbols as road signs. One may be moved to immediate action in either case – to put on a brake, or to change one's life (in however slight and intangible a way). Or, in either case, one may simply 'understand': I can 'take in' a street sign without 'reacting' to it ('Oh, there's a school hereabouts, is there?'), just as I can be aware of a picture of a sunset or a bowl of roses without being moved to act. The aesthetic attitude to art is equivalent to maintaining that you don't put your brakes on because you 'understand' the sign, but merely because of a mystically 'significant' arrangement of black and white enamel. The forms of painting are just as informative and instructional as those of road signs, and we should not allow their immeasurably greater complexity – the greater complexity of life as an instructor over the Highway Code – to blind us to the fact. In literary, as in pictorial texts, it is these forms, this material, we must study to understand their meaning.

When we say that it is the material of a work of art we must observe for the secret and the meaning, finally, we should always bear in mind that 'material' should not be allowed a qualitative meaning. I mean that 'material' has no flavour, and if I talk of the material of a work of literature I do not necessarily mean to indicate 'words' as such: although when I speak of the material of lyric poetry, for example, I do indicate the words, I may not do so in the same way when I speak of the material of the novel. I take it as axiomatic that the artist uses a language, a language articulating 'meanings' far beyond the reach of discursive faculties. Just as what a discursive symbolism can express governs the forms and syntax of that symbolism, so the symbolism of art takes its forms from what it is capable of expressing. Thus, tautologically, the capacity of a language to express is conditioned by its success in expression. Discursive language as we use it (of course there are many discursive languages: sign-language, symbolic logic, deaf-and-dumb talk, ordinary discourse, mathematics, morse) has no capacity for expressing what we can only call logical contradiction. When we contradict ourselves, our language tells us so. We cannot express the idea of a thing as both being and not-being, or being something and the negation of it, or as both having and not-having a property at the same time. We can only try to start to say what it would be like: then we contradict ourselves. Our language has failed. And indeed if it did *not* fail then anything would go, and it would fail in every other respect. We have no way of referring to what we cannot express: 'Wovon man nicht sprechen kann, darüber muss man schweigen.'[11] Is not art a set (infinite in number, potentially) of languages whose purpose could be expressed by saying, 'Wovon man sprechen kann, darüber muss man schweigen'? Art languages, that is, might be termed symbolisms of unique representation. We have taken it as axiomatic of ordinary language that anything that can be expressed can be expressed differently. I take it as an axiom of art-languages that anything that can be expressed *is* expressed, and that anything that is expressed cannot be expressed differently.

(ii) OBJECT-LANGUAGE AND META-LANGUAGE

All this and much more must be understood when I say that beyond the materials of art there is nothing. So that when I say that there is no such thing as content in art, I mean that a work of art expresses what it expresses. Thus we cannot strictly use the language of expression when talking of art: yet we use it frequently. And how could it be otherwise? The sentences we use in talking about the world and objects in it constitute our language. This language can be described in the meta-language – but we do not imagine when we use the meta-language that we are, or can be, doing the same as the job we are doing with the object-language. We do not, that is, imagine that we are speaking about actual objects and things: or at least only about a special set of objects and things (the grammatical categories of the language) which cannot *ex hypothesi* be expressed in the object-language itself. When we speak about works of art, therefore, we are not talking about the objects that are the subject of the work (death, love, pain, sunsets), but are using the meta-language. This is the key to most dispute about art-objects and idealism. If we get used to the idea that we are talking about an object-language when we talk about works of art, we shall see that we are not, and cannot be, speaking about a special set of *meanings*, and that to talk about these meanings would be to use the object-language, that is, to create. The 'meanings', that is to say, are hidden, or as I prefer to say, incarcerated in the form of the object-language.

Thus, the critic's outlining of an artist's symbolism, for instance, has nothing in common with the artist's own use of it. Essentially, I might describe a novel or a play in the same way as I describe a film. In neither case would I claim to be doing more than merely indicating lines of stress and emphasis in the work. I do not claim to describe the work as I might describe a photograph. Still less do I imagine that I am capable of rendering the *quality* of the work. Literary critics might well borrow a distinction from symbolic logic in this area. Philosophers distinguish between the structure and the content of propositions. Propositions can give us the logico-factual structure of an experiential entity, but only our sense organs can give us the flavour of the experience. Some philosophers have held that content is 'inexpressible' – Moritz Schlick, for example[12] – so that this is not a shortcoming of language at all. But on the whole, it seems true that 'green' cannot be communicated in the way that information about the shape and weight of a leaf can. The spurious distinction in criticism – form and content – is almost exactly the opposite of this; the flavour of the work is the form; the structure (in the philosopher's sense) – that is, what can be communicated in propositions – is the content.

Now, we can see that in the case of literature, to describe is to describe content (in this philosophical sense). I mean that the 'form' of a literary text is indescribable. Content is what can be communicated in words. Descriptive statements can be applied to literary works in the following ways:

(1)   The *theme*, plot or development (more dubious) are described. This clearly applies to content: 'this play is about regicide' is no more objectionable a statement than 'this is a portrait of a king'; thus far, content is an admissible postulation in the meta-language, and Barthes is merely odd to deny it.

(2)   By quotation or summarisation of types of image; for example, 'this poem contains three flower images, two animal and one abstract'; this also clearly applies to content; it is what Erwin Panofsky calls iconography;[13] this also is unexceptionable.

(3)   By evaluation: 'This poem is good, bad; beautiful, ugly, sincere-sounding, inauthentic', etc.

So long as we remember that *form* and *content* are terms belonging to different areas of discourse, and that our critical meta-language allows us to refer to a work's content as above defined, but *not*, except by *pointing*, to its form, we are safe. The fallacy is to regard form and content as differentiable entities causally related within the text, rather than as simply different ways of talking about the same thing, and therefore as indicating separate areas of discourse, the language and the meta-language.

The view I am putting forward here is sharply distinct from the classical structuralist view as set out by Claude Lévi-Strauss. Lévi Straussian structuralism depends upon an essentially Cartesian dualism; to reach reality, 'one has first to reject experience, if only to reintegrate it into an objective synthesis devoid of any sentimentality'.[14] Thus, phenomena – what we actually live – are distinct from their own 'meaning', 'meaning which is formulated in terms of structure'.[15] This kind of philosophy – it is to be found in both Descartes and Hegel – is essentially fatalistic and inherently despairing: 'It is hopeless to expect a structural analysis to change our ways of perceiving concrete social relations.'[16] Man is divorced finally and ultimately from the source of significance, and can only guess at it by patient enumeration of structural relations. Yet there is an inherent contradiction in the kind of rationalism represented in Lévi-Straussian structuralism: and it derives, precisely, from failing to distinguish between form and content in the manner I have suggested above. Lévi-Strauss derives his 'models' of reality from observation of reality; the binary oppositions and repetitions that are reproduced in these structural models are 'there', otherwise his models are inaccurate. There is, therefore, no basis for differentiating between the structure revealed in the models from those existing in reality. The error is to think of the 'meaning' of phenomena as a property separately existing from them, and attributable to them instead of as a property of our discourse about reality. Here again we see that Lockean substratum theory exposed by Berkeley. Empiricism merely asserts that the latter derives from the former and that 'meaning' is a property of discourse, not of the world of things. If the world of things is organised in a particular way (by means of combinatories or binary oppositions, for instance), then our discourse should say so. This does not mean that the 'meaning' is (tragically) hidden from us, and only disclosed through our scientific researches. One of Lévi-Strauss's apologists has fairly summarised his view of representation by saying that 'there is a discontinuity, a break between the diversity of the real and the formal abstraction of the structure that signifies it, the movement from the one to the other implying a *passage* from diversity to simplicity, from the concrete to the abstract'.[17] Of course! World is world and language language, and language could not work if it did not respect the difference. 'It follows', Arthur Danto puts it, 'from this general requirement upon explanation that the world described by scientific theories *has* to be different from the world to be explained with reference to it. If they were the same, then there would have been no explanation.'[18] It is therefore difficult to see the force of Lévi-Strauss's critique of formalism: 'For the former (formalism) the two domains (the abstract and the concrete) must be absolutely separate, since form alone is intelligible, and content is only a residual deprived of any significant value. For structuralism this opposition does not exist. There is not something abstract on one side and something concrete on the other. Form and content are of the same nature, susceptible to the same analysis.'[19] Lévi-Strauss is right in censuring formalism for pretending that the items of semiotic furniture it describes have no significance outside the texts in which they occur, and that, as Josué Harari puts it, structural analysis places itself 'at the level of signification'.[20] Yet his own critique of formalism, as we have seen, can be turned against himself. His structures are derived from phenomenological research, from experience; yet they are allowed to become independent entities, with a meaning separate from the objects and processes which properly constitute them. This error is reflected even in his very proper critique of the characteristic formalist ignoring of the fact that forms have meanings: Lévi-Strauss speaks of form and content as if they were actually describable entities within texts and processes, where in fact they really refer only to ways we *talk about* texts and processes. It is not 'form' alone which is intelligible, but rather content alone which is *expressible*. What is intelligibility? Is an apple intelligible? An apple can be eaten, seen, touched, smelled or savoured: all these are sensory activities. If we want to discuss or tabulate the apple's *properties* (its structural coherence with other fruit and phenomena), we step outside the ring of the experienced (*le vécu*). In doing so, we acquire a certain power, but at the same time we lose cogency – the cogency of experiencing. I shall be returning to these questions later. Here let us note only that to differentiate, on the lines I have suggested above, between the form and content of works of art is not to distinguish two types of property within the text – one intelligible, the other merely residual, in Lévi-Strauss's words. It is to say, on the contrary, that the distinction is a mere convenience – though a crucially important one – which enables us to discuss certain aspects of the way works function without committing ourselves to the dualistic fallacy. *Vis-à-vis* the meta-language of criticism, the work *is* a world: as such it can be experienced, and it is our experience we formalise in criticism.

(iii) CONSEQUENCES OF THE FORM-CONTENT DUALISM

Let us examine a common version of the dualistic fallacy: 'If what is said isn't worth saying, it must be said better than *that*.' The speaker implies that if 'it' had been brilliantly expressed, the work would have been good. This view – dependent as it is on the form-content dualism – leads to certain consequences. One is that it implies that the writer could have another shot, that is, if he took what he said and had another crack at saying it, he might produce a great work. Another consequence is that it puts writers in the place of actors: that is, we can imagine content, since this is divisible from form, being offered to the writer for him to 'express'. If this is so, then it becomes irrelevant to criticise an artist for the content of his work. That is to say, the form is divorced from the content, the content is only by accident part of the work. It is obvious that the form cannot entail content: there is no necessary connection between what he says and how he says it. The less naïve version of this view is that the content governs the form such that one *does* entail the other. But it is always possible that another artist should have the *same* content; and that unless the two works are identical, it seems to be true that no given content entails any particular form. If this consequence is to be avoided the two contents will have to be differentiated little by little so that we can say that the content of one work is only *similar* to that of another. However, it is still possible to find an artist whose content was not thus differentiable. So the contents would have to be yet more finely differentiated. However, this process clearly cannot be continued indefinitely without in the end offering a set of propositions equivalent to the propositions of the original work's form, rather than of its content. Thus this distinction cannot reasonably be held. The more closely we try to describe the alleged content of a work, the more closely we approximate to a description of its form.

If the critic accepted that his discourse is in the meta-language and that there is no real difference between the criticism of literature and that of, for instance, painting; that the art-object can be referred to and described in the meta-language of criticism, but that its *quality* cannot be conveyed, then he would be spared the anomalies of form-and-content dilemma. The critics invented form and the critics invented content. In reality there is only the art-object: we can say things about this, as we can about the weather, but we cannot separate its elements into form and content, any more than we can differentiate a thunderstorm's form from its content. There is no part of the work which is not subsumed under the heading of form. In a painting, 'form' is every brush-stroke, in a symphony every bar, in a poem every word. The fallacy of dissolving the deeper themes and meanings of literary texts into skin after semiotic skin would be avoided by re-phrasing the nature of literary form in this way. Since there is no part of the literary text which is not form, and – by the same token – no part which is not content, it follows that the content is precisely what is being peeled away in Barthes's model. No wonder he found nothing at the 'heart', when the heart was everywhere! This is no logical trap but the fact of the matter.

Directly, then, the 'feeling' symbolised by the poem – I mean what the poem 'is' – is inseparable from the words. I do not mean inseparable in the way that rain is inseparable from the clouds. I mean a sense of identity. That is why, for instance, translations depend for their success upon an immense act of will by the reader in concentrating on the imagery. Even the best translations wear an air of lifelessness. The lines and phrases seem self-contained. In the original language, the sense of feeling suffuses the whole thing, welded together.

(iv) DESCRIPTION, INTERPRETATION

Granted that he is using a meta-language, how is the critic to describe a poem? If the form of a work is its every word, it follows that there are properly speaking no skeletons separable as *'the form'*. Thus, it is clear that any criticism that is relevant is about form since there is nothing else to criticise.

If there is only the work, the thing itself, we can speak of its themes and skeletons not as isolable entities sunk in other matter (the form-and-content fallacy), but as a means of convenient reference in the meta-language. Now this view, strictly speaking, commits us to the concomitant view that the role of the critic is not interpretation, but description: what the critic should do is not interpret the work, but familiarise the reader with its language. To interpret means to *find out* its meaning, as if that meaning lay elsewhere; yet we have seen that the work of art has no paraphrasable content: it is unlike other forms of discourse in that its elements refuse translation into equivalent terms. If this is so, what do we mean when we say that we understand an art-work? Why isn't merely to see (hear, read) it the same as to understand it?

There are, to start with, undeniable elements in a work which are strictly speaking non-physical. There are tensions and emphases in the work which some people feel and others do not. These are empirically testable, and seeing them is always a matter of understanding the artist's language. The proper concern of the critic is the description of these empirically testable but not-physically-given elements 'in' the text. Now, in speaking of the 'language' of the art-work, we have committed ourselves to the view that art-works – symbols of unique representation – are to be regarded as statements of some order. Language makes statements, and the concept of a statement is one which implies a certain order among its elements. 'A painting', wrote Rudolf Arnheim, 'is a particular configuration of forces.'[21] We have rejected the idea that there are isolable skeletons within art-works: the form is the whole thing. Yet this form *is* a configuration, in Arnheim's sense. This configuration is the statement, the 'inner' shape, the lie of the elements at work. The critic's task is – where necessary – to describe the nature of that shape or configuration, to make the statement intelligible, if it is not already clearly so. Thus, although there are no isolable skeletons in the work, there are certain organisations, configurations: some elements are given more prominence than others. They lie *in relation to* each other.

The critic articulates these relations, these configurations, and by so doing familiarises the reader with the artist's language. How? It is possible, for instance, to give an exhaustive description or catalogue of all the elements in the work: 'Matisse's "Le Colière d'ambre" contains a number of vertical lines, the following colours', etc. Does such a descriptive catalogue even begin to shape a judgement of the work? Has it even begun to make the painting intelligible? We can see that it is a representation of a woman: what call has it on our attention? What do we mean in short by speaking of the painting as a statement, as a 'particular configuration of forces'? Doesn't Arnheim's formulation imply that something more is involved than the mere recognition that this daub is a representation of a woman with a necklace (and a rather bad one, if Ingres is our model)? A serious theory of criticism must begin with a recognition of the fact that the descriptions that are the critic's stock-in-trade must go beyond the merely physical description to that 'particular configuration of forces' which *is* the work of art. This in turn rests upon a theory of art – one that accepts that, whatever else we say about them, art-works are objects of a peculiar sort. If they are *'dinglich'* – 'thingly' – in Martin Heidegger's odd yet useful term,[22] they are *dinglich* not as stones are: they are *shaped*, and our perception of the shapedness is as integral an element of our perception of them as it is of our perception of a pair of shoes. They are, furthermore, *dinglich* not as shoes are, for our perception of shoes tells us that they are not self-sufficient, as paintings and poems at least partly are. We cannot hide behind the 'thingliness' of art-works, therefore, and pretend that we are doing something worthwhile if we merely relay back descriptions of them as we might describe shoes or stones. Shoes don't have to be described, paintings don't have to be used. What is the presuppositon behind our constant and persisting feeling that art-works often need to be described? It is surely a sense that these forms have a certain value, and that if the statement or configuration made up by the shapes of the art-work isn't picked out, the work is 'missed'. We can't 'miss' a pair of shoes; but it is a fundamental fact about our experience of art that we (or other people we know) can miss or fail to 'get' art-works.

A description which does succeed in picking out the work's internal form, its inner shape or actual 'configuration of forces' we can validly enough call an interpretation. The relationship between 'mere' descriptions and genuine critical acts (interpretations) is the subject of the following pages. In particular, we shall be considering the relationship between our sense of the value of a work and a 'correct' interpretation of it. The relationship is a deep and integral one, yet it is fashionable nowadays to duck the value-judgement, and leave it to Leavis, the implication being that this is strictly for the moralists, beneath the attention of the lofty philosopher-critic. Nelson Goodman, for instance, writes that 'Estimates of excellence are among the minor aids to insight'.[23] Thus, if 'a connoisseur tells me that one of two Cycladic idols that seem to me almost indistinguishable is much finer than the other, this inspires me to look for the significant differences between the two'.[24] Professor Goodman's instance is almost satanically ill-chosen: as we shall see, there are crucial differences between the problems involved in judging pre-civilised art and those involved where more urban and sophisticated art is concerned. Moreover, Goodman takes for granted that 'connoisseur' raises no problem; but, what is a connoisseur a connoisseur *of*? Doesn't the use of the term imply certain strata of experience mere familiarity can't supply? Some wines are not merely different from others, but better. This too we shall come to in due course. More troubling than these matters in Goodman's observation is the phrase – blithely thrown off and uninspected – 'significant differences'. What is the basis of this 'significant' difference? Isn't this precisely what the problem of criticism is? How are we as critics to describe art-works so as to locate the significant differences which, we agree, separate not only more and less distinguished, but *different* examples of the same form? The critic's problem is to describe the 'differences' in art-works so as to satisfy us as to their significance – to describe the 'inner' form of the work, elucidate its stresses and tensions, the nature of that particular configuration we recognise as its 'inscape' – these stresses and tensions which are empirically testable, yet not *there* in quite the same simple way in which the physical marks are there. Briefly, the problem for any critical theory is, how to describe the art-work so as to entail an interpretation – a convincing statement of its 'significant differences', without offering us a mere transcription of the work's words or a description of its marks and signs. The sting in the tail of this question is that unless we answer it, we have not merely worthy but dull descriptions that fail quite to generate interpretations, we have no descriptions whatever; for the 'mere' description is a description of something else – the *dinglich* object, which we can align with the pair of shoes or the wallpaper, but not know as art. The identifying caste-mark of the modernistic critic is his desire to describe the art-work's significance without reducing it by an inferential cross-relation to some order of discourse – history, psychology, morality – extrinsic to the work. How has modernism succeeded in this aim of locating significance by attention to the textual facts alone? That is the question.

3 Stylistics and Structural Poetics

(i) INTRODUCTION

The determination to analyse literature with no reference to any factors outside the text is so widespread as to be all but synonymous with modern literary criticism. There have been many riders and qualifications to, and outright dissensions from, such an approach. But the wealth and prestige of those schools acknowledging the primacy of the facts of the text, the words on the page, are so great they still dominate critical procedure. So various have its manifestations become, indeed, that some terminological clarification is necessary before any attempt to survey its results can be made. In the first place, we must refer to the fact of a general movement towards a text-oriented criticism at about the time of the First World War. What I have called symbological and stylist criticism derived from the rejection of the referential nature of literary statements: they asserted that works of art constitute only pseudo-statements, which are crucially different from actual statements, so that literature is to be valued for its style or its symbolising capacities. By the 1920s there had appeared the Cambridge criticism in England (Richards, Empson and T. S. Eliot, in his capacity of lecturer as well as publisher-poet-critic) and, in Russia the school generally known as formalism. Both these 'schools' concentrated their attention on the 'literariness' of literature. The text in Richards was a self-consistent system of forces balancing each other; in Jakobson and Shklovsky a totality of verbal units to be analysed with the instruments of linguistics and interpreted exclusively on the basis of their interrelations.

The American New Criticism, which is often cited as the forerunner of later developments, followed in the footsteps of Empson, Richards, Eliot and Leavis. In particular, in Wolfgang Iser's words, it valued the 'harmonization of ambiguities',[1] exactly as Richards had laid down in his *Principles*, and in general consolidated what Empson, in a flattering review of Brooks's *Modern Poetry and the Tradition*, called 'the intellectualist position'.[2] After the Second World War, textualist literary analysis developed in two main thrusts – structural poetics, and what has become known as stylistics. There is considerable overlap between the two movements, but they should not be confused. French structuralism stems from Claude Lévi-Strauss's *Structural Anthropology*, with its expressed aim of reducing the diversity of phenomenal appearance to certain binary structures which could, in turn, serve to anticipate and clarify our understanding of hitherto inchoate laws. Lévi-Strauss based his methodology on Saussure's theory of the sign, but it should be emphasised that his persistent preoccupation with dualistic oppositions and pairings is not anticipated in Saussure, and represents his own mental bias. The aims of literary structuralism have been described by a later apologist – J. V. Harari – in terms that apply and could have been applied to the Cambridge criticism of the 1920s: 'Structural analysis . . . bypasses the problems associated with the figure of the author as well as other criteria exterior to the text, and instead focuses its attention on the text, understood as a construct whose mode of functioning must be described.'[3] It is no accident that Harari's formulations could be found in so many different critical places over the last forty or fifty years. Harari's rejection of the claims of the author's life or the historical world-picture could be found repeated in F. R. Leavis's long campaigns against that mode of 'explanation' in terms of the current 'world-picture' associated in England with Basil Willey. It is as well to remember how widespread and interchangeable the fundamental aims of many critical schools are, despite the differences in methodology.

The school generally known as stylistics, lastly, is based on the work of the Prague formalists. Like structuralism, it avails itself of the methods of Saussurean linguistics. In many instances, the work of structuralist and stylisticist critics is indistinguishable. The contributors of Barthes's *Communications* of 1968[4] attempt to derive rules for explaining the transformations of narrative forms. The work of Tzvetan Todorov and A. J. Greimas is frequently cited in stylisticist works and could be termed stylisticist as well as structuralist. But we must remember that Lévi-Strauss sharply differentiated himself from the Prague formalists, who made the mistake, in his view, of regarding the signs of a literary work as bearing no relation to anything outside the text. Classical structuralism bases itself on the Saussurean concept of the *signe* – the union of signifier and signified, and therefore is implicitly committed to the world of the signified. We should therefore be on our guard against identifying structuralism with stylistics.

(ii) STYLISTICS

It is stylistics which has most rigorously striven to validate the right of criticism to base itself on the text and nothing but the text. 'Style' consists in systems of signs established within a given text, 'a recurrence', in Donald Freeman's words, 'or convergence of textual pattern'.[5] Much has been made of the diversification within stylistics studies nowadays, but constant to all its varieties is the notion that literary analysis should confine itself to the text, eschewing extra-textual information and reflection as rigorously as the old New Criticism.

Now formalist and stylistics critics claim to describe works of art precisely in such ways as to entail interpretation, as I have suggested above is necessary; yet such claims are, as I think I can show, extremely dubious. As much has been suggested from within the pallisade on a number of occasions. In a famous and humorous critique of the claims of stylistics, Stanley Fish has shown, with the expertise of a practitioner, that stylisticist analyses characteristically fail to generate the hermeneutic conclusions they lay claim to. No student of philosophy would be surprised by Mr Fish's conclusions, but they are significant as coming from a dedicated stylistician: he points to the serious defect in stylistics, the absence of any constraint on the way in which one moves from description to interpretation, with the result that any interpretation one puts forward is 'arbitrary and unverifiable'.[6] This is of course a version of the slide Hume noted in ethical treatises, from *is* to *ought*, and it is precisely the problem I have been discussing above. What we are concerned with is the internal dimension of the 'real' work of art within the mere phenomenal arrangement of its elements. It had often been urged against Roman Jakobson that his complicated descriptions of the surfaces of literary texts did not seem to throw any light on them: one was left with a pile of *bric-à-brac* which did nothing to change one's view of the poem. Fish applies this criticism to stylistics as a whole; he takes examples where different stylisticians use the same grammatical phenomena as evidence for entirely different arguments. What the stylistician habitually does, Fish argues, is run a text through the machine so that its parts are disassembled, 'then retrieved and reassembled into exactly the form they previously had'.[7]

Unfortunately, Fish is good only negatively. His own belief in the possibilities of stylistics is alarmingly indicated in his statement that 'stylistics was born of a reaction to the subjectivity and imprecision of literary studies'.[8] Now such a dream of complete critical objectivity invariably – and, I shall show, necessarily – takes the form of an impoverishment or simplification of the literary text, a surgical removal of the text's organs of complexity. The really problematic parts of text and criticism disappear at a go, so that an entirely different and far more damaging imprecision results. Whatever follies traditional criticism accomplished out of 'subjective' imprecision pale by comparison with the absurdities of stylistics with its pseudo-objectivity.

To move from description to valid 'interpretation' is the perennial task of literary criticism. It was Stanley Fish's virtue to have seen the illusoriness of stylisticians' claims to have done this in their complicated-yet-not-complex descriptions. Having competently and entertainingly shown up the falsities of other stylisticians, however, he proclaims his faith in speech-act theory, and thereby places himself in the same position as those he has discredited. His new 'affective' stylistics merely shifts the focus of attention from 'the spatial context of a page and its observable regularities to the temporal context of a mind and its experiences'.[9] To the difficulties of justifying an interpretation of a given text, in other words, is added the much greater difficulty of describing the mental world each reader brings to the text and 'negotiates' *in* the text. It is, of course, just as hard to say what a particular word of a text is 'doing' as to say what it 'means'. And there is still no indication of how stylistics would set about justifying its interpretation. Granted that an Austinian theory of locutions provides a more complete objective description of the text, Fish cannot say how he would move from this more thorough description to an interpretation. Fish thinks that the more subtle reading-theory suggested by Austin and Searle automatically crosses the gap from description to interpretation, but this is a delusion. Certainly, speech-act theory allows us to dispense with the more naively formalistic accounts of literature: we shall no longer have to account for the meaning, say, of a Chekhov story or a George Herbert poem entirely in terms of a verbal icon which possesses magic qualities of lexis or sound. Instead, we can go through our Austinian rigmaroles to show that the effect of a question in a story, or an exclamation in a poem, depends upon the various ways in which such language-functions work in ordinary speech. When Donne begins a poem 'For God's sake hold your tonge, and let me love', speech-act theory will enable us to dispense with the more solemn 'rigours' of Jakobsonian analysis in terms of phonemes balancing each other, and couples of lines pairing off with other couples, and so on, and to explain its effect by considering the pre-suppositions behind a question. What situation is presupposed in a certain speech-form? What are the rules for the deployment of this or that mode of utterance? What audience is assumed, what condition of use? And so on.

Yet Fish's conclusion, that such considerations show that the reader, in the act of reading the text, is also in the act of interpreting the language of the text, and therefore that the gap from description to interpretation has been crossed, is totally invalid. All that we have is a more judicious description of the text, one that allows of a more flexible and realistic attitude towards language than that allowed by the Prague school: we have still not moved an inch towards justifying an interpretation of this reading. Nor could we, without a change of ground so radical as to amount to an abandonment of the stylistics stance altogether.

It is worth noting in this context that mainstream literary criticism – that of F. R. Leavis in particular – has always assumed the essentials of speech-act theory in its practice. It has, in other words, acknowledged and honoured the writer's familiarity with the subtleties (tone and inflection in dialogue, for instance, or nuance of authorial commentary). In this respect, as in so many others, stylistics merely elaborates the working methods of mainstream literary criticism: it is, in other words, not so much the literary-critical wing of linguistics as the linguistic wing of literary criticism.

What has been said of Stanley Fish applies, *mutatis mutandis*, to Michael Riffaterre's well-known tilt at Jakobson's and Lévi-

Strauss's structuralist readings of Baudelaire's 'Les Chats'. Here the problem is more particularly that of establishing literariness. It is all very well relaying a poem's linguistic features; what makes them specifically literary? Riffaterre's often-quoted demolition of Jakobson's analysis can be extended to cover the entire stylisticist enterprise: 'No grammatical analysis of a poem can give more than the grammar of the poem.'[10] Now the satisfaction with which stylisticians are apt to cite this piece of *samokritika* in fact hardly seems justified: the assumption behind the stylistician's analysis of a poem's grammar is that the peculiar grammatical features in the given poem can be related to its *meaning*. Riffaterre hasn't said anything that might not be extended to language or to any other concrete form of analysis: you might as well say, the linguistic analysis of a poem can give no more than the language of the poem. True: but the stylisticist's claim is that both language and grammar *described aright* illuminate reading. This hit surely misses. What, Riffaterre then asks more pertinently, establishes the contact between poetry and the reader? What makes the fragments isolated by analysis poetically effective? Which of the bits tabulated by Jakobson *work – are poetic?* 'Can we not suppose', he asks, 'that the poem may contain certain structures that play no part in its function and effect as a literary work of art, and that there may be no way for structural linguistics to distinguish between those unmarked structures and those that are literarily active?'[11] Riffaterre, that is to say, acknowledges precisely the problem I have been concerned with in these pages, and we can see that the problem is not merely that of choosing between a value-judgement criticism, with all its aura of subjectivism and impressionism, on the one hand, and a purely objective criticism, concerned only to describe the text, on the other; the problem is rather that of recognising and experiencing the text *as literature in the first place*. Riffaterre's emphasis on the importance of locating the 'literarily active' part of a text concedes that the question of describing a text so as to shape an interpretation is indistinguishable from that of describing a text so as to produce a value-judgement, and that the question of the value-judgement, haughtily shelved by Northrop Frye in a famous context,[12] lies at the very root of the critical venture and can never be ignored. To carry out an act of literary criticism, is properly speaking to have made a value-judgement: by the same token, to produce a value-judgement is necessarily to have made a successful interpretation.

Unfortunately, Riffaterre's commitment to the kind of criticism he presents – highly structured, quasi-scientific – is as limiting as Stanley Fish's. He has no answer to the criticism he makes of Lévi-Strauss and Jakobson – the criticism that, properly speaking, the mass of data and 'structural' commentary or transcription they produce fails to make contact with the poem *as poem*, and therefore fails to comment on it at all. Like Fish, he falls back on a solution that solves nothing, but only introduces fresh difficulties and therefore makes a coherent theory still more unattainable. He introduces the old rhetoric, to point out that the features described (or transcribed) by Jakobson are also *effects*, and that effects are meant to affect hypothetical readers in certain ways. Again, no rules are given to elucidate why it is that some parts of the poem affect the reader more than others, and the solution of arriving at an interpretation is as distant as ever.[13] Traditional rhetoric had always acknowledged that the devices used by poets are instruments for producing effects: that if certain things are done, for instance, the dramatist loses the audience's credibility; that such-and-such figures take the poem too far from the reader's or hearer's sympathy and hence strain his sympathy, and so on. Edmund Burke's *On the Notions of the Beautiful and the Sublime*, for instance, is a close description of the ways in which the laws of visual perception can be exploited to produce certain effects: great size and darkness produce an effect of awe, smooth lines and gentle gradations are pleasing, etc. There is, in other words, nothing new in the New Stylisticians' introduction of the audience-factor into criticism: it has been assumed since Aristotle that every rhetorical device is what it *is* in virtue of what it *does* to the reader. The problem remains, how do we interpret or evaluate the particular use by the poet of these devices or effects so as to produce a significant commentary?

Impatient with Jakobsonian minutiae, and afraid that the whole stylisticist enterprise might be sabotaged, Tzvetan Todorov inserted the notion of 'pertinence' into the programme: 'Literary works organise themselves around a pertinence which is unique to each of them, linking grammatical and thematic elements in their own unique way.'[14] Who would disagree? Yet who can fail to see that this amendment to the descriptiveness of a Jakobson lets in the 'intuitive' value-judgement by the back door, and so sabotages the entire enterprise of stylistics and structural poetics? 'Pertinence', like 'significance' in the Significant Form theory, begs the questions it was meant to answer: how are we to establish 'pertinence', except by admitting the role of that necessarily subjective intuitive faculty that lies within a more honestly value-oriented criticism?

The reader doubtful of the necessity of a rider such as Todorov's need only turn to the 'interpretation' which Roman Jakobson added to his famous 'reading' of Shakespeare's 'Th' expense of spirit in a waste of shame'. The poem 'means', Jakobson says, 'in action, lust is the expenditure of vital power (mind and semen) in a wasting of shame (chastity and genitalia), and until action, lust is deliberately treacherous, murderous, bloody, culpable, savage, intemperate, brutal, cruel, perfidious, no sooner had'[15] and so on. This 'tentative explanatory re-wording' is proffered as 'interpretation'. It is no more than a paraphrase of the poem, such as any schoolboy would scorn to produce.

It had seemed possible 'just' to describe works of art, as Jakobson has 'just' described the Shakespeare sonnet ('such-and-such a number of rhymes, such-and-such pairings, etc., etc.'). This seemed an honest enough programme. But such a description, it appears (even if theoretically exhaustive), does not even begin to shape a judgement or an interpretation. We have always to add the rider 'this is "literarily active" ' or 'this is "pertinent" ', or 'this is the *real* shape of the work, that real or internal dimension within the mere describable physiognomy'.

Characteristically, stylistics and structural poetics sought the principles of organisation within a given text, not outside it, in history or biography. They tried to describe it in a number of different but related ways, either as deviation from the norms of the language in which the particular text is written, or as recurrence of linguistic features, as the 'foregrounding' of 'certain' elements. Now, of course, these are ideas which no literary critic can feel comfortable refusing: it has been a working principle of criticism for most of this century – indeed since Coleridge – that the reasons why a poem is such and such should be sought within the poem, not outside it. The truth is that it was only the extreme views of certain early stylisticians, together with the bogey of the computer under the bed, which caused the furore about the subject in the pages of *Essays in Criticism* in the late 1960s.[16] It was inevitable, and indeed salutary, that this debate should have been held, and it was conducted with admirable vigour and energy. Roger Fowler and F. W. Bateson were excellent representatives of their 'schools'. Interestingly, Fowler bent over quite a long way backwards towards a 'liberal' posture about the subject, while Bateson adopted a far more rigorously textual posture than was natural to him. This was surely appropriate, the value of the debate being precisely that it fertilised each of the 'schools' with some of the spirit of the other.

Yet the truth of the matter was that there was really only an illusion of difference between the positions held by each critic. It is one of the most irritating characteristics of collections of stylistics essays that the introductory chapter, and, often, a majority of the offerings within, declare in ringing terms the emancipation of literary criticism from the 'subjectivity' and 'impressionism' (these two terms occur with monotonous regularity) of traditional criticism. Usually it is stated that the stylistician, aided by Chomsky or Saussure, is going to furnish the reader with finer instruments, and set the subject on a scientific basis. And so on. We know this screed by heart. And indeed stylistics, we have seen, is committed to some such doctrine: it purports to put that valid descriptive criticism I have sketched above, on an objective basis. Traditional liberal criticism rarely if ever adopts this tone, yet in essence the spirit of criticism after Empson and Richards is similar to that of stylistics. Stylistics must be seen as the inheritor of the 'New' Criticism. Modernist criticism, like stylistics, really depends upon the assumption that it can pick out certain significant patterns, congruences, convergences of image or inflection, and thereby reveal to the reader the 'inscape', the deep structure or simply – to use the formalists' term – the *literaturnost'* of the text. Modernist criticism tried to detect and lay bare the work's principles, which it described in those 'organic' terms first articulated by Coleridge, the real father of modern criticism.

Seen from this point of view, the heated reaction registered by F. W. Bateson was unnecessary and even unreasonable: surely stylistics, whatever its inflated claims, was only trying to do what all modern literary criticism was committed to attempting? But if this means that mainstream literary criticism is no less textualist than stylistics, it also means that stylistics is committed to precisely that subjectivism which it affects to deplore in mainstream criticism. This is a point which, though it is sometimes paid lip-service to by stylisticists, does not seem to have been grasped in all its force. Bateson, in fact, was quick to throw the fact as a 'taunt' into Fowler's face. What stylistics *ought* to do,

Bateson pointed out, is merely *describe* the text, break it down, with its so-called scientific instruments. What we in fact get in a representative bit of stylistics is smuggled-in evaluation. Speaking of Sinclair's analysis of Philip Larkin's 'The Whitsun Weddings', Bateson observed 'the accidental intrusion of evaluation' in 'almost the only passages where Mr Sinclair appears to be concerned with the poem itself rather than with the grammatical system that it enables him to demonstrate'.[17] As evaluation, Bateson went on, 'seeps into description, so description oozes into evaluation'. Now it is interesting that Fowler – on the whole fairer and more balanced in the exchange than his literary opponents – completely fails to grasp the force of this objection: 'Mr Bateson words this spurious distinction [between scientific and objective language] as "description" vs. "evaluation".' Fowler goes on to reject Bateson's model along with the 'slur'. More interesting still is Bateson's blindness to the force of his own objection that the linguist should have no truck with evaluation, which 'seeps' and 'oozes' in. What we must do, Bateson says, is 'resist the mating of the language of description with the language of evaluation'.[18]

Neither man seems to have understood that the debate in which they were involved had brought them to the brink of the most troublesome and fundamental fact about literary criticism: the gulf between the discourse of description and that of evaluation. The failure is the more striking in Fowler, in that he, earlier in the controversy, had stated that he considered the 'hunch' essential to the formation of a critical judgement, and the 'linguistic analysis . . . a subsequent process, explanatory and confirmatory'.[19] This seems to be an exemplary statement of critical intentions. But later observations of Fowler's make it clear that he regards the confirmations and explanations of the linguistic analysis, if subsequent, none the less soundly based: 'mere description', he observes, if 'unselective and insensitive', should 'rarely' be the concern of the linguist *qua* critic, who 'must compare and evaluate and go beyond his professional techniques if he is doing anything more than practising or displaying his methods'.[20]

Just how the linguist goes beyond his professional techniques without 'seeping' into evaluation is, of course, *the* question, and it is just what Fowler doesn't answer. Not only does he not answer it, he seems oblivious to its importance: in his eagerness to establish his literary humanism he adopts precisely the pose of the literary critic which the 'science' of linguistics was supposed to have made impossible. Stylistics is nothing if not description of the text: and the value it can have is precisely its showing up of what I have called the text's shapes and tensions (empirically testable but not, as it were, physically 'there' as the actual vocables or brush-strokes are 'there'). But this is, as I have suggested, exactly where the difficulties start: what constitutes a valid description of a text? Is it a mere repetition of the text? Is it an amassing of 'all' its stylistic, grammatical, syntactical, rhetorical features? What is it that tells us that a 'shape' or tension picked out by the critic is really 'there'? What, in other words, turns the pile of data amassable by the New Critic or stylistician into 'valid' delineation of significant structure?

These questions remain unanswered. Indeed, they remain largely unaddressed. Nowhere in stylistics or structural poetics – in 'poetology' in general – have any principles begun to emerge which enable us to place the interpretation of literature on a scientific basis. The fact of the matter is that stylisticist and structuralist approaches base themselves on a model of analysis which cannot really serve the case of literature. It was the aim of the formalists to isolate a literary text from its extra-textual background, ignore the author's psychology and the text's history, and thereby to isolate the text's *literaturnost.*' But in this, as we have seen, neither they nor their stylisticist followers were successful. Granted that the value of the text – its 'literariness' – must lie in its forms, it appears that to isolate this value it is not enough merely to enumerate all its properties. This will result in the heap of bric-à-brac characteristic of the Jakobsonian analysis. The feeling persists that Jakobson's analyses are based upon the implicit criterion of complicatedness: the more internal interrelations can be demonstrated within the poem, the more highly organised it is, and therefore the better it is. In this, Jakobson's presuppositions are close to those of William Empson, and there is probably a degree of truth in them. Yet neither Jakobson nor Empson produced criteria for judging the 'significant' degree of complexity, or arguments to show why an exceedingly complicated academic work, for instance, might not be inferior to an apparently simpler masterpiece by an original artist. Without making complexity a criterion of excellence, and thereby tailoring the requirements of complexity to fit the (premade) judgement, it is difficult to see how the idea can help us.[21] Academic critics frequently confuse subtlety with complexity, and tend perhaps to value complexity above subtlety. More frequently still, they tend to find things subtle (or complex, or whatever their particular hobby-horse happens to be) whenever they find them successful: what we approve of, in other words, we smother in our critical terminology, apposite or not.

4 The Analysis of Value-Judgements

(i) INTRODUCTION

In view of the theoretical and practical confusion we encounter in criticism of which the avowed intention is to eliminate subjectivity from the critical act and place the whole discipline on a scientific basis, it seems a matter of some importance to inspect the language of criticism a little more closely than is usually the case. The logical analysis of critical terminology may well reveal the intrinsic nature of criticism itself. For underlying all criticism is a theory of literature (or art in general) and it is this basic theoretical structure we are really concerned with in modern claims to have eliminated the 'subjective' and bypassed the 'intuitive'.

Philosophical aesthetics, when it has concerned itself with these matters, has generally tended to conclude that the language of aesthetics (by which I mean criticism here) must be aligned with that of ethics. Wittgenstein's dictum that 'Ethics and aesthetics are one' has its roots in Hume's observation that aesthetic statements are like ethical ones in being expressions of approval ('taste') rather than about matters of fact, and English philosophy has in general favoured this approach. In recent years, however, a number of 'ordinary language' philosophers have sought ways of placing the logical analysis of aesthetic (critical) terms on a sounder basis. William Elton's excellent anthology, *Aesthetics and Language*,[1] brings together a number of critics and aestheticians who collectively and individually show a keener awareness of the real nature of the problems of aesthetics and of critical language, than it is usual to meet with in philosophical aesthetics. A number of these critics and philosophers – Stuart Hampshire, Arnold Isenberg and Helen Knight in particular – revealed certain tendencies in the logic of criticism which had not hitherto been understood. In particular,

43

they were concerned with the logical processes by which a critic came to his conclusions about a work. Can we, these philosopher-critics asked, make the analogy between the process by which we come to judgement about practical matters and that by which we arrive at aesthetic or critical judgements? Are statements such as 'This is a good poem' similar, in the respects that matter, to statements such as 'This is a good bicycle'?

Helen Knight sought to establish such a parallel on the strength of the similarity of the ways in which we reach decisions about poems and about bicycles. In both cases, we refer to relevant sets of criteria: 'the meaning of "good"', she concludes, 'varies when we use different criteria'.[2] Many critical anomalies vanish when we admit·that the criteria relevant to judging one work are irrelevant to judging another. These criteria, however, often overlap, giving rise to the troubling generality in 'good', and making it seem as if we contradict ourselves when we say that two quite different poems are both good. Thus, in the cases of both practical and aesthetic value-judgements, the process of coming to a decision is the same: we select the relevant criteria and use them to come to rationally accountable decisions. (Mrs. Knight uses the term 'good-statements': I shall call these v(alue)-judgements.) Knight uses the example of a tennis player.[3] The rating of this player, according to the theory under discussion, is determined by the qualities he displays: he is good because he is fast, powerful, serves well and so on. Thus any v-judgement about him is to be explained by the elucidation of the criteria-relations holding. This is taken to be the model of practical judgements; as such is carried over into the realm of aesthetics. This is, I believe, a mistake due to her failure to analyse more closely the criteria-relations in practical v-judgements.

(ii) PRACTICAL VALUE-JUDGEMENTS

In my analysis I shall distinguish between descriptive propositions (d-propositions), as in 'this top is round', and propositions about performance (p-propositions), such as 'this top spins well'. Both these types of proposition are to be considered as involved in the analysis of practical v-judgements. The failure to observe this distinction, I believe, vitiates Knight's attempt. Broadly speaking, my analysis can be represented by the following diagram:

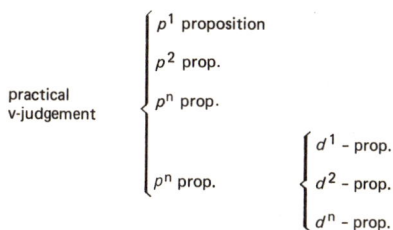

$$
\text{practical} \atop \text{v-judgement}
\left\{
\begin{array}{l}
p^1 \text{ proposition} \\
p^2 \text{ prop.} \\
p^n \text{ prop.} \\
\\
p^n \text{ prop.} \quad
\left\{
\begin{array}{l}
d^1 - \text{prop.} \\
d^2 - \text{prop.} \\
d^n - \text{prop.}
\end{array}
\right.
\end{array}
\right.
$$

It may be formulated in the following way. V-judgements are analysable into sets of p-propositions, each of which is analysable into sets of d-propositions; theoretically, the analyses are exhaustive. There is nothing in the practical v-judgement, therefore, which cannot be expressed in terms of p-propositions.

At first sight, it seems that a sufficient number of p-propositions entails a given v-judgement; but in fact it is always possible to deny a v-judgement, even given all available p-propositions, without falling into logical contradiction. This is why experts are needed, even when no further facts are forthcoming. Let us imagine two men, A and B, discussing tennis player X. A agrees that X is strong, but thinks he is too slow; thus he may be led to say that the player is not very good. B may agree that X is slow, but he thinks he has such control that his lack of speed is counterbalanced; thus B thinks X is good. The example may be ever so much more complex, but the final disagreement will be the same. It is in this sense that criteria-statements need interpreting. Now the argument may be settled definitely by X's next match in which his good service wins more points than his slowness concedes. It is precisely the possibility of this kind of verification which makes v-judgements objective, such that it is not merely a matter of opinion or of personal interpretation. In actual fact, this kind of interpretation is not long in coming to v-judgements. We feel that a certain number of p-propositions have only to be asserted for a particular v-judgement to be undeniable. (This kind of analysis, in which the expert puts sets of p-propositions before us, is of course sharply distinct from analysis the other way, in which we give p-propositions to say what we *mean* by a v-judgement.) The reason for this is that some kind of interpretation has gone on prior to the emergence of p-propositions. This relates to the status of d-propositions. It may have been noticed that in the appraisal of the tennis player, the reasons given divided easily into physical (fast, strong, lots of stamina) and technical (serves well, volleys hard, accurate in ground strokes). It is this natural bifurcation which suggests the distinction between d- and p-propositions, of which I shall now give a fuller account.

It will perhaps be to our advantage to use a simpler example, though what I say of this example will hold good of any more complex examples. I shall take for my example, instead of a complex organism like a tennis player, a bicycle.

I shall wish to claim that when someone says 'This is a good bicycle' he would agree in asserting a number of propositions which refer to the performance of the bicycle and that if *no* such propositions are intended in this sense, then the person is either talking nonsense, misusing the language or saying something of whose meaning he is ignorant. In this sense, I propose to say that these propositions constitute exhaustively any value-judgement, v, and that in this sense, we can say that v *means* p v p^1 v p^2 v p^3 v p^n. This must be interpreted in the following way. Any one possible p-proposition may not be intended by the speaker. (A p-proposition will be said to be intended if it was in some degree instrumental in the formation of v.) Further, two v-judgements will be said to be the same if they are constituted by the same p-propositions. Thus, if A calls the bicycle good, but intends p-propositions which B regards as non-decisive, then B's sentence 'The bicyle is good' will not be regarded as expressing the same v-judgement. Clearly no rigid rule exists for deciding when and when not two sets of p-propositions subtend the same v-judgement. Some clarification of the situation is possible, however. The key word is 'decisive', which I have introduced into the structure of evaluation. One sentence ('The bicycle is good') has been said to express two different propositions (v-judgements); B agreed in asserting 'The bicycle is good', but he denied the truth of A's proposition. In these circumstances we feel like saying, 'Oh yes, I agree with you, but for different reasons', implying that there is a common proposition which can be held or denied for different reasons, by different people. The fact is, however, that there is no such common proposition. That A *means* one thing and B another, precisely because v-judgements are constructions out of p-propositions. From this it follows that the proposition expressed by the sentence 'The bicycle is good' is itself neither true nor false, that is, to B, A is wrong; to A, B is wrong. 'Good-statements' are odd in this way.

This seems to come close to a Humean view of art and ethics which express approval rather than matters of fact. Yet on the face of it, such statements as 'This is a good bicycle' are certainly not merely emotive; they are backed up by testable statements about performance, and we acknowledge the status of experts, that is, people whose opinion is simply worth more than others who have not acquired their expertise. Nevertheless, our analysis has shown that there is something different about practical judgements ('This is a good bike'), something setting them apart from grammatically similar propositions such as 'This is a blue bicycle', about which such expertise is neither necessary nor acknowledged. It is this difference in logical status which concerns us here: practical judgements are, as I have said, constructed out of d- and p-propositions, and this is not true of statements which simply reduce to sensory evidence. What is of interest here is the relationship of practical judgements to aesthetic v-judgements: we shall see that there are certain crucial differences.

(iii) AESTHETIC VALUE-JUDGEMENTS

In the first place, this difference is apparent if we imagine putting to an art-critic the question, What qualities do you look for in a good painting? And at the same time imagine a comparable question put to a tennis coach. The tennis coach's answer to the question, what qualities he looked for in a good tennis player, will be of real practical value. We should be able to leave him to put his advice into practice, improve our ground strokes, work on our volleying, safe in the knowledge that more or less any other coach would give us the same sort of advice (though two coaches might obviously differ in the methods they prescribed to go about it). It is certain that the art-critic, assuming that he knows his job as well as the tennis coach knew his, will be able to give us an answer of no practical value whatever. For a practical answer would have to include statements of two logically different sorts. Helen Knight establishes, to her own satisfaction, a parallel between v-judgements in respect of tennis players and of works of art. In her view, to ask for an elucidation of such statements is always to ask for statements about the criteria-relation involved. That is, if I want to know why McEnroe is thought a good tennis player, I will be given a list of qualities which normally serve as criteria in the judgement of tennis players, much as the coach in my own example gave us tips equally sanctified by practice and experience. Knight carries this structure directly into aesthetics. The qualities involved in painting, for example, are realism, poetry, brilliance in colour, balance of design, harmony, etc. Now what I should like to argue is that in making such a parallel between the two sorts of v-judgements, Knight is making a serious error, the nature of which I intend to elucidate by enquiring what is involved in the making of aesthetic as opposed to practical v-judgements.

First, I wish to separate aesthetic characteristics into two categories, (a) and (b). (a)-characteristics include words like 'balanced', 'striped', 'polytonal', 'contrapuntal', 'metaphoric'; (b)-characteristics include such words as 'noble', 'moving', 'profound'. What I wish to assert is that it is only the (a)-characteristics – which are in fact purely descriptive – which can be equated with the criteria involved in evaluating a good tennis player, and that the second order of characteristics, (b)-type, are quite different, are not really involved in evaluation at all, but are so freely intermingled with (a)-type in critical discourse that most philosophers and critics fail to notice the difference. That they are different, I shall try to show by revealing that they fulfil different functions, and that both these functions in fact are different from the practical v-judgements we have been concerned with hitherto.

I shall deal with (a)-characteristics first, since they are, *prima facie*, similar in type to the criteria-explanation of the tennis coach. The tennis coach's answer to our enquiry was, we remember, of distinct practical value: his answer was couched in terms of (a)-type characteristics. The art critic's answer was useless, we can now see, because it was couched, like most critical pronouncements, in terms of both (a)- and (b)-characteristics. A genuinely helpful practical answer would need to be framed purely in terms of (a)-characteristics, that is to say, purely descriptive ones. The difference between the two situations now emerges. There is simply no guarantee that pictures containing all the (a)-characteristics the critic can mention will be good art, or 'art' at all. No amount of practice on our part at painting with correctly mixed colours, or observing all the rules of perspective and balanced masses, will yield the kind of results that the tennis player gets when he successfully works up his speed, service, backhand, and drop-volley. In point of fact, as I have said, the critic approached for helpful advice would probably freely mingle his (a)- and (b)-characteristics; and (b)-characteristics are, practically speaking, useless. Moreover, it was precisely the (b)-characteristics we wanted clarifying when we put our question. Having beforehand heard the critic expatiating on a great painter's work in (b)-characteristics, we asked him for an explanation in terms of (a)-characteristics. This means in fact that we were asking for a series of causal connections between the physical features of a painting (or poem or sonata) and the critic's expressed approval of it. And this was precisely what was not forthcoming.

That this discrepancy indicates a radical difference in such subject-matter will be clear from the following example. Let us again switch territories from human performance to mechanical. We shall imagine two salesmen, one of bicycles, the other of paintings. (I mean real paintings – works of art – not drawing-room furniture.) The first salesman's sales-talk consists of a simple enumeration of the bicycle's qualities: 'Easy to clean, simple construction, three-speed gears, guaranteed brakes, finished in blue acrylic paint.' If we assume that the prospective buyer is able to know for certain that the salesman tells nothing but the truth, then he will have no doubt that the bicycle described is the one for him. He will know that a bicycle with these qualities is simply good. He will probably insist on a translation of these d-propositions into p-ones, will want to go for a spin on it. But such a test is not essential. What about the picture salesman? He also gives an enumeration of (a)-characteristics – 'Bright colour, balanced masses; balance of horizontals and diagonals; subject: girl in sunset.' He may try to describe the physical characteristics in d-propositions at least as detailed as the other salesman's. (This, I should add, is the way Knight says critics talk about works of art in general.) The difference is that the sophisticated art-lover (we will assume an equal expertise with the bicycle buyer) will by no means be satisfied with this. He needs to know one more thing of the critic: he must be assured that the painting, as well as being possessed of all these properties, is also good. For in the nature of the case, a bicycle with the qualities ascribed to it by our salesman just *is* a good bicycle, and it would be absurd for the buyer to say, 'Yes, I accept all that, but is it a *good* bike?' To say that a bicycle is good is, as we have seen, simply to say that it is possessed of such and such a list of qualities – and nothing more: to ask for an elucidation of the value-judgement is to ask for a list of these or similar qualities, that is, for an explication of the criteria-relations involved. It is quite evident, on the other hand, that any or all of the qualities ascribable to the painting may equally well be present in bad painting or even in a kaleidoscope. We acknowledge in fact a distinction in art which has no place in the world of practical judgements: the bad-good painting, and the good-bad one. On the one hand, the academic work which follows all the rules, was judged good by those who ought to know, but now seems simply dead, dull, even absurd; on the other hand, the work which breaks all the known rules, yet is great: like Beethoven's *Grosse Fuge*.

There is no place for the 'academic' bicycle or the bad-good lawnmower – the mower which has blunt blades, wonky wheels, rusty finish yet is somehow 'great'. A 'great' bicycle is merely a very, very good one. Practical v-judgements have no place – even in the world of the Rolls-Royce – for the distinction between the merely good, competent, and the great or sublime.

(iv) IDEAL QUALITIES

It is the failure to distinguish between (a)- and (b)-characteristics which involves Knight in error. Just as the critic in our example might have replied to the question in terms of (b)-characteristics, so the salesman might attempt to sell the painting by speaking of its profundity, 'sublimity', even 'beauty'; in fact by simply praising the picture. This is just what the prospective buyer needs, and it is noteworthy that the very thing the bicycle salesman did not need to do was praise his product: 'it sells itself' – ideally, of course. It speaks for itself, at least, or rather the qualities speak for themselves.

Thus, to explain what he meant by saying that he had a 'good' picture to sell, the picture salesman had really no alternative but to reiterate (in so many words) 'I mean good', that is, to utter a tautology. There is one more point to be made here which underlines the difference involved in the two types of statement. If, having made our exhaustive descriptions of the articles involved, two salesmen still disagree about two kinds of bicycle, there is one sure way of ending the argument (though it is in practice useless). If one kind stands up to months of hard wear and severe weather successfully, and the other kind decays in a short period, then one of the salesmen must either relinquish his position or accuse himself of pigheadedness. In other words, practical value-judgements are constructs out of performance and test-propositions. There are certain tests which themselves justify or fail to justify practical v-judgements. In the absence of such tests the question must remain open, and it is in the expectation of such tests being possible that we make lists of qualities 'explaining' these v-judgements. Thus, practical v-judgements refer not to any primary quality which subsumes the primary qualities, but to performance. To say that X is a good tennis player is to talk about his past performances and make predictions about his future ones.

Because such performance-tests are possible, the elucidation of practical v-judgements consists in the enumeration of ideal qualities. No such ideal qualities are relevant to the judgement of works of art. There is no such thing as the ideal painting, although it seems relatively easy to conceive of the ideal tennis player. (This holds good until we enter that realm where sport shades off into art, where Drobny's drop-volleys and Nastase's 'touch', like George Best's swerve and Brady's left foot, simply seem unanalysable values in their own right – unteachable, and unquantifiable: these, of course, confirm my point by being exceptional.) Knight tries to explain the underlying somewhat-ness of aesthetic and practical 'goodness' by pointing out that a player may be fast but not good, or slow but good (like V. Krishnan, for instance) so that the goodness of a player is not wholly determined by measuring him up against ideal qualities. This schema she applies to works of art. There is again a great difference, however. Although it is true that speed will be included in our list of 'ideal' qualities for tennis players, we can and do say, 'X is good, *though* slow', 'Y is erratic *despite* his speed'. This fails completely when applied to works of art. Knight takes the example of a Cézanne, in which the v-judgement is explained in part at least by describing its depth-effect. This example is intended to illustrate the way the explication of the criteria-relation involved serves to justify the v-judgement (that is, 'the Cézanne is good because of the depth-effect'). If I am approached and asked to explain why I think this particular Cézanne is good, I reply by pointing to the effect of three-dimensionality and solidity Cézanne here achieves. But Dali's 'The Font' also achieves an effect of depth. The figures have great solidity, the whole has a convincingly deep atmosphere. But I none the less think it a bad picture. Moreover, I do not say that it is a bad picture *in spite of* the effect of depth achieved, any more than I say that the Cézanne is good *because* of it. In criticising Dali's picture, I will probably say that the harshness of the figures is unexplained by a central vision, the diagonal line takes us far into the distance and nowhere in particular; in fact that the depth effect is 'used badly'. I do not wish to treat the depth-effect as something concrete common to both Cézanne and Dali, but used well by Cézanne and badly by Dali, in the way that the volley is used well by X and badly by Y because, for instance, Y plays it perfectly but to the wrong sort of ball. A good volley is always a good volley, and Y's fault can probably be rectified by better timing. But there is no way in which the depth-effect can be said to be good or bad. In fact, the true nature of critical judgements is well indicated by this use of pseudo-criteria.

(v) PSEUDO-CRITERIA

Helen Knight[4] gives an instance of a film, *After Office Hours*, which A praises for its smartness, slickness and technical competence but which B condemns, not accepting these as criteria at all. This makes it seem that there is a real disagreement about the nature of criteria, since B acknowledges the presence of these qualities on the film, but rejects them as inartistic. The disagreement is illusory, however, B's irrelevant rejection of the criteria being prompted by A's irrelevant praise for them. Such disagreements should not occur in the discussion of works of art, and if B had been more perspicacious, he ought to have replied, 'I agree they are present, but they aren't used artistically'. Aesthetic judgements do not refer to bundles of commendable qualities. What then do they refer to? We have seen that there are no objectively testable standards, yet there is surely something authoritative in the critic's pronouncements? When we pick teams to judge works of art, we go to critics rather than to economists, and we strengthen this by referring to such qualities as 'sensitivity' and 'insight'. Clearly these words refer to something, just as to say that a man is a good judge of bicycles is to assert that his predictions about its performance will by and large be accurate. In practical discourse there are objective standards – ideal properties in the absence of which v-judgements would be impossible. (These properties, as our analysis has made clear, are related directly to performance: round wheels run smoothly, and are 'good'.) In art there are no such standards. For these reasons, the criteria-relations of ordinary practical v-judgements do not apply to aesthetic v-judgements. By practical v-judgements, I mean those to which empirical tests can be applied, and in which the rejection of these tests is generally taken to be a refusal to 'see reason'. We found that if B still demurred about the qualities of a player, the question could be settled by watching him play. Unless it was agreed that the player was off form, most disagreement would be dispelled by the player's flowing drives or consistent double faults.

In this, as in other important respects, the language and procedure of criticism are unlike those of practical discourse, and it is a fault of certain critical schools that they fail to see this. In practical discourse, giving a reason for a judgement will concern supporting a preference with descriptive propositions. 'This is a good bicycle' will entail a number of d-propositions which must hold good in order for the judgement to have any sense. Obviously there is no fixed rule governing when we decide that the bicycle is good, and when only 'quite good'. Thus, some practical v-judgements will entail more of the relevant d-propositions than others. However, a certain number must be entailed, otherwise no v-judgement can reasonably be made. I can't say, 'This is a good bike but I can't give you any reasons for it.' Thus, giving reasons in practical discourse is describing the object. From this it follows that certain d-propositions always tend to entail v-judgements, or certain properties support approval.

Here we have in a nutshell the distinction I wish to draw between practical and aesthetic v-judgements. Briefly, of no aesthetic v-judgement will it be possible to say that it is entailed by any d-propositions. As we saw in the case of Beethoven's

Grosse Fuge, it is always possible for a work to contravene every rule of 'good' construction – even of good taste – and remain a masterpiece. Thus, there are no aesthetic descriptive propositions which automatically support approval or denigration.

In speaking of works of art, therefore, we have found that we only speak of 'good'-qualities by a liberty of usage. In reality we find that when we refer to these supposed good-qualities, we are in fact referring *to a quality behind them* in the work which gives them what value they appear to have – value that we think we have traced to the existence of good-qualities. Thus when we speak in praise of a particular art-work or literary text, we imply something beside the quality itself: 'The diagonal of the table-cloth in this Cézanne still-life sets off the vertical of the table leg.' We always have to back this – which sounds like a reason-giving procedure on the model of the practical v-judgement – with an implicit or explicit 'And this is well used by the painter'.

Now it is clearly not a tautology to say 'This painting is good', yet there is something tautologous involved when a person, asked to explain why he thinks a painting is good, gives as his reason that it is good. And as we have seen, this is what the analysis of aesthetic reason-giving shows to be going on. The confusion among critics and theorists alike results from the practice of freely mixing (a)- and (b)-type judgements – evaluative with descriptive ones. The role of criticism is, therefore, more complicated and tricky than may at first appear. It is principally concerned with elucidating the nature of the subtensive goodness. Basically, the critic tries to make clear the structural skeleton (internal dimension, real form) of the work, its various tensions and emphases. This kind of description has led various critics to think that it is evaluation. This is due to the failure to distinguish the two types of statement involved, and to the critic's professionally odd mixture of exhortation and explanation. He either exhorts us to share an experience, or he mingles these exhortations with descriptive-sounding statements. But this 'explanation' is radically different from giving lists of properties. What he is explaining is the subtensive goodness, and goodness here won't be analysed into bundles of qualities. The goodness here subtends the qualities used in the actual explanation. The elucidation of this relation of subtension must be regarded as the only serious task of criticism.

My thesis then has been there is no set of characteristics which determine that a work is good or bad. Or rather that there can be no answer to the question, 'What is the reason for the expressive quality of works of art?' Or to the question, 'What and how does art express?' In other words, I am rejecting as futile the wholly metaphysical questions 'What is art?' and 'Why do we react as we do to it?' and 'Why are some works of art greater than others?' Art is a kind of knowledge; to the question 'What is knowledge?' the only answer is 'What we know', or a catalogue of every fact that we know. Thus, the misguidedness of seeking a key to the art-mystery will be shown up. There is no 'artness', no 'literariness'. 'Art' and 'literature' are simply labels for referring to the body of works we value. Too much recent criticism has taken advantage of the theoretical confusion rampant in traditional aesthetics and theory to show that, since 'literature' cannot be satisfactorily defined (as it cannot, since it is the name of a class rather than a member of one),[5] there is no such thing as 'literature' at all. This is simple sleight of hand, a counter-fallacy born of a fallacy. There is no 'literary quality', no 'artness'. But there are works (paintings, poems, sonatas) which have certain effects on us, and say certain things. Criticism must satisfy our sense of these values and meanings: it must be adequate to its object. Much *avant garde* criticism is misguided not because it disbelieves in 'literature', but because its analyses fail to do justice to their objects, either simplifying them into ideology, or using pseudo-criteria – fake descriptive-evaluative standards such as 'complexity' or 'interrogativeness' or 'ironic consideration'. There are many other such in use. There is, for instance, the concept of 'wholeness'. The literary concept of wholeness is paralleled in philosophy by the 'organic wholes' of G. E. Moore, such that all the work of criticism and aesthetics seems to be taken over by these wholes, which become a kind of shibboleth of good art. In fact the concept of wholeness is as little descriptive as any critical concept. There is no way of applying the standard of wholeness to a work of art and finding it wanting or not wanting in wholeness. What happens is that we choose to adopt the discourse of 'wholeness' (Langer's 'spatially resolved', like her 'virtual experience', is another) as a more explicit means of presenting preferences or evaluation.

Almost any genuinely critical work will provide us with similar examples. I shall give just a few. The philosopher Arnold Isenberg, for instance, presents Ludwig Goldscheider's analysis of El Greco's painting as if the critic had offered us terms which are both descriptive and evaluative. He says that the role of the critic is to narrow down the field of possible visual orientation by describing some of the actual qualities of the painting, and thus guiding us 'in the discrimination of details'.[6] But, again, such description is meaningless without the suppressed 'good' or 'well-used' statements. Think of the critic on a bad work. If he merely describes the thing as Goldscheider 'describes' the El Greco, the reader may well imagine the work is being praised. So the critic intersperses his writing with words like 'imitative', 'feeble', 'insincere'. Without this explicit or implicit evaluation, the critical description is useless. Actually of course the physical descriptive statements are meant to *reveal* the structural skeleton of the work, as I have said critics often have to try to do. Thus, evaluation shades off into interpretation, and the task before the critic is as great in the one area as in the other, if not in fact identical.

Often the critic will present an instrument of evaluation as if it were a distinction existing in the natural world. Coleridge, for instance, called Imagination 'essentially *vital*, even as all objects (*as* objects) are essentially fixed and dead'. Fancy, on the other hand, has no other counters to play with, but fixities and definites'; it is 'no other than a mode of memory'.[7] He claims to be discrimating two actual faculties, where he is in reality doing no more than giving us ways of distinguishing good from bad, Milton from Cowley.

All this may seem somewhat over-fastidious. But logic here does not merely trap the unwary; it also serves to elicit the somewhat confused hinterland to many critical statements. What has been argued with respect of Dostoevsky's apparently repetitious and obsessional novels could be applied, for instance, to Bruckner's symphonies ('too long'), or Whitman's poetry ('formless, repetitive, uneconomical, sprawling'). These considerations might well make us more aware of the actual decisions – moral, sometimes political – that underlie our seemingly value-free critical procedures. This is especially the case in criticism which, as it were, ideologically eschews the value-judgement as a sign of bourgeois elitism, yet covertly practises it at the very base of its own operations. Neo-Marxist criticism in particular likes to sabotage the positive contents and stylistic certitudes of 'bourgeois' realism by implicitly favouring a literature of 'rupture', fracture, or absence. Catherine Belsey, for instance, distinguishes between 'declarative', 'imperative' and 'interrogative' texts.[8] No great acuteness is required to guess that the 'interrogative' texts are the good ones, and that the 'declarative' and 'imperative' ones the bad, because they bully us and are too obvious. Literature, for Belsey, is recognisable by its capacity for disrupting our unity 'by discouraging identification with a unified subject'.[9] But how do we tell a lying declarative text from a truth-inspiring interrogative one? The answer is not, of course, forthcoming, for Belsey's 'criterion' is a pseudo-criterion, based upon the very judgement it is meant to provide. Much the same is true of Terry Eagleton's 'good' text which '[flexes] and [compacts] its senses': this is supposed to be different from the bad text which comforts, assures and lies.[10] Like Belsey's 'interrogative text' it can only be recognised after the event, when the v-judgement has been made.

We could follow an unbroken line back through Richards's 'ironic' texts to Coleridge's 'organic' ones, and thence back to the origins of criticism in Plato and Aristotle. The message is always the same: responsible literary critics are those who, acknowledging the true nature of what they are doing, exhort and persuade us to accept a vision of life, through literature; irresponsible critics, pretending to base themselves upon scientific or philosophical certainties and to have eliminated the subjective and the irrational from their work, in effect work a confidence trick upon us.

(vi) CONCLUSION

Critical pronouncements, then, are of two sorts. First, the simple affirmation or approval ('good'-statements, in which it is illogical or logically odd to say that 'I approve what I know to be bad'); this may be the helpful classification of a new work, and is in fact an indispensable part of the tradition of literary criticism in every culture: the critic persuades by being right. Alternatively this kind of statement may elide with the second type, in which the critic gives the kind of reason described above as (a)-type, but backs his explication (which may be indefinitely elaborate, as in structural poetics and stylistics) with an explicit or smuggled-in approval-judgement, (b)-type. Naturally a critic, when asked to explain or justify a preference or judgement, should not merely repeat it in the same words, or merely give up the ghost. Thus, for instance, the critic uses descriptive-sounding formulae as if he were 'explaining' his v-judgement. In fact, they do not really do so, they merely *point*. One may say, in justifying an adverse judgement on a Carlo Dolci madonna, 'Don't you see how sentimental it is?' or, in explaining a low opinion of a Swinburne lyric, 'There's no depth or density, no intellectual grasp'. One may even attempt a Leavisite analysis and try to *show* that the poem is bad. However cleverly this is done, it will always be possible to analyse the analysis in terms of either evaluative or descriptive words – never both. Leavis himself acknowledged this in his well-known methodological formula, 'This is so, is it not?' – 'Yes, but . . . '. In his own criticism, reasons are constantly given, yet they are not more frequent than quotations from the author in question. We are asked to test for ourselves the quality of the work under the influence of Leavis's evaluations, yet these reasons of his are always given names which themselves are more than just that reason. His vocabulary includes words with a moral ring like 'strong', 'weak', 'concrete', 'not fully realised'. Here the giving of the reasons and the backing with approval are elided, and so it must be in all good criticism. There is no such thing as a fully objective or intrinsic criticism. No critical utterance both describes and entails evaluation. What the critic does is to recommend a particular judgement or to describe the work in the hope of laying bare some of its suppressed (unperceived) material. Sometimes this procedure is called supporting a judgement with reasons. This is dubious, as we have seen, but it must be allowed, since a critic who purely gives his own opinion (that is, uses only (b)-type propositions) is useless; only the mélange described above is of any use whatever.

It must not, however, be supposed to be any more than pointing, describing and recommending. There can be no 'therefores' and 'it follows thats'. If this does not sufficiently demean or deflate the currency of criticism (as perhaps any inflationary currency requires devaluing from time to time), let it be observed that because of their intrinsically unstable mixture of description and smuggled-in evaluation, a proper term for critical statements would be tautology: they really assert, ever so subtly, 'It's good because it's good'. A further variety of this statement is the rather odd but possible one, 'This painting is a work of art'. There are plenty of contexts in which such a judgement might have to be asserted, and some in which it would be equivalent to 'This painting is good'. A really cruel classifier then might reduce the dignity of critical judgements still further: they are ejaculations or tautologies. And this would still leave criticism intact and important. Few of the thousands of so-called art-works produced every year have the quality of real art or literature. Yet they have the physiognomical resemblance to the great. The critic learns to speak the language of the present on the many, so that he shall be ready silently to admire the few.

5 Critical Witness and the Evolution of Culture

Logical analysis has shown that the critic's sense of value in a work must be subjective: no analysis of the text's qualities will generate or necessitate a judgement, in the way that an analysis of a bicycle's qualities produces certain judgements. To many critics, this will be a welcome conclusion, seeming to confirm a hostility to the use of value-judgements in criticism, and thereby to support the case of an 'objective' value-free criticism. Yet, as we have seen, the reverse is the case: far from eliminating the value-judgement from criticism, our analysis insists on emphasising its absolute indispensability, its intrinsicness to the whole enterprise of criticism. The critic's role emerges as that of witness to the text's literariness (or artness, in other forms). Ultimately the critic merely *points to* the text's configuration of forces, internal dimension or *literaturnost'*. To isolate the text's structures so as to identify its literariness was early seen as the goal of a formalist criticism. Stylistics in particular claimed to eliminate those impressionistic or subjective elements supposed to vitiate mainstream criticism, and therefore to obviate the value-judgement altogether. Now it appears that all criticism is condemned either to be merely descriptive, with no guarantee of interpretation, let alone evaluation, or to rely precisely on that confusion of descriptive and evaluative elements so much despised in the rejected criticism.

It is important to recognise that this is not a matter of a vague sense of appropriateness – a deep-seated misgiving about reducing to science what should be left to loftier or more soulful faculties. It is a matter of logical fact: any literary criticism which hopes to make proper contact with literary texts, in Jakobson's sense of outlining or locating their *literaturnost'*, has to employ the language of the value-judgement, which means in the end that he is reduced to gesticulation, or pointing, or witnessing.

This assertion is not gainsaid by what we may call taxonomic or rhetorical criticism. Granted that all criticism is in the meta-language, taxonomic criticism is meta-criticism. Thus, its intention of cataloguing effects (rhetoric) or operations (structural poetics) in no way absolves it from the necessary impurity, the ultimately incoherent, exclamatory witnessing role of all criticism. Indeed, its capacity to describe and catalogue in a quasi-scientific spirit is only afforded it by the assurance of a society of values and collective responses which, being predictable, bring into being the apparently objective instruments of rhetoric. Thus, Burke's contrasting of the beautiful and the sublime, Frye's broad catalogue of the forms and modes of world-literature, Aristotle's more limited description of the properties of Attic drama – all these taxonomies in fact rest upon the incomputably numerous acts of value-judgement, appraisal and 'sensitive' response which they appear to obviate. Burke could only impute an effect of 'grandeur' and 'awe' to certain orders of pictorial device because of the 'effectiveness' of certain works by Michelangelo, Milton and Claude. It was an early criticism of Frye's *Anatomy* that he did indeed appear to disdain the value-judgements he in fact assumed all the time in dealing only with accepted master-works. In so far as he was concerned only with the description of these works, Frye's later claim to have 'misled no one' can be accepted:[1] there was no need for him to do other than he did. But in so far as he claimed to base his *Anatomy* on quasi-objective grounds from which the exercise of the value-judgement was eliminated as by a superior wisdom granted to Frye by God, then he was gravely in error – in ignorance, indeed, of his own critical methods.

There may be no need for a taxonomic criticism to do other than taxonomise – whether it be the properties many different works or even genres have in common, or the 'effects' isolable within a particular work. But a taxonomic criticism which does not know or acknowledge that it acts only by courtesy of the intersubjective, transindividual world of agreed values and responses, acts in darkness and will certainly run into error. The expert taxonomies of a Propp or an Arnheim depend very much upon the acceptance of genres which in turn presuppose a general, intersubjective act of recognition. Recognition, as we have said, is the prime quality of the critical act. Let us take, for instance, the famous analysis Propp made of Russian folk-tales.[2] This highly structured 'description' of a locally delimited range of texts (the 'laws' do not seem to apply outside the historical and geographical area selected by Propp) is made on the assumption of the acceptance of these texts. Presented theoretically, indeed, Propp's case would be hopeless: offered as a theory of narrative it can work only by refusing to accept other sorts of text. As such, the tales offer themselves with their more or less unvarying formal characteristics. But they are endorsed, agreed upon, both by the society which chose to retain them for its children, and repeat their 'meanings' under variation throughout a more highly evolved culture, and by the original audiences which both made them up and listened to them and abstracted the key features for use in its own production. In other words, the selection of the field of study in this case is itself an implicit value-judgement: Propp recognises the texts and, implicitly, the values enshrined in them. Thus, his mere description of them is an interpretation. Moreover, these tales were 'written', as it were, without cultural forethought – that damaging and possibly disqualifying competitiveness by which professional writers, in a society which grants a living and perhaps an immortality to those who go through certain motions, approximate to the shape, tone and quality of existing work. An analysis such as Propp's could proceed as it did because the peculiarly rich and subtle epistemes within the folk-tale remained, for all their having eased themselves into existence without the apparent mediation of the individual creator, innocent of the audience-conscious falsifications of the metropolitan creation which will end in a signature. The folk-tale represents a resting-place – an end-stop guaranteed by need and a collective of drives, fears and hopes, which will only be confirmed by the fancy calligraphy of a Perrault or an Anderson. Thus, the tradition of the folk-tale – it is a closed file, which will not be re-opened, in spite of the occasional escorted inspections of a Propp – affirms the values always implicit in the literary venture itself. These values are founded on man's humanity itself, and they can never remain far from our preoccupations.

Propp's analysis, then, this description which seems so objective, so scientific, itself assumes and affirms the value-judgement it appears to eschew; the implicit assumption throughout is that these thirty-one functions, in their given order, *work*. It is not necessary for Propp to add 'And they work . . . ', of course, any more than it is necessary for Frye to interlard his lofty commentary with nudges and winks of appreciation, in order that his readers will get the point: no audience is quite so sleepy that it needs to be told that Shakespeare, Homer and company show forth good examples of the literary text. Thus, it may appear that a simple act of description is in progress. In fact, the literariness apparently disdained by the critic supports the 'value-free' taxonomy as an invisible property. It may not be useful – to return to Nelson Goodman's observation – to say that one folk-tale is better than another; it may be that such distinctions and contra-distinctions belong to a later phase of literary development. Yet this should not blind us to the fact that the serious part of literary evaluation – the part that is concerned with arriving at a proper evaluation of the text's literariness – is exercised no less in the long anonymous process of selection and solidification that results in the establishment of a folk-tale than in the articulations of a modern critic. We must, at the very least, discriminate between the taxonomising of a folk tradition and the description of the literariness of a modern novel. In the first sort of criticism we are describing the convergences of a style which has, as it were, already been witnessed. In the second, we accept it as the important part of the critic's task to establish the text's authenticity, to witness what we can later at leisure describe.

We approach once more the question of stylistic inheritance. Primitive art is distinguished by its form-free creativity. That is, the primitive artist had no style, no tradition to 'read' into his imagery. It is this style-conscience, this secondary reading-in or carrying-over of past shapes and forms in other art, that characterises the art of civilisation. Thus the comparison between some twentieth-century art (Rousseau, Dubuffet, and so on) and primitive art is not irrelevant. But primitive art is no less characterised by what we can call its archaism. That is, a stiffness, an inflexible rigidity betokening the narrow emotional repertoire of primitive man. Art is equal to its needs. What Harold Bloom calls the anxiety of influence is also an enabling, flexibilising force, releasing more and more minutely subjectivised expressiveness. This being admitted, we can say that the forms of primitive art leap at us in their spontaneous freedom from stylistic norms: they are fresh because they are, as it were, instinctually adequate to their ritualistic and magic purposes.

Certainly, we can acknowledge in the last analysis that no sign is without its history (otherwise it could not be a sign), and that the primitive art that has come down to us (or across to us from surviving cultures) itself represents a previous history of signs and representations. So that ultimately we shall have to admit that the Altamira cave-draughtsmen also were working within a tradition. The question is, what is the nature of that tradition? Primitive art must, we are obliged to accept, have 'served its purpose'. Propp's folk-tales were equal to theirs. Otherwise they would not survive. But how are we to talk about the innumerable works that pour out of the presses and studios of the modern world? Though we cannot reduce any art or ritual to its practical purposes, we can at least deduce the *necessity* of primitive, religious or folk art from its role in the ritualistic and social life of primitive or ancient man. We do not, that is, have to set about establishing the superiority of one Cycladic idol to another: the task becomes an irrelevant and distorting intrusion from a different cultural era (our own) – an era in which, precisely, the difficulty is to be able to recognise what *is* 'relevant' or 'real'.

To put the matter simply, we can say that difficulties multiply as the social and economic organisation of society both encourages the production of 'art' (by rewarding the artist with money, prestige or security) and at the same time lowers the status of the art from the level of a sacrament to that of a technique or an entertainment. We may assume that the gifts, flairs and genius-like abilities we admire in our modern artists – our Shakespeares and Michelangelos – existed also in primitive man, and exist indeed in surviving Stone Age societies. We may also assume that some tribes were without any man of such flair, but that, since the gods had to be propitiated, and the rituals gone through, somebody had to carve the idols and paint the cave walls. But, this being allowed, may we not also assume that the process of selection in simpler societies was simply more efficient than it can be in our own? That, to sum up, the religious nature of the artistic enterprise surrounded it with a certain awe, such that the man of spirit (the artist in this case) knew himself selected, and that the 'phoney' by definition could hardly exist? Mircea Eliade's account of the selection of the shaman throws light on the situation.[3]

There is something shamanistic about every artist. It is interesting that even primitive societies know of false shamans and are in the habit of distinguishing between shamans selected by natural gift and those chosen because they belong to a family with a shamanistic tradition. Yet still, the impression persists that ritualistic and artistic matters were in better hands in primitive societies than they are in more advanced ones. The reason why literary criticism begins to exist in more sophisticated societies is not merely that there is more literature to criticise, more self-consciousness, more leisure. It is because in such societies the over-production of 'art' begins to take on something of the luxurious air so abhorrent to critics of the Frankfurt school. Decadence in art is less a matter of degenerate moral attitudes and disbelief in the gods (though these are significant symptoms). It is rather a matter of the non-necessity of the art: the art is produced to satisfy the needs of the audience, and these needs are simply less serious than those of primitive man: the need to be entertained and diverted is scarcely a need at all. And if it is allowed as a serious need, we must at least take leave to point out that the particular form of satisfaction (one play or film or another) is so free, so undirected, as to make the instrument of that satisfaction (the work blessed by popularity) more or less fortuitous, and hence less necessitous.

This applies to the society of the ancient Greeks as well as to our own – as well, but not as much as. In the semi-ritualistic dramas of Aeschylus, with their narrowly prescribed rota of themes and treatments, their severe limits of expression and performance, we see perhaps the most interesting case of art between the archaic and the modern stages. The audience comes to judge, to discriminate: but the emotions and functions of the half-ritualistic dramas they applaud and reward are still deeply implanted in the psyche. They are still only imperfectly released from the world of religious ritual. Seneca and, following him, the Elizabethans, thematised the actions of Greek tragedy as revenge. Yet it is not revenge that stalks through the Oresteian trilogy, but transgression and pollution and the need to atone. The main theme of Greek tragedy is religious, not psychological.

In keeping with this situation, the great Greek poetics is both a taxonomy – a simple and severe catalogue of the properties of ritual and myth – and at the same time an act of critical witness. Aristotle's purpose is to describe Sophocles and Aeschylus, but it is also to tell you how to spot a phoney, the poet who is all flowers and no blood, the dramatist who surprises but does not move. The element of value-judgement criticism in the *Poetics* has perhaps not been recognised quite as much as it should.

Obviously, the circumstances which made for the Athenian culture must be studied before its features are to be understood. A large and affluent leisure-class will always generate a high percentage of superfluous art: the rewards of vanity and kudos are high in a society where many men have a lot of time to ruminate and digest what is offered. Hence, the form of the yearly drama festivals, which were not merely a shadow of a ritualistic past, but a way of guaranteeing standards. It is significant, I think, that although such competitions do survive in our own time, they play a minimal and marginal part in cultural life: the confidence to hold a festival of plays and choose the best from the offerings has been lost with the proliferation of artistic modes and the elimination of public themes. For the narrowness of the subject-matter and the relative stringency of formal requirements must have made for a concentrated and intense experience at the Athenian festivals: in a sense, the audience was saying, 'No, not that, not that. . . . Ah, *that*.' In this way, the witness of the audience and the judges ensured the continuity and the purity of those themes and contents which were spiritually important to the Greeks, in an age of increasing scepticism and secularisation.

Leibniz expressed the horror of an overproducing culture: 'the indefinite multitude of authors will shortly expose them all to the danger of general oblivion; the hope of glory animating many people at work in studies will suddenly cease; it will be perhaps as disgraceful to be an author as it was formerly honourable.'[4] Leibniz's emphasis is on the triviality of the new literature: maybe, he says, we must accept the ephemeral books, which have 'the effect of a useful conversation, not simply pleasing and keeping the idle out of mischief but helping to shape the mind and language'. These little books, Leibniz says, are like 'the flowers of a springtime or like the fruits of an autumn, scarcely surviving a year'. If we lower the level of the useful ephemera sufficiently at least to include the TV play and the well-reviewed respectable novel, we can see our own time distinctly foreshadowed in Leibniz's despair. The deeper and more serious the aim of the author, according to Leibniz, the greater will be his survival-power. Conversely, the more superficial the intention – to instruct on the higher level, to please on the lower – the shorter will be the book's staying power. By the same token, the less important the aim, the more easily will it be achieved. For every one *Paradise Lost* there are twenty honourable satires; for every honourable satire a hundred lampoons.

It was the sense of some such devolutionary process at work in Western culture which prompted T. S. Eliot to formulate his dissociation-of-sensibility thesis in the first place. Earlier critics and philosophers, from Schiller and Hegel onwards, had expressed the feeling of loss, of impoverishment and absence in modern civilisation. Marx made it possible to give this a quasi-scientific justification in terms of capitalism and its vitiating effect upon the organisation of social machinery. Yet does not Leibniz's lament suggest that Eliot's explanation, in terms of a much wider and more inevitable process within the very movement of modern history itself, in spite of class-organisation, is more plausible? And hasn't Eliot's thesis – for all the scepticism with which it is now held – been imitated and varied by numerous writers since, from Erich Heller to Michel Foucault? What we are concerned with, in short, is the devolution of the necessitated, sacred origination of culture to its secular, socially motivated forms. The sense of value – however pale it now seems – is the vestigial life of this sacred origination, and it is this which requires preservation. The entertainment industry will take care of itself.

This means that literary criticism, in its fundamental sense of discrimination between the value of different works, is endemic to any culture that has advanced beyond the level of the primitive – beyond the time, that is to say, when work may have been supposed to be produced according to need. Note that we need not say that the work was produced in order to *satisfy* the need – a view which would certainly be reductive of artistic value and indeed, as Wittgenstein saw, of religious experience itself. The ritual act Wittgenstein observes, does not '*aim* at anything: we act in this way and then feel satisfied'.[5] We have noted already that the descriptive and the evaluative are mixed freely in Aristotle. They will be found similarly mingled throughout the Renaissance: the forms and genres of poetry, say, are regarded as available to the poet in the Italian rhetoricians of the sixteenth century.[6] Their *value* is always contingent upon the genius or seriousness or holiness of the poet. In general, we can say, however, that the need to insist upon value in particular works increases as the idioms and conventions become less and less fixed. In Johnson's *Lives of the Poets*, the poet's life is retailed in simple outline: the end of each life is followed by a rapid survey of the work, in which its value is assessed according to its performance of certain tasks which remain more or less fixed, as they were in the Renaissance. Milton's 'Lycidas', to cite a familiar example, is found wanting because it confuses its genres, pastoral and elegy.[7] A later critic than Johnson might have found this a fusion rather than a *con*fusion and hence located the work's value in its successful creation of a new form, even if a form of only one instantiation.

It is with Coleridge, and Romanticism in general, that the new criticism begins in which the principal object of the enquiry is to locate the work's literariness. In the old world the literariness was given in the genre: not the *value*, note, but the *literariness*. A bad set of rhymed couplets celebrating the king's birthday was bad literature: a recognised task has been performed, but performed badly. This is in line with general critical practice from Aristotle to Johnson. Such procedures depended upon the acceptance of rhetoric as a more or less strictly definable set of weapons: the arsenal of a cultural hierarchy. Now of course it is a long time before the weapons of 'classical' literature, with its clear typologies and taxonomies, disintegrate into the world of free verse and abstract painting. But essentially, the new situation is crystallised in Coleridge's observation that 'a poem of any length neither can be, nor ought to be, all poetry'.[8] This was developed by Poe into the idea that a long poem is mostly prose: 'For this reason, at least one half of the *Paradise Lost* is essentially prose – a succession of poetical excitements interspersed, inevitably, with corresponding depressions – the whole being deprived, through the extremeness of its length, of the vastly important artistic element, totality, or unity of effect.'[9] Poetry is now being treated as something pure, divorced from the moral and the didactic, even from the public and thematic. Shelley – another prime influence on Poe – had already made the break from didacticism: the line leads thence directly to Rimbaud, with his contemptuous rejection of all but a few couplets of Racine and Baudelaire.[10] We are now on familiar ground, of course, well within the territory in which a poem is what it is, not what it allegedly 'says'. And this, we might feel, is where we came in. Let us observe some things: first, the 'classical' poem (that is, the poem which was supposed to have *said* something, and pointed to something beyond itself, as opposed to the symbolist poem which 'is' something), *was* no less something than the symbolist or romantic poem. The speech into which the moral or religious axiom or code was woven by the poet constitutes a new speech, which in turn needs interpreting. In this sense Aristotle was doing for Aeschylus and Sophocles precisely what F. R. Leavis did for Pound and Hopkins – sorting the wheat from the chaff. This means, in a sense, that Aristotle too is concerned with locating literariness. Nevertheless, we must observe the differences here. There is a profound difference between the critic for whom the principal task is to ascertain the excellence of the performance, because the themes themselves are holy, and the critic who, on the other hand, needs above all to recognise the poetry within the prose, in Poe's words. We may ascribe the emergence of a new kind of literary criticism in the nineteenth century to the need for criticism to adapt itself to new literary contents: to do justice to the modern poet's power of creating scenery that could be 'the embodied symbol' of feeling,[11] clearly demanded different tools from those used by Johnson or Dryden. We are no longer concerned with the varying skill of renditions of accepted tasks, but with the presence or absence of literature at all. In Verlaine's 'Art poétique' this is expressed in the contrast of 'musique' and 'littérature':

De la musique avant toute chose.
Toute la reste est littérature.

'*Musique*' is clearly Poe's 'poetry' (and indeed Coleridge's); '*littérature*' is the unredeemed mass of literary discourse, mere dead theme and attitude. In time, of course, this way of thinking led to the so-called literature without contents: if everything that can be described in other words (that is, content) is dead, clearly the valuable in literature – Verlaine's '*musique*', Coleridge's 'poetry' – must eschew the stateable or paraphrasable altogether and hence approximate towards nonsense or sheer language, or silence.

In fact, such a situation was an inevitable concomitant and constituent of the general evolution of modern society. What is now required of the critic is something much closer to that intuitive response the Japanese *haijin* expected of their critics: the good critic 'responds' to the good poem – to the image with grace or spirit, that has really captured the effect. In a sense all criticism had always in part been concerned with this. But, again, there is a crucial difference between the tradition which expects of its 'best' listeners and readers an accurate critique of performance, from the tradition which had eliminated everything else from its critical armoury. In point of fact, classical Japanese criticism, like our own value-judgement criticism, is no less and no more 'subjective' than that of the classical and Renaissance rhetoricians. All that has happened is that the new realism of language, and the new democratic culture in society, has obliterated the profile of the old rhetorical forms and themes, throwing more emphasis upon the value-judgement element which had always been part of the critical act.

In our own time – I mean the past twenty years – the importance of the value-judgement element in criticism has increased. Now more than ever, with a whole society of academic writers steeped in the methods of modern criticism, we need to be able to 'tell' who is genuine and who is phoney. No longer will it do to wait for the *avant garde* signs – the alienation, the rejection of success and the material, which were definite signs of quality in the old *avant garde*. These have been mastered, even by Hollywood. How can we know whether the new novel, jangling with archetypes, sophisticatedly aware of its own illusoriness, self-conscious, consciously ambiguous, and conscious of being consciously ambiguous, 'about' its own genesis – in a word, fulfilling all the requirements of the 'serious' novel – how can we tell whether the given offering is the real thing, or in Verlaine's word, *littérature*?

It is in this context that we must consider the role of the critical witness.

6 Meaning

The emergence of an essentially 'valorific' criticism, then, is characteristic of modern society – by which I hasten to add that I mean nothing but Western society over the past two hundred years or so. Tolstoy, to my knowledge, was the first critic who sensed in the increasing emphasis on beauty as ultimate criterion in aesthetics a significantly modern development. In *What is Art?*, Tolstoy specifically relates the rise of aesthetics (the 'science' of beauty) to the decline of that 'religious conception' which, he says, 'decides the value of the feelings transmitted by art'[1] in any age. Modern man invented beauty, in other words, to fill the gap left by religious belief. A valorific literary criticism is an obvious concomitant of such a development. More recent criticism has tried to explain 'bourgeois' aestheticism and its valorific criticism in ideological terms, as the effort of a class to sustain itself upon a system of values which are supposed to be 'universal' but are, in fact, designed to meet its own aims. I shall come to this matter in due course. All I want to stress here is that the question of beauty as ultimate aesthetic criterion, and of the emergence of a characteristically valorific criticism are both symptomatic of a general condition. The most signal characteristic of this condition is, in turn, the preoccupation with meaning in all senses of the term.

In a culture sure of its 'values', and more or less coherently organised in the form of a hierarchical pyramid – a culture such as existed, that is to say, roughly until the middle of the eighteenth century in Europe – the question of the meaning of artworks or literary texts hardly arises. I do not deny that an ancient tradition of hermeneutic criticism did exist: indeed, I shall be talking about this myself later (Chapter 8). But older ways of systematically 'deep-reading' texts, translating one set of facts (the words and images of the poem) into terms of another (the 'meaning' – Christian symbolism, Gnostic or Platonic ideas), differ in important respects from modern hermeneutical modes. The most important of these differences is the fact that,

71

in the older society, the meaningfulness of texts was as undoubted as the meaningfulness of life itself. And it is just the sense that literary texts share the meaning*less*ness of modern life (or might share it) that is so deeply characteristic of Romantic and post-Romantic civilisation. The most interesting expression of this development is the Baudelairean idea we have had to refer to more than once already, that a poem does not *mean* something, it *is* something. Older texts (classical texts) were supposed to have their meanings attached to them, as if by an invisible cord; modern texts to be somehow cut adrift from meaning in this sense. This has become the hallmark of specifically modernist criticism – a denial of 'meaning' in the sense of content. When I suggested above that we should call art-works symbols of unique representation, I certainly did not intend to deny them meaning in this or any other sense. It seems important, then, to examine closely the word *meaning* and the ways in which it is habitually used by critics. For to say that a work does not *mean* something but *is* something seems to be equivalent to saying it 'has no meaning'. This formulation suggests that meaning is something which can be had, or contained, like a fluid. It is certainly the misleading implications of our ways of expressing ourselves that have led many critics astray. In the first place, we must accept that *meaning* itself has many different meanings, and that these are often used interchangeably. Our first task, then, is to try to separate the different uses of the word *meaning*.

(i) THE MEANINGS OF 'MEANING'

We can in the first place distinguish two broad uses of the word. English, in its richness of reference and its overlayerings, has provided us with a signal test-case in giving *meaning* two basic meanings. The central problem of meaning is clarified rather than obscured by the fact that where French, German and Russian, for instance, have two distinct expressions for the ideas of *wanting to say something*, on the one hand, and *signifying* on the other, English has but one – *to mean*. English *to mean* means, or wishes to say, both *vouloir dire* and *signifier*; *meinen* and *bedeuten*; *khotit' skazat'* and *znatchit'*. This linguistic fact makes the problem of interpretation more, not less, clear; it obliges us to remember all the time that we cannot speak simply of 'the' meaning of a work, or that it 'means' something. We must bear in mind all the time that meaning is a complex, not merely complicated, business. Before we consider what a particular critic says of the meaning of a particular work, we must be sure what he means or intends to say: which of the meanings of the word 'meaning' is he drawing upon? Is it *signification* (*meaning*₁) or *intention* (*meaning*₂)?

This primary ambiguity of meaning is not to be resolved by merely agreeing to use either of the two basic meanings – *vouloir dire* or *signifier* – in different situations: we find that *meaning* is intrinsically ambiguous. We find, indeed, that even in its more narrowly defined meaning of signification, *meaning*₁, meaning is a complex notion. We can break down *meaning*₁ into six broad categories:

(1)   'Table' *means* 'table'
       signifie 'table'
       bedeutet 'Tisch'
       znatchit 'stol'
This is the translator's 'meaning'.

(2)   'Monkish' *means* 'of monks, monastic; characteristic of monks'.
This is the lexicographer's 'meaning'.

(3)   'Table' *means* a finite number of sense-data which will be encountered if certain sensory conditions are fulfilled. This is the phenomenalist philosopher's 'meaning', and it is a logically tightened version of the empiricist's 'meaning' in which we can say that 'table' *means* – and then point to an actual table. In this sense a table is a content of 'table'.

(4)   'Clouds mean rain';
'An ambulance means an accident';
This is the hermeneutic 'meaning', in which evidence is interpreted to yield a picture of events hidden from the eye. This category really includes (4*a*) – the superstitious meaning: 'Queen of Spades means death', in which an intrinsically unrelated phenomenon (the turning up of a particular playing card) is related by magic to another series of events. It is possible that certain forms of literary criticism fall into this category: critics like Harold Bloom and Kenneth Burke in effect say this kind of image *means* that kind of psychological process. The basic example of this 'meaning' is Freudian analysis.

(5) 'His presence means much to her';
    This is the sentimental 'meaning', and it is not to be set
    aside as a mere linguistic accident, a turn of phrase
    divorced from the primary *meaning*. We may find in the end
    that the importance of art in general is to be explained as
    sentimental meaning.

(6) 'He really means it'; the sincere 'meaning'.

These, then, are the six broad categories of *meaning*₁. Our concern is with the application of these categories to literary texts
and works of art in general. But a few preliminary observations
will be appropriate.

In the first place, we observe that although a great deal of
criticism and philosophy in fact assumes that by *meaning* we
mean only a kind of equivalence-giving, only two out of the six
categories – (1) and (2) – resemble the fluid/container account of
meaning: the word is a vessel to be filled with the content
divulged by the dictionary. It is generally this kind of *meaning*
that is assumed to be fallible and in the end dispensable: the
imprecision of actual usages is frequently held to discredit the
effectiveness of meaning and thence to discredit meaning itself –
Roland Barthes, for instance, observes that 'the dictionary can
be expanded, the grammar can be modified',[2] as if this were all
that were required to hole a belief in specific meanings below the
water-line.

Yet this view, appealing as it is, has its limitations. The young
linguist wants to know 'What does "bijou" or "Berg" mean?'
This is to ask for a word-for-word translation. (It is interesting,
incidentally, that this request is often cast in the form 'What *is*
"bijou" or "Berg"?' There seems to be a distinction between
these two modes of expression.) Later on in his language-
training, he wants to know if he can use 'aveugle' in the sense of
blind with rage or jealousy, or whether 'innocent' can be used in
this or that context. These questions want to know 'how', not
'what'. The request is for linguistic behaviour, not one-to-one
identification. The fluid/container theory, then, is already
breached: even lexicographic meaning is a matter of behaviour,
of *how*, not *what*. However, it is worth noting that 'jaune' is
always just *yellow* (never red or blue), and 'avoir' always *to have*,
never *to be* or *to know*. A complete relativism therefore is theoretically unsound. Our request for greater sophistication of linguis-

tic behaviour is a request for manoeuvrability, for the rules by which we can transfer contexts and levels of application. It does not imply a total rejection of contextual definiteness. On the contrary, we could not have linguistic contexts at all unless we first had a fixity of reference establishing primary contexts later to be interchanged. Thus, for instance, on the level of the vibrations of certain light waves 'yellow' always *means* 'jaune'. It is only when we want to try the word out in a different context that we start asking different sorts of questions about it.

This is important, since the questioning of meaning or the possibility of meaning, so common among more 'advanced' literary theorists, often takes the form of denying the existence of this primary level of more or less rigid reference. Language is like 'total science' as William van Orman Quine described it – a field of force, steady, but needing hemming from time to time.[3] In the end we shall find that everything depends upon our basic attitudes towards experience and language, and that our theoretical disagreements about language reflect deeper disagreements in world-view. In the present context, we have noted that though we start with an apparently simple fluid/container theory of meaning ('yellow' *means* 'jaune'), we very soon begin to talk about linguistic behaviour. Let us imagine the young lexicographer's or linguist's question, 'What does *le phagocyte* mean?' – 'It means "phagocyte".' 'Oh, what's a phagocyte?' The linguist would be irritated at the irony of the first answer he received, since obviously to know the English meaning of phagocyte would have been to know what 'le phagocyte' meant. But the sequence is illuminating. Both this question and the young lexicographer's 'What does "polyphiloprogenitive" mean?' illustrate that the giving of meanings shades off into a slightly different sort of meaning, that of our third category, the phenomenalist philosopher's, in which to ask what a word means is taken to be equivalent to asking for an account of a logical entity. We note that a certain slide has taken place: the young linguist's desire for linguistic behaviour is not quite the same as the lexicographer's desire for an account of a logical entity. But the linguist could 'use' *jaune* (when informed of the equivalence-rule) only because he knew what *yellow* was. So there is really no difference in essence between asking for the rules for the use of a word and asking for a breakdown of its logical structure. In both cases, certain situations of experience have to be assumed.

Thus the question 'What does "diaphragm" mean?' may be answered by ostension, by pointing to a diaphragm or the area where it is known to be. But what if the questioner persists, 'What's that?'? Could he be said to know what 'diaphragm' meant in that case? Is to say 'He knows what it means' the same as to say 'He knows how it works', 'He knows what its function is'? Further, can a medical student be said to know what 'diaphragm' means *better* or *more* than a lecturer in philosophy? Sometimes these questions are answered in the form of 'knowing how' to use a word. But this isn't very satisfactory either. Captain Boyle in O'Casey's play *Juno and the Paycock* knew how to use 'consols' when he said 'Consols is down half a percent', but he didn't really know what he meant. Structurally and in every linguistic way – even in the socio-linguistic way of appropriateness to conversational context – Captain Boyle was using the word correctly, yet, though what he said was in this case meaningful and might (let us say if Bentham, to whom the remark was addressed, had acted upon the tip) have resulted in appropriate action, we feel that the basic prerequisite of meaningful utterance is absent. It was just such a feeling – applied to words like 'God' and 'cause' and 'innate ideas' and 'self' – that motivated the various linguistic researches of Hume, Locke and Berkeley. The medical student doesn't – we feel – know the meaning of the word 'diaphragm' better than a philosophy lecturer, yet a certain minimum expertise is required before we can be said to know what any word means. The example of Captain Boyle's consols seems to indicate the direction of interrogation: he can't answer any questions about consols except that they are down half a percent: when Juno asks him reverently what consols are, he just says, 'Oh, Consols is – oh, there's no use tellin' women what Consols is – th'wouldn't understand'. He could use the term, as he had understood its usage linguistically when he came across it in the *Irish Times*. Yet beyond its grammatical and linguistic usability, and its vague applicability in the realm of finance, the term was devoid of meaning for him: he didn't know what he was saying, we say. Does this shade off into the case of the philosophy lecturer whose acquaintance with diaphragms is more limited than that of the medical student, and therefore whose stock of satisfactory answers to Juno-esque questions would run out sooner, making him seem Captain Boyle-like in respect of diaphragms? We feel uncomfortable answering these questions affirmatively: the philosophy lecturer *does* know what 'diaphragm' means. He could answer a number of crucial questions about it, stating that it was an organ of the body (or is it?) whose function is necessary to life, and so on. But the example does indicate an important and hazy area of enquiry: at some point the rules governing the correct use of a term shade off into those determining meaningful utterance; the two areas are not co-extensive, and this fact is philosophically worrying. What linguists call linguistic competence is more profoundly involved with what we know and understand in experience than is generally acknowledged inside technical linguistics. It is more than some basic aptitude for recognising well-formedness that is involved in the mastery of language: it is also a matter of grasping a common stock of experiential concepts.

It is clear, even from this brief set of remarks on some of the problematic aspects of *meaning*₁, that theories of meaningful utterance very early on establish themselves as theories of linguistic usage, but that theories of linguistic usage themselves depend upon certain fundamental facts about the human condition. It is rare that we can say, the meaning of X is Y, or even that X means Y. Even in the context of early language-learning and vocabulary-acquisition, requests for definition turn into requests for knowing *how* terms are used. Empiricism basically is a theory of meaning based upon a theory of experience – and vice versa. The only fundamental difference between a classical empiricist theory of meaning and a purely linguistic theory is that empiricism always insists that in the last analysis we have to define our terms as simple equivalences for experiential data.

Yet in spite of this, *meaning*₁ is still habitually approached as if it *were* a matter of fluid contents and exact equivalences, the argument being often that as soon as you have undermined belief in the exactitude of the equivalences, you have disposed of meaning *per se*. *Meaning*, that is to say, haunts our language as a spectre of plentitude.

We shall see that much of this mischief derives from setting up a fall-guy *meaning* (definitional, lexicographic, fluid) and then proceeding, from its manifest inadequacy, to a theory of signs which leaves meaning out altogether. Such fall-guy accounts of meaning ignore entirely the next three categories of meaning given above – the hermeneutic, the sentimental and the sincere. When we ask what does something mean, we are not merely asking for definitions (even of the enlightened sort just discussed, in terms of usage) but for something else. 'What does it mean?' we ask of a modern painting or poem. Our question is fair and valid, and ought not to be ducked by those qualified to answer. But it is a little more complex than is often understood, even by the questioner.

(ii) MEANING IN ART

In the context of modern art-forms, the question is often treated, even by experts, as if it could be answered purely in terms of our first three categories. Or rather, since it obviously *can't* be answered in those terms, it is treated as a foolish question: 'It doesn't *mean* anything, it *is* something.' The assumption has been so general since Flaubert and Poe that it is almost synonymous with modernist or *avant garde* critical thinking. The spectral notion behind it is that we can speak of a 'meaning', an equivalence, behind *some* works (classical ones), and that this relationship of equivalence no longer obtains. Wolfgang Iser, for instance, bases a whole theory of interpretation on a supposed 'classical' mode of interpretation which assumed that 'the work of art was a representation of a whole, if not the actual form of truth itself'.[4] (Hegel is behind this formulation, with his despair at the ability of the spirit to appear through the forms of Romantic art.) In point of fact, one may take leave to doubt whether art was ever really thought of in this way. The function of art in a world-view which assumed a certain meaningfulness in human life and its logical place in a benevolently ordered universe is surely not accurately defined as its being 'the representation of the actual form of truth itself'. It was more likely to have been thought of as illustrating the truth, reflecting its spirit, being part of it. It is a convenient Hegelian fiction that art ever was a reflection of the 'totality'. It is easy to see how, accordingly, Hegel found it relatively easy to write art off the map entirely.[5] In fact, art was never really what Hegel pretended he thought it was, so that, by the same token, its fragmentary modern equivalent was not really as invalid as he thought. Taken by itself, Iser's Hegelianism is not particularly misleading: it clearly reflects something of the alienated art of the post-Romantic period. Yet in conjunction with his description of alleged classical methods

of interpreting art, it becomes mischievous: classical interpretation, we are told, habitually and characteristically reduced art to
the representation of a 'hidden meaning'.[6] Nowhere does the
confused or uninspected use of the idea of *meaning*₁ wreak more
havoc than here. According to Iser, classical art represented
totality; it could be explained by the meaning it concealed – *the*
meaning, we note. There is no plurality here, no complexity, just
a simple embedded 'meaning'. This is the lexicographic *meaning*
and it has no right, I submit, to be here. The basis for Iser's
opinion that it has, is Henry James's story, *The Figure in the
Carpet*. In this story, a writer and a critic vie with each other for
the meaning of the writer's latest story: the story has a secret, a
meaning which, once understood, 'solves' the riddle of the
story's surface, and thereby in a sense cancels its reality. The
critic possesses the story's meaning, much as a savage might
possess someone's soul by finding out his secret name. Now it is
a good story, one which poses a good many interesting questions
about the relations of art and criticism. But its theory of meaning
is essentially rhetorical: no critic ever looked for 'the' meaning of
a text as Corvick seeks and finds 'the' meaning of Vereker's story
in James's tale. Apart from certain types of poetry (the riddles of
the Welsh bards, for instance), no art, classical or modern, is
really possessed of 'a' meaning, like the meaning of a riddle or
the multiple 'meanings' of a crossword puzzle. To base a theory
of interpretation upon the rejection of this supposed mode of
classical interpretation is surely mischievous. Iser implicitly
bases himself upon a postulation – and subsequently a rejection,
in the name of modernism – of meaning as a specific, definitional
thing, something which once could be grasped through classical
texts but can't through modern ones.

In point of fact, the critical quest, or the interpreter's quest,
has not traditionally been for meanings in this sense – answers
to riddles, invisible counterparts to figures in carpets, once
grasped, never forgotten. According to James, the text articulates in itself a meaning (the meaning that *is* itself, in modernist
terminology), but the critic goes on looking for something that
explains what in effect needs no explaining, since any explanation would cancel the new thing that has been created by referring it to another frame of reference. This constitutes an admirable critique of inferential criticism. Where Iser goes wrong is in
supposing that his distinction between meaning-as-effect and

meaning-by-explanation or interpretation enables us to describe modern texts accurately: 'It would not be unfair to say that, at least since the advent of "modern art", the referential reduction of fictional texts to a single "hidden" meaning represents a phase of interpretation that belongs to the past.'[7] On the contrary, I think it would be not only unfair but totally misleading.

The reaction to modern art is still, Iser rightly says, 'What's it supposed to mean?' But what does the 'average man' really mean when he asks this? Does he really expect explanation in terms of a hidden meaning? Because modern art-works have no total meaning, as classical works are supposed to have had, Iser is driven to postulate the necessity for a reading-theory to make up the gap in meaning: the modern work's meaning has to be made by the reader. This view is only necessary if we accept that modern texts have 'no' meaning of the sort Iser postulates in so-called classical works. If we deny the existence of such a meaning in classical texts, and suggest that the question of meaning really has to be answered in a different sort of way, we shall avoid this anomalous de-construction of the modern work into its various readings. Iser indeed postulates the need for 'readings' to compensate for the alleged lack of 'meanings' in modernist texts, much in the way that Barthes moves from *works* (classical, readable, authoritarian, pinned to one meaning) to *texts* (writable, modernist, confined to no meaning, do-it-yourself).[8] In each case, an over-simplified model of the so-called classical work which has a 'meaning' dictates a still more over-simplified model of the modernist text which hardly exists apart from its interpretations. In fact, if we keep clear the various kinds of *meaning*$_1$ that can be attributed to works of art, we shall see that classical and modern texts are less different than either Barthes or Iser suggests.

We can begin by pointing out that when the 'average man' asks 'What does it mean?' (where 'it' is, for example, a painting by Jackson Pollock or Mondrian), he really wants to know why the painter placed his pigment the way he did. This *may* take the form of asking 'What objects are represented?' The mistake often, of course, is to confuse the first type of question with the second. The confusion arises often because different sorts of modern painting are involved. The question 'What does it mean?' is more likely to be asked of a non-figurative painting than of a figurative one. In the case of the abstract work, the viewer-questioner implicitly assumes that paintings are basically representations of something and that the primary task of 'understanding' pictures is to work out 'what' is being painted (that is, represented). Thus, the question assumes *meaning*₁ in its phenomenalistic sense – the painting is constructed out of certain visual data. Yet this is due to conservatism of taste rather than to a radical misunderstanding. If this were not so, then clearly all figurative paintings of the same object or set of objects would be felt to have the same value, as photographs do. They would all 'mean' the same thing – Napoleon or a city street or whatever. Yet even an unexceptional man, whose taste stopped short at post-Impressionism, will probably make sharp distinctions between a portrait by Velazquez, for instance, and one by Reynolds, a Virgin by Raphael and one by Carlo Dolci. When tackled on this, such people normally admit that there is a quality present which they call 'beauty' or 'greatness', only they insist that it must be associated with recognisable images and objects, not with squiggles or abstract shapes. But whether they prefer Velazquez or Dolci, or are just bored by them both, these people rarely if ever ask 'What does it mean?' or, on the other hand, declare that these paintings that they admire *mean* the king or the Madonna depicted. The question of what these old masters 'mean' is certainly not one the hypothetical average viewer would answer simply, in terms of the identity of the subject, or in any way as if there were a 'key' which explained the picture. He is likely to insist, on the contrary, that it does not *mean* anything in that sense, but is beautiful or ennobling to look at, and that this is its function. Neither would he be so very wrong at that.

Thus, the average man's question, 'What does it mean?' needs a little more attention than is commonly given it. Among figurative painters, Picasso also provoked this response: the viewer felt that he did not know what a Picasso portrait with both eyes on the same side of the nose 'meant' because he did not understand the degree of the distortion: he did not understand why Picasso did *that*, and therefore did not know what the painting 'meant'. Anton Ehrenzweig postulated the operation of a different, wiser organ of vision (the unconscious, or remaining childhood element in the grown man) to explain why it is that Picasso portraits which seem on the face of it wildly unreal somehow don't seem odd.[9] Ernst Gombrich distinguished two main drives behind visual representation: first there is the 'matching' of design with external reality; then there is the complex tradition of inherited schemata of representation which is known as style.[10] It is the failure to admit the element of 'matching' — mimesis in literature — which vitiates so much recent literary criticism: in point of fact, the styles or discourses of art never detach themselves from the constant process of matching and re-matching. Ehrenzweig shows that a Picasso portrait — that of Ambroise Vollard, for instance — is not a rejection of the notion of matching (representation, realism) but, on the contrary, a refinement of it — a means of saying 'it' more truly than the inherited mode of realism would allow. We can verify the truth of Ehrenzweig's perception by turning to the example of Cézanne's portraits: what modern viewer — no matter how simple and uncultivated — even notices, much less is disturbed by, the fact that Cézanne's self-portrait of 1880 is full of wildly unrealistic colour-patches — tints of green and purple where it should be one simple flesh colour, for instance? This should not be accepted as a demonstration of the power of conventional seeing (the viewer doesn't notice these things because his vision is dulled and conditioned by socially imposed frames), but, on the contrary, as the proof of the convincingness of Cézanne's vision: it just doesn't look odd.

Neo-modernist criticism has built an entire theoretical edifice upon the modern artist's 'experimental' or anti-realistic devices, as if these did nothing but draw attention to themselves, and thereby destroy the usual realism of effect. From this, it deduces the self-referential nature of all significant modern art. Still more radically, Derrida has turned the recurrent sound-effects of poetry against themselves: they become evidence of language's intrinsic self-referentialism, and thus testify to our inability to refer to externally existent realities. Yet on neither the plane of ordinary language nor of art-language is this view justified. We could add to Ehrenzweig's examples innumerable others to prove that modern artists habitually use distortion to create a more-true-to-reality effect. What seems whimsical self-referentialism to the academic critic or the bemused layman, to the poet or to the discerning reader is penetrating accuracy:

In Midas' garden the simple flowers
Laugh, and the tulips are bright as the showers,
    For Spring is here; the auriculas

And the Emily-coloured primulas
Bob in their pinafores on the grass
As they watch the gardener's daughter pass.

Edith Sitwell explains the bright and exhilarating effects in these
lines in the following way: 'Emily is a countrified name, and pink
primulas remind me of the bright cheeks of country girls. Obviously I could not mean yellow primulas, since nobody is of that
bright yellow colour.'[11] Modern poets often expect a high standard of selection from their readers ('Obviously . . .') but the
modes of selection are not dissimilar from those required by
classical poets.

If the viewer wants to know 'what' is represented in an abstract painting, therefore, it is not this demand that really underlies his question. The Picasso portrait puzzles him, even though
he knows it 'means' a woman or a man. He is also nonplussed by
more recent figurative painters – by Willem de Kooning's red-
hot mommas, for instance, or alternatively by a whole range of
surrealist pictures. Salvador Dali frequently evokes this
response. His gift is precisely connected with the fact that he has
brought figurativeness (realism, in a simple sense) to this point:
his canvases are dramas without plot, allegories without keys,
rather like the novels of Kafka, about which similar questions
are still consistently raised. The same is true, in a slightly different way, of photo-realist and conceptualist painting, in which
the meticulously delineated objects and scenes seem devoid of
purpose. The puzzled viewer wants to know why he was cajoled
off the streets, where there are thousands of real cars and motor
bikes, to see a Max Parrish 'depiction' which is so 'real' that you
want to touch it – though without the wonder and joy of Giotto's
contemporaries. Here the question 'What does it mean?' shades
off into 'What's the point?' It was precisely this gap which was
exploited by the conceptualist and photo-realist painters and
sculptors of the 1970s. Here again, Iser's model of 'meaning' as a
key, or extra-textual signification, leads him astray. The point of
pop art (an earlier example of this sort of art) is, says Iser, that
'by explicitly refusing even to contain a hidden meaning, it
directs attention to the origins of the very idea of hidden meanings, that is, historically conditioned expectations of the
observer'.[12] It is true that pop art, like conceptualist painting,
plays its images off against assumed cultural expectations; but

Iser's postulation of a tradition of hidden meanings still leads him to distort the point of the bemused viewer's questions, and therefore of the art itself. It is not a 'hidden meaning' that the viewer misses in pop art, it is simply a purpose: why has he painted *that* like *this*? And this is a very different sort of question. Iser's error is complemented by one of Susan Sontag, which he himself cites: 'Abstract painting', Sontag asserted, 'is the attempt to have, in the ordinary sense, no content; since there is no content there is no interpretation. Pop art works by the opposite means to the same result; using a content so blatant, so "what it is", it, too, ends by being uninterpretable.'[13] In fact, it is simply not true to say that abstract painting has no content, any more than it is true to say that Mallarmé's poetry or Joyce's prose has no content. It is precisely this kind of false modernism which the present book is intended to oppose. Admittedly, Sontag's qualifying phrase, 'in the ordinary sense' is vague enough to allow any kind of interpretation of 'meaning'. But it is plain that *meaning* is being identified with subject or realism here, and again this won't do. The meanings of traditional works of art are certainly set forth through the medium of recognisable things and persons, and therefore deeply related to their identities. But in no sense can we say that their meanings reduce to these identities.

In point of fact, not even a photograph can be said to 'mean' the things caught in it. A holiday snap doesn't *mean* Uncle Joe, Auntie Lil and deckchairs on the beach at Brighton. It is nonsense to say that it does. The only sense in which I could meaningfully ask what a photograph means would be in sense (4) or (5) of our list of *meaning*₁, the sentimental or hermeneutic ones: 'It means that you're a liar' or 'It means a lot to me'. The only other relevant questions about the 'meaning' of a photograph would be circumstantial ones. Who was the lady sitting there? and other questions relating to matters of fact. To transfer this already false picture of meaning (a photograph can't really be said to mean anything) to trees and cars and other objects is worse than obtuse. Trees and cars don't have their meanings in themselves, they have no 'meaning' at all. The world is everything that is the case, as Wittgenstein said. But this doesn't mean that it means only what can be expressed. The means of expression are severely restricted, and we cannot say that the world means anything, or that it is true, only that it is.

The meaning, therefore, of even the most photographic of paintings cannot be decided purely by reference to the identification of what it represents. Even the simplest observer will feel that the difference between a great portrait and a merely accurate likeness involves us in reconsidering the question of what either 'means'.

The next step is to see that when the difficult modern picture has been unravelled the onlooker will not say, '*Now* I see what it means' but rather 'Now I get it' (which in fact means, interestingly enough, 'Now I get something out of it'). In fact, it is obvious that no question of *meaning*₁ in the first, second or third senses given above is intended in this case: there is no question of the painting's being *equivalent to* anything else. In other words, it is not the significative sense of meaning (*bedeuten* or *signifier*) that is really involved in the question, 'What does Picasso mean by this?' but the second general sense of 'intends'. People who ask the question of the Picasso-apologist are generally triumphant when he begins to hedge, 'Well, he means what he says', or evasively counter-thrusts, 'What does it mean to *you?*' or concedes 'He doesn't actually *mean* anything in the sense that . . .'.

In point of fact, the embarrassed apologist would be quite justified in asking, 'What does Leonardo's "Virgin on the Rocks" *mean?*' The question is no more answerable of Leonardo than of Picasso, and the strategic manoeuvre would or should have the virtue of reminding everyone that putting questions in the wrong form often puts us off the scent. The puzzled viewer's question is – if it is in good faith – a request for enlightenment, and it really means what my analysis above suggests it means: 'What is the artist up to? Why does he paint it that way? What is the point of it all?' He could be made to see that perhaps this was the purpose of the painter's using these devices. But anyway such questions would have the value of re-directing attention from meaning in the sense of equivalence, or paraphrasable anterior 'content', neither of which notions are useful in describing art-works, to meaning in a more complex sense – a mixture of *vouloir dire* and, perhaps, hermeneutic or superstitious meaning. If the questioner could see that his question would be just as difficult to handle in respect of Leonardo or Rembrandt as in respect of Picasso or Kandinsky, he might have learned something valuable about art in general. For it should by now be obvious that the question 'What does it mean?' about a painting is itself incapable of being answered. Obviously, the answer to this question 'What does it mean?' must begin 'It means that . . .' and clearly the 'It means that' formula cannot apply to paintings. What does Christ mean when he says, 'Know thyself'? 'He means that we should do such and such.'

Similarly, what does the theory of relativity mean? 'It means that certain errors of Newton's can be accounted for; that we are no longer warranted in making such-and-such assertions.'

What does this sentence from Wittgenstein's *Tractatus Logico-Philosophicus* mean? 'It means that a fact should be correspondent with a situation in the world.'

What does *Teufel* mean? 'It means *devil*.'

It is evident that there is no possible sense in which such *meanings* could be predicated of a painting.

It is doubtful that any serious human error or fallacy with regard to the most serious matters that confront human beings has ever derived *entirely* from a mistaken use of language, as logical positivists, linguistic analysts and ordinary language philosophers have from time to time asserted. There is obviously some profound disturbance at the root of the attacks upon meaning – as traditionally understood – which figure so prominently in modern literature and criticism, and I don't wish to spirit this away by logical analysis. Yet there seems no doubt that a great deal of confusion has been caused, and a good deal of nonsense generated, by the mischievous use of the word 'meaning'. Wolfgang Iser – a notably serious and responsible critic, of considerable sensitivity – provides an example that could be repeated more or less endlessly. In treating 'meaning' as an entity which once lay within receptacles called works of art but which was rejected by modern works of art, Iser and others have obscured the real nature of works of art themselves. For my suggestion is that all art-works, literary and musical, aspire in this respect to the condition of painting, and that meaning is no more to be predicated of sonatas and poems than of portraits and landscapes. Yet like portraits and landscapes, the epics, dramas and lyrics of literary tradition are inescapably *meaningful*, and no account of their nature or functioning can begin to be given without this fact being accepted. It has never been the case that a work of art could be explained in terms of *a* meaning existing in relation to itself: yet equally, it has never been the case (in the fifth century BC or the twentieth AD) that a work of art has been *meaningless*.

A look is meaningful; a present means something; a person's presence means something else; what does 'The Wreck of the Medusa' mean?

(iii) ART-WORKS AS SIGNALS

Our difficulties begin here. Art-works are nothing if not meaningful, yet, resisting translation into equivalent propositions, and therefore being in effect undiscussable, they appear to want to behave as if they had no meaning. I have called them symbols of unique representation, with deliberately paradoxical intent. For a symbol is something which essentially isn't unique, in the sense in which we have to call art-symbols unique. Perhaps we need some terminological clarification. C. S. Peirce – to whom we owe the general structure of modern semiotics – distinguished between symbols, indexes and icons.[14] By symbols Peirce meant what Locke meant when he called words signs of 'general ideas'.[15] In Peirce's view, words, sentences, books and other conventional signs are symbols. If we think of a symbol as a very highly conventionalised sign we shall not go far wrong. An index, in Peirce's understanding, is a part of a natural event or process or phenomenon, which nevertheless functions as its sign; this corresponds exactly to my third category of meaning, 'Clouds mean rain'. His icons, finally, are of course representations, pictures, bearing a structural and evocative resemblance to the reality they mirror. This afforded Wittgenstein the meat of his picture-theory of meaning in the *Tractatus*. Peirce himself suggested that an index, for instance, could also be iconic – a barber's sign might be a picture of a barber or a razor, for instance. Peirce's tripartition was simplified by Susanne Langer into a dichotomy of symbol and sign,[16] and it is this dichotomy I prefer to use myself. The symbol, as Langer defines it, is conceptualised, as it is in Peirce. The sign, on the other hand, is tied to its situational occurrence, and has no use outside it. Thus, a sign (in this Langerian sense) is like Peirce's index: it is part of an action-situation and has $meaning_1$ in my fourth sense. It can 'stand for' danger, for instance, and can act as a stimulus. This sort of meaning may be described as sign-meaning. It is noteworthy that such signs have a history, and thus a certain degree of conventionalisation. Indeed, they could not have their type-(4) meaning if they had not. A road-sign, for instance, might be thought a symbol, since it is conventionalised. But although the two converging lines on a white field *mean* narrowing of the road ahead *on all British roads*, this sign doesn't work off the road, that is, out of the context in which it functions. We can't make up a sentence using this sign, for instance. That is, such signs require a context of understanding or agreement to function at all. In animal situations, we find this context made by agreement or perhaps (though this is semiotically as well as biologically contentious) by instinct: animals have innumerable ways, for instance, of scenting danger – an unusual quietness, or a particular smell. Thus far, the 'neutral' element – the stillness of a glade, or the contrary movement of a branch or bush – is de-neutralised by the animal's understanding: they play a semiotic role, they are no longer neutral elements. Alternatively, human beings can grant such a semiotic status to things by the de-neutralising effect of an agreement. This is meaning by convention; we must respect the peculiar quality of this sign-agreement, with its more natural affinity to the animal danger-situation. 'Your visit means a lot to me', 'Clouds mean rain': like the road-sign meaning, this kind of meaning is non-transferable, and does not give us general propositions and rules. It is not possible to combine them beyond their actual or possible occurrence into discursive forms. It is worth noting that symbols used in discursive forms are sometimes used in this way: a word – which is correctly speaking a symbol – may be used to do the work of a sign, but only by a special agreement or by a contextual de-neutralisation of the symbol's 'correct' usage. Thus, 'When the word "box" occurs in a sentence I use, it will be the sign for you to leave'. In this case, 'box' is gutted of its usual, symbolic meaning: it is de-neutralised by agreement. Symbols are combined according to grammatical rules and in accordance with their rules of being, that is, with the laws of logic. We notice that in the case of the word being de-neutralised, it does so by joining the universe of *things*: the word becomes a mere thing, a trigger or signal, in leaving the world of symbolic discourse and joining that of animal signs or local agreements.

Is it too remote to suggest that the symbols of art are symbols which are de-neutralised, and thus are being used in a *signal* way? This would help to explain their unique, untranslatable quality, and also their deep-reaching associations with layers of the mind inaccessible to rational discourse. It is clear that with these qualities – untranslatability, untransferability, signal quality – art-works and literary texts approach the condition of non-linguistic signs: that is to say, the condition of objects. The poem is a palimpsest, an old stone dug up in a field. As such its words may sometimes appear terribly simple. After the exciting explications of the critic – his language bristling with absolute terms and ultimate solutions or with technical schemata filched from psychoanalysis or linguistics such as the writer himself can often hardly be supposed capable of understanding – the student may be disappointed to turn to the actual words themselves, which may be no more abstruse than 'My heart aches and a drowsy numbness pains My sense' or 'Tomorrow shall be my daunsynge day' or 'My life closed twice before its close'. The experiential facts of the poem are likely to be basic and simple: a man is bored, or frustrated or missing somebody, or feels guilty. The poet is – unlike the god-critic – a man like ourselves. Yet his words have the power to call us to the edge of consciousness, and listen, suspending the wandering agitations of normal consciousness. They are both simple and complex. This complexity is quite different from the critic's complicatedness: the proliferation of verbiage produced under the illusion that the more he says the more scientific he becomes, by which the critic seeks to disguise his own failure to respond to the poem. The delicate powerful facts of the poem sunk in the continuum of human experience in human culture in human history are complex: we can never say enough about them and yet the little is always too much.

Yet the poem cannot be consigned to the realm of the non-linguistic: they are *not* just signs and warnings, any more than sighs and groans – betrayals of interior emotion to be de-coded in terms *of some other meaning* – are symbols translatable into different equivalents. They are essentially themselves. They are eloquent, even in their dumbness. It is not for nothing that we feel most fully liberated through these unique object-like signs which refuse the civilised mode of free linguistic commerce. And this eloquence (the very existence of good taste and of literary criticism itself) can be learned: it *is* daily learned. We reject the ignorant man's I-know-what-I-like claims because we know that experience and familiarity with these signs-that-are-not-signs alters our sense of their 'meaning': the feeling persists that they are to be understood, not merely reacted to, as an animal reacts to a danger signal, or a driver to a Stop sign.

Now, it is significant that we so often use the language of signs in describing our experience of works of art: we speak of how we reacted, how we responded, not merely of whether we understood. This is a significant difference from the ordinary language situation: we do not speak of reacting to a sentence, unless the meaning of the sentence acquires another complexion, unless, that is, it functions as a sign, is de-neutralised, and acquires a signal property. Ordinarily we do not speak of responding to a sentence but of understanding it. Admittedly, there might be the makings of a *langue-parole* dispute here: those who distrust Saussure's distinction (as I do myself) might be inclined to say that in fact there was no occasion ever to suppose language in a vacuum, and that understanding is always understanding in a particular situation. Nevertheless, I shall maintain that the essential property of discursive statements is that they require to be understood and that their modality is that of understanding, not responding: they can be understood without being responded to. They must be understood before they are responded to.[17]

If it is the defining characteristic of all discursive symbolisms that they are to be understood, and of signs that they are to be responded to, or acted upon, is it not the defining characteristic of art-languages that they require both to be understood *and* reacted to, and that the act of comprehending them is not sufficiently defined unless both things are taken into account? That is to say, the statements of art-works are neither to be analysed purely for their 'meaning' in the first three of our senses above, nor purely in terms of their cash-value in sign-terms. Any hermeneutics which takes the art-work merely as a semiotic or a semantic unit to be dissected for its unravellable significations is neglecting the signal quality of art-works. Any criticism, on the other hand, which adopts a wholly rhetorical approach – regarding them as incomprehensible icons, which are somehow responded to but not understood in the ordinary sense – is neglecting the essentially symbolic quality of art-works: they are to be understood, as well as responded to.

In this respect, all art aspires to the condition not of music, or of painting, but of literature. If it is the temptation of the literary critic to treat literary texts as if they were all signification, it is the cardinal temptation of the music critic to treat music as if it were 'pure' sound, and the art critic painting as if it were devoid of signification and merely representational, or organic or sound-or-shape in themselves. It is, of course, the nature of the respective idioms that creates these temptations: literature is *like* the ordinary language which traffics in significations, just as painting, for instance, is like the world it represents (being, that is, purely visual, with no symbolism or semantics), or music like the world of pure sound, with no assignable meanings. Modern theory has been eager to push these resemblances to the utmost. It still seems important, therefore to emphasise that the respective idioms of literature, music and painting *are* languages, and that their products cannot ever be reduced to pure sound or pure icon. In each case we must work to understand as well as to see or hear: seeing and hearing, in the case of painting and music, are in fact faculties of understanding, as well as ocular and auditory sense modes.

What this amounts to, in respect of literature, is that we are obliged to *interpret* the various signs that make up the text, both in themselves and in the ensemble they help to make up. I have already declared myself against an inferential criticism – one which interprets the text by referring it to some order of meaning outside itself: it is in the nature of literary texts that they shut off the symbol's lines of communication with exteriority in constituting an art-surface taut with a perpetual two-way pull. This does not mean that the symbols have no meaning. It means only that to understand their meaning we have to learn the artist's peculiar language. The essence of this language is that it functions signally: the text creates a danger-situation of its own, and it is only within this situation that it can be responded to. But to grasp this situation we have to understand the symbol. That is to say, its meaning has to be negotiated. This is where criticism comes in (and in this respect every reader is a critic). For the work seems helpless, unable either to refer to or interpret itself. It forms no situation to tell us how to read it. The natural sign (the cloud that means rain, the moving twig that means danger to the bird, the agreed-on word that triggers an action) is able to function because of the contexts of convention, instinct or experience within which it has its being. It would be a very foolish as well as a very remarkable bird which stopped to wonder whether the moving branch in the sinisterly silent glade *necessarily* meant a hunter behind a bush. (In fact, that is what a great deal of literary criticism consists of – the superfluous debating of remarkable, foolish birds.)

Now one conclusion to be drawn from this helplessness of the literary text is that it is up to the critic or the reader to furnish the context that in turn supplies the meaning. This conclusion has been drawn by whole schools of modern critics and I shall return to it in due course. Quite the reverse conclusion is that the work in fact does tell us how it is to be read, and that it does this purely by the particular configuration of its elements. We have come to the frontier of this highly contentious issue at last: unlike discursive statements, art-statements require to be read in particular ways, since they cannot be simply analysed for their signification. They are neither, as we have seen, purely symbolic nor purely iconic.

Broadly speaking, modern criticism and philosophy set out to analyse not what we do mean but what we could mean – the sense-capacity of speech and not the intentions of speech. Russell's theory of descriptions, for instance, sets out certain lines along which the implications of utterances are to be pursued, and it enables us to distinguish between intention and import. What is interesting or useful in utterances is not what I intend to say, but what conclusions can be drawn from what I say, what are the implications of my utterance. If a man were to say, after people's replies and remarks on every sentence he utters, 'No, that is not what I meant at all', his listeners would very soon conclude not that their understanding was inadequate, but that he was not using language properly.

That is to say, the things we say have import: what we intend is only what we succeed in saying. This means that intention only has relevance so far as it helps us to grasp import: what he says is what matters, not what he means to say: what he means to say is relevant only until we grasp through it the import of what he says. This import can be structured, it is not free; and so we can reasonably say that once a man has committed himself to utterance, his utterance is not his, it is not an intention but an import. And if, in our earlier example, the man who kept protesting finally did manage to get through to his questioners, either they would have to admit that they didn't understand what he had said, but do now, or that he had earlier said something different, which their questioning has now modified into something else which they do understand. In this sense they could say that if his new statement *B* was what he meant when he uttered *A*, the import of *A* did not mean *B*, so that he had misused the language.

It is this attitude towards utterance which distinguishes the work of the New Critics and the other formalist schools of the century. The question they seek to answer is, 'What does a text mean?' That is, 'What is its import?' The sentence-structures and semantic rules to which we commit ourselves have certain ranges of import, which we are not at liberty to break. The text is what it succeeds in saying, not what the writer/speaker might later protest he *meant* to say. It is this fact which led Paul Valèry to say that a poem once written no longer belongs to the poet. Unfortunately, however, it is not always easy to establish this import. The literary text, we have seen, has no precisely specifying context; it constitutes its own danger-situation; it seems helpless and dumb. What are we to make of these complex signs or symbols? Can we confidently set about the matter of establishing import merely by attending to signification? Or must we look beyond-signification-(*meaning*$_1$) to intention-(*meaning*$_2$)? Must the poem mean everything and anything the commentator wants it to mean? Is the question, what does the poet mean to mean, relevant? This is the next question we have to examine.

7 Intentions/Intensions

To ask the question, what does the poet mean to mean? is to run foul of the Intentional Fallacy, of course. Much as this key concept of the New Criticism has been bombarded in recent years, its essential spirit remains with us, and probably always will.[1] The feeling that the reasons why a poem is so-and-so and such-and-such must reside, we agree with Coleridge, inside the poem, not outside it in history or biography: we are so far right in refusing to let the poet's otherwise expressed intentions of meaning influence our judgement of what he succeeded in saying. Yet when we inspected the word 'meaning', as it is applied to artworks, it was to find that it is unprofitable to ask, what is the meaning of a literary text or a painting, as if that question could be answered simply by unravelling the significations of the elements it is composed of. These elements 'mean' in a slightly different sense: they are meaning*ful*, and this may remain the irreducible quality of all art-works. They are meant, they are uttered and they matter to us. It was the fault of formalist and structuralist criticism that they assumed only a single meaning for 'meaning', and thus assumed that modernist works are absolutely different from classical works, since modernist texts cannot be 'explained' as classical ones can. In fact, classical works too refuse to be deciphered for their import without reference to their intent and meaningfulness. Of both sorts of work we need to ask, what does it mean, in this more complex way.

The feeling of dissatisfaction with pure formalist readings, therefore, derives not from any deep disagreement about what literature is, but from a fundamental dissension from its view of the act of reading or apprehending texts. We found that strict formalist or textualist criticism habitually imported its value-judgements and its modes of understanding, while claiming to be simply unravelling the formal interrelations of signs. This meant in effect that these critics were cheating not only about the nature of what lay before them but about the way what lay before them was read: if texts are something more than, other

94

than, sets of interrelated signs bearing only semiotic significance, reading itself is more than, and other than a reaction, passive and infallible, to these sets of signs. In fact, these errors are related: the error of regarding the text merely as a semiotic construct is the obverse of that of regarding reading as mere understanding, in the sense of understanding a proposition in logic. It is the use of the word 'meaning' that often promotes these errors: texts do not merely *mean* in the sense of signification, they mean in the sense of intending and warning and simply being meaningful. We have found that speaking of poems as being meaningful might well help us avoid many of the mistakes made by critics who speak of meaning and conceive of it as a definite, fluid-like thing which is or is not present 'in' the work.

(i) SCANSION-THEORIES: CONTEXTUALISM, TEXTUALISM, DE-TEXTUALISM

The question 'What does the poem mean?' therefore, is more complicated than is often assumed. Formalistic answers – and those related answers basing themselves on the semantics and semiotics of the text-and-nothing-but-the-text – require to be expanded: no account simply in terms of the text's signification will do. A great deal of recent criticism has concerned itself with modifying quasi-formalist approaches. Broadly speaking, there have been two major kinds of exploration. The first bases itself upon the need to relate the text to its origination out of social, political and historical factors: the text cannot be read in isolation. The contention is no longer that we need to know some of the 'background' to the text, but that the text itself is constituted by its surrounding and preceding history, which can therefore no longer be regarded as extrinsic and irrelevant to analysis. This general contention I shall call contextualist, since it expands works into their contexts. The second mode is inverse in movement: essentially it diminishes texts, concerning itself with the act of reading or apprehending the text. It begins from an acknowledgement of the necessity of taking account of the fact that texts require to be 'realised' (and thereby released) by the act of reading, and that therefore they cannot be considered as if they were inert or autotelically meaningful. This general mode I shall call de-textualist, since its attack basically is upon the idea of the 'text' as self-sufficient construct. If we distinguish between these two modes of enquiry, a middle position – the more traditional text-oriented view or set of views I have variously, and I'm afraid rather loosely, referred to as formalist or structuralist – we can fairly enough descry three broad theories of scansion which are also theories of meaning: contextualist, textualist and de-textualist.

These three theories are by no means mutually exclusive. None is independent of the others, though some proponents claim them to be. In particular, there is considerable ambiguity in the role of structuralism. Structuralism is generally presented as a textualist movement, using Saussurean linguistic procedures to establish the autonomy of texts on purely semiotic grounds. Yet because its purpose, at least in the classical Lévi-Straussian form, was to purify texts of their phenomenal individuality by relating them to pre-existing laws of structure, structuralism must really be classed as a contextualist mode. As if to confirm this view, it leans towards the determinism which is so generally characteristic of contextualist modes. On the other hand, many writers often associated with structuralism – Barthes and Foucault, in particular – have produced work of a marked de-textualist bias, and the relations between classical structuralism and what is fashionably known as post-structuralism or de-constructionism are, as we shall see, close and intrinsic. Foucault (who, it is true, generally disowns structuralism) attempts to place texts in an 'exteriority' of discourse which has the effect at once of contextualising and de-textualising them. No suggestion is made here, therefore, that these three broad modes of approach can be treated in isolation.

Neither, on the other hand, do I suggest that any one critic practises any of these modes with complete purity and rigour. On the contrary, the effectiveness of much of the work produced by critics who could reasonably be called contextualist, de-textualist or textualist derives precisely from the actual impurity of their practice. It is nevertheless necessary to present each of the modes in a harsh, somewhat humourless light, in order to bring out their implicit shortcomings. Fundamentally, my contention is that the enlightened act of reading partakes of some of the spirit of all three modes, and therefore that any critic who exaggerates an allegiance to any one is likely to run up against its limitations in an inhibiting form.

If the pure textualist insists that the poem always carries its information on the surface and that no other information is required to understand it, de-textualist theories begin from the belief that the act of reading a poem is not posterior to and extrinsic to the poem itself, but is intrinsic to it. In this view, the poem is realised and released by the reader's attention and understanding. Now this has produced a whole series of critical modes which have the effect of de-materialising the work, which becomes a mere occasion for the reader's fantasies. The best example of this tendency is perhaps the *opera aperta* of Umberto Eco.[2] In Eco, the work is 'expanded' beyond the limits of a textualist reading, but only at the expense of its own reality: it becomes nothing, in seeming to be the occasion for everything. Pierre Macherey's verdict on this tendency seems worth repeating: '[The work] has not one meaning but many: though this possible indefinite multiplicity, a quality or effect accomplished by the reader, has nothing to do with that real complexity, necessarily finite, which is the structure of the book.'[3] Macherey is right, surely, to insist that texts are not infinite, and to suggest strict bounds to the room available for interpretation. All theories which allow the work to become a mere template for the reader's fantasy disintegrate the work in the act of expanding it. Such is the case with Barbara Herrnstein-Smith's theory of the poem as merely 'fictive', a mere accidental obstruction creating infinite numbers of poems by the odd shapes it happens to cast upon the ether.[4]

The more rigorous and scientific de-textualist modes have recognised this danger. This is particularly true of those de-textualists who adhere to Husserlian phenomenology. Wolfgang Iser, for instance, wishes to tie the reading to the text, much as Macherey does: a literary text, Iser asserts, 'initiates "performances" of meanings'.[5] And yet this very reasonableness of Iser's, in so honestly limiting the scope of phenomenological reading, in fact undercuts itself. What is the difference between saying that texts 'initiate performances of meanings' and saying that they formulate meanings in themselves? It was this latter idea of the self-contained 'meaning' in the text which Iser had intended to discredit by showing that it is the act of reading which creates the text. But if any statement about a reading must be checked back against a fact in the text, what is the difference between text and reading? Why not simply transcribe or describe the textual facts, with the understanding these facts are also effects (something always understood in rhetoric) designed to bring about certain responses in the reader? I do not say that it is never relevant to study reading. It is a question simply of being aware of what is happening, and of the significance of what is being claimed.

What phenomenology claims is that an adequate explanation of how texts mean must derive from the analysis of the act of reading, because without the reading, as it were, there is no text. What it achieves is largely the re-stating of the problem that needed to be solved – a collapsing of reading into textual pre-structure. This is in accordance with common sense, and it should also be pointed out that, the theoretical palaver over, there is no real difference between, for instance, the way Wolfgang Iser analyses a novel like *Tristram Shandy*, and the way Ian Watt analyses *The Ambassadors*, or Leavis *Heart of Darkness*. This is important, because it is often claimed that criticism cannot or should not proceed without a theory behind it, the implication being that critics like Watt and Leavis didn't really know what they were doing. This is pernicious nonsense: there is no demonstrable relationship between the possession of a 'theory' and the practice of criticism. I have tried to show that the authentic act of criticism is recognisable by its violation of theoretical rules, by its reliance upon the intuitive and the inexpressible. Whether the critic chooses otherwise to indulge himself in something called Theory (as I am doing here) is quite beside the point.

Whenever phenomenological analyses have any value, there is always present a theoretical impurity, an implicit trust in unspoken modes of cognition. In *Qu'est-ce que la littérature?*, an influential proto-phenomenological work, Sartre states that 'the process of writing . . . includes as a dialectical correlative the process of reading, and these two interdependent acts involve two differently active people. The combined efforts of author and reader bring into being the concrete and imaginary object which is the work of the mind. Art exists only for and through other people.'[6] Now it is clear from this classic de-textualist statement that the phenomenology of reading was for Sartre a philosophical desideratum. He is opposing the 'bourgeois' notion of the autotelic work, self-contained and indifferent to the rest of the human race. But Sartre's eminently sane philosophy of literature as a meaningful and teleologically purposive activity is one thing; his brief sketch of the reading-experience quite another. He does not, any more than Wolfgang Iser or Roman Ingarden, succeed in making the analysis of the reading-process seem indispensable to the understanding of literary texts.

Now Sartre's case is especially interesting, since the implicit de-textualism of his phenomenology is adulterated by an equally implicit contextualism: he places the phenomenology of reading in a greater context, that of man in society, and it is this greater context which raises *Qu'est-ce que la littérature?* so far above the mere technicalities of phenomenological analysis. This greater context was later to clarify itself into an overtly Marxist theory of history. If Iser's work shows how closely related are textualist and de-textualist theories (Iser ties the reading so closely to the text that a symbiosis takes place), Sartre's demonstrates another type of kinship – that between de-textualist theories such as phenomenology, and contextualist theories such as Marxism. As phenomenologist, Sartre was inherently a de-textualist: the work was released from non-being by being realised through the act of reading: as crypto-Marxist, he was implicitly contextualist; the work acquired significance only as its relationship to history was understood. As crypto-Freudian, on the other hand, he was later to interpret works in terms of their provenance from the writer's early family history.

Marxist and Freudian modes of reading are both implicitly contextualist, in that they dissolve the work's independence into the immediately preceding psychic or social history. By far the greater number of significant contextualist theories have been Marxist, however. All psychoanalytic theories tend towards a structuralisation of the text: they tend, classically, to 'reduce' the text to the psychoanalytic structures, types and traces that can be detected in it. And this is a different activity from the Marxist one of relating the text to its historical surrounding. I shall therefore take Marxist theories as being definingly contextualist. The broader implications of this will be considered later. Here I wish to take a particular instance of a genuine theory of reading which is also specifically Marxist, that of V. I. Voloshinov.[7] Voloshinov introduces the notion of 'intonation' to explain how it is that we make sense of textual data. A literary text, he argues, is something like a conversation between two friends in a closed room, which we are permitted to overhear. He gives the example of a single syllable, 'Well . . . ' (Russian '*Noo* . . .'). The vocable is spoken by one friend for the benefit of his only listener. The interloper (the reader here) can make no sense of this, unless he has prior knowledge of the preceding situation, and can therefore catch the 'intonation' of the syllable pronounced. The effect, and therefore the *meaning*, of the syllable therefore depends upon the context in which it is pronounced. This is not entirely true, in fact: even in the situation outlined by Voloshinov, it would make a difference if the syllable spoken had been 'Damn! or 'Rubbish!' or 'Darling . . .'. The language in which the syllable is spoken supplies us with some information, but – Voloshinov is right in stressing – not enough. Textualist theories assume that all we need is the words used and a knowledge of the language they are written in. Contextualist theories such as Voloshinov's point out that this information is, on the face of it, inadequate: we could lay claim only to a very partial understanding of 'Well . . .' if we knew nothing of the immediately preceding emotional or social history of the speaker and his listener. All literature, Voloshinov asserts, is like such a conversation, not in being private, but simply in requiring a great deal more orientation and information before its texts are to be properly understood. It is the writer's task, says Voloshinov, to supply us with as much contextual information as is needed to understand the vocables that make up the text.

For such a purpose a purely textualist analysis would obviously be inadequate. Let us imagine that a stylisticist with a particular interest in phonetics tries to account for the meaning of the single syllable 'Well . . .' entirely in terms of the combination of syllables involved – the opposition of bilabial frictionless continuants and dental non-fricatives. Subsequent reading of the situation tells him what the state of affairs is, but he pretends that he has arrived at his interpretation of the syllable purely on internal or phonetic grounds. It is because of such absurdities that Fish proclaimed the new 'affective' stylistics. If a pure linguistic analysis is inadequate, speech-act theory might help us eke out these implausible rigmaroles with a more reasonable theory of utterance. But this, too, as we saw, is inadequate. Speech-act theory can give us the speech-rules of ordinary language as exploited by the writer in a given situation. What Michael Riffaterre said of grammar applies also to speech-act interpretation: it can give us only the speech-rules of the poem's linguistic elements, not their interpretation.

Voloshinov's concept of intonation offers us a more plausible model for the process by which we do in fact read poems. We note that his theory is potentially de-textualistic: the 'meaning' of the work is locked away in the relationship between text ('Well . . .') and knowledge of the situation. But instead of following this possibility into de-textualism, Voloshinov explains intonation by the historicistic concept of context. To understand a poem, we need the means of evaluating the entire set of contextual factors *as which* the poem is uttered, just as we need to know something of the preceding emotional situation to understand the word 'Well . . .' in his imaginary conversation. Context, then, is given a historical meaning. More, it is given a specific historical meaning – that of Marxist-Leninist materialism. The context we need to know to understand the text is nothing less than the text's economico-political provenance. And this is not *background*, it is foreground and form – intension.

Voloshinov's suggestive model suffers from the narrowness of this interpretation, I believe. In the first place, context is confined to socio-economic forces. Certainly, such factors enter into texts and may even be said in part to constitute them. But so do many other sets of factors – cultural, spiritual, personal, psychological. The consequence of adopting so narrowly economic a definition of context is the reduction of texts to a shallow determinism, an impoverishment of their richness and a confinement of their reach. It is worse – a positive distortion: often enough the reading-in of socio-economic factors where they are not operative falsifies our conception of those texts.

Moreover, Voloshinov expands the text *via* the amorphous notion of intonation into everything synchronically surrounding and diachronically preceding the text. In this sense, it would be impossible to interpret the poem, since there would be no way of establishing a cut-off point – the point at which the text itself ceases to exist or begins to exist. Here context has absorbed and invaded text. This is a difficulty Marxist criticism has yet to overcome in its dealings with literature. It is also the defining fault of all pure contextualist theories: to cancel the text by over-objectivising it, letting the work bleed out into its context so that we are left with nothing that is *it*. It is the exact equivalent of the defining fault of de-textualist theories: over-subjectivisation, injecting ourselves into the text, so that nothing is left in it which is not ours. De-textualism dissolves the text into the readings; contextualism into its provenance. Basically all theories which explain the text in terms of its 'production' or generation out of sets of forces (usually socio-economic or ideological, though it may be, as in Foucault, simply discourse) are contextualist and their hallmark is over-determination – the reduction of text to context without remainder.

Thus Voloshinov's 'context' both includes and excludes too much to be useful. It includes too little in that it fails to take account of different sources of meaning (psychological, spiritual, cultural). It includes too much because, as Voloshinov defines it, context subsumes the entire social history surrounding and preceding the poem, thus dissolving the poem's frontiers into history. Obviously, such considerations take us out of the sphere of scansion-theory into that of interpretation proper. Yet is is important to remember that Voloshinov provided a theory of reading and a theory of interpretation which are mutually dependent, and this is as it should be. My concern in this chapter is with the scansion of texts. The way we conceive of textual scansion is obviously going to influence and be reflected in the way we conceive of the broader and deeper demands the text makes on us. Scansion establishes the text; interpretation tells us what the text so established means.

Generally speaking, pure textualist theories of scansion depend upon an interpretation-theory which eschews the broader historical and psychological processes and functions literature might be supposed to serve. Voloshinov's scansion-theory is fully consistent with his Marxist interpretation-theory. In textualist criticism (whether New Critical or structuralist), the critic is usually uninterested in such extraneous matters as history and psychology. Thus, Michael Riffaterre argues for 'the self-sufficient text'.[8] Riffaterre insists that the text must be protected against various fallacies we could call contextualist – biographical, psychological, historical, political – very much in the spirit of the old New Criticism. This insistence removes the text from the world. Such thinking is still deeply typical of our literary culture. Afraid that literature will be reduced to something else – propaganda, ideology, parable – the critic clings to the spirit of the Bergsonian distinction between extensive and intensive manifolds, between art-speech and ordinary speech. He thereby effectively cuts art off from the reality it must both serve and express.

(ii) GETTING THE POEM

This intention to treat the work of art 'purely', as an artefact in a special sort of language (non-discursive), is perhaps the most striking characteristic of Western criticism in this century. Susanne Langer, for example, stringently keeps apart the discursive and the non-discursive uses of language, so that while literature is 'saved' from the excesses of Harriet Beecher Stowe, it is also denied the emotional reality and power of Gerard Manley Hopkins or D. H. Lawrence. Now in point of fact it is simply not true – and this may be important – that ordinary speech (discursive language) and all other forms of discursive symbolism are absolutely different in their operation from the operation of so-called art-speech. It is only so long as we can satisfactorily ask 'What did he say?' that explication in terms of equivalent expressions really applies to discursive speech. In speech, much is conveyed through and beyond the actual 'meaning' (that body of equivalent propositions said to explicate its import satisfactorily): we read between the lines. And very often it just won't do to give a 'translation' such as I have suggested is adequate for such speech. This is not important to logic. But in so far as logically-minded people apply themselves to the semantic elucidation of art, it is important. For the icons and symbols of art have much in common with ordinary speech, in which context, idiom, expression, delivery and phrasing play as important a role as truth-values. Rhetoric lies between discursive and non-discursive symbolisms: we can only up to a point summarise what the political speaker says. We can't in this way account for the effect Hitler, for instance, had on his audiences. Classical rhetoric acknowledged this by dividing the properties of the subject up into two main groups: those pertaining to meaning (that of which summary can be made, which was called *inventio*), and those pertaining to delivery (*locutio* and *pronunciaio*).

Art also is gesture, idiom and manner. Works of art belong properly to a realm of utterance, declaration and commitment. It is useless considering them purely as symbols to which there is a 'meaning'. As well analyse a pithy saying, a witticism of Wilde or Whistler, in the context of utterance brilliant, apart from it dull. The philosopher or formalist critic who carries out an analysis of the poem and accuses the poet of mysticism when he says 'No, that isn't it . . .' is very likely forgetting the importance of this context of utterance, or forgetting that a poem *is* uttered within a context, and that it is never merely a text. It is this series of considerations which is neglected in Voloshinov's concept of intonation. Voloshinov is right to insist that the theory of reading which pays no attention to any factors outside the words on the page is inadequate. He is wrong in that he pays no attention to the subtle relations that exist between the author's words and the contexts which the author knows he can persuade his reader to assume as operative. He ignores, in other words, all those factors relating to the author's intentions or to intentionality in general.

All three theories of scansion and meaning considered above – contextualist, textualist and de-textualist – ignore the question of the poem's intentionality, its built-in, self-declaring interpretation. Contextualism ties the poem to the whole mass of world-history, whether the author was conscious of it or not; textualism concerns itself with the 'meaning' of the text in a purely semiotic or semantic way; de-textualism treats the poem as the more or less accidental occasion for the reader's fantasy – a trigger in a random psychological process. Are not these apparently different theories of scansion allied in their refusal to let the text or the author stipulate the way it is to be read? In other words, to *mean* one thing (no matter how ambiguous or multivalent) rather than anything at all? The purpose of a proper theory of scansion must surely be, in contrast to these theories, to establish that texts have at once import and a specifying intentionality, which is in fact decisive in establishing that import. Import, as we saw at the end of the last chapter, can be loosely defined as what the text succeeds in saying, so that it is, in the end, irrelevant for the author to say, 'But I didn't mean that . . .'. This perception was the basis of the Intentional Fallacy theory, and it contains a residue of truth. But it neglects both the process by which the text establishes its import and the process by which we, as readers, come to know that import. If we call import intension, we can say – with pardonable slickness, merely to point up the issue – that the critic's task is to establish how the poet's intentions are realised as intension, or how his intensions are created by intention.

Intentions in the sense of prior draughts (still often taken to give real insight into the meanings of achieved texts), remarks in the author's correspondence, 'explanations', prefaces, lectures –

all this not only can but must be ignored: it is not part of the text. The poet's interpretations of his own poems are given from a privileged position, with inside information, but *qua* interpretation they have no absolute claims on our attention. The poem has import, and if the poet says 'No, that is not what I meant . . . ' we can ignore him. What he said *means* something, in that it amounts to something, has import; if it can be shown that its import is other than the speaker later claims, then either he has expressed himself wrongly, or we failed to understand him initially. Everything that can be said about the poem must be referable to the words on the page: so far the Intentional Fallacy critics are right. But the way we read those words depends upon a number of decisions not describable so simply. Intentions can be ignored if they do not form part of the text; as realised in the text, as intension, they cannot be.

A useful model of the process by which intentions become intensions is offered by Barthes in his analysis of mythologies.[9] Barthes distinguishes between the meaning of a given sign (poem, poster, stamp, dress) and what the mythic use to which that sign is put obliges us to make of it: Barthes calls this mythic level the 'form'. I find his terms confusing. I prefer to call what he calls the meaning of the sign its content. Thus, the image of the Negro in uniform saluting the tricolour on the front of *Paris Match* in Barthes's example I shall call the *content* of the cover: what the editor obliges us to accept of this image (the implied willing self-subjugation of black Africans to white colonial superiority) constitutes its *meaning*: that is what the cover *says*. What Barthes's suggestive analysis reveals is that the surface contents of a sign (= text, poem) are as it were *used by* the mythic intention. They are impoverished, in that we do not attend to the Negro's personal characteristics, the shape of his eyes or whatever; but at the same time they are enriched in being put at the service of another meaning: 'The presence [that is, the content as I have just sketched it in] is tamed, put at a distance, made almost transparent; it recedes a little, it becomes the accomplice of a concept which comes to it fully armed, French imperiality: once made use of, it becomes artificial.'[10] I am not concerned with the actual theory of myth in itself. What is interesting is the notion of a perceived intention Barthes makes use of: he is saying in effect that the intention signalised in the artefact (poem, text, poster) tells us how to read the contents of the artefact, and thereby gives it a meaning. Of course, if a stupid or obstinate person were to object to Barthes's analysis, and insist that he couldn't *see* the implied and proffered myth of imperialism Barthes has revealed in the cover – 'It's just a photograph of a Negro saluting' – there is really no answer but the shrug, or the persuasive argument beginning 'But surely . . .'. My contention is that this is really the nature of all critical disputations, and that the proffering of myth through the content of an image as Barthes describes it, affords us a model of the entire process by which the individual signs that make up the larger sign of a poem are to be read. The poem really *means* something just as Barthes's *Paris Match* cover *means* something. The question we should ask of it is not so much 'What does it mean?' as 'What does it mean to mean?', 'What is it trying to say?' This is exactly as we say in daily life, 'Are you trying to say something?' All art-works are trying to say something to us and when we understand this we shall be on the way to avoiding the fallacies of pure textualism, pure contextualism and pure de-textualism.

Textualist theories will always have a certain hold over the literary mind because literary texts are in words. A number of errors spring from this fact. If it were remembered that the object-language of poetry is, in this respect, in the same category as the languages of music and painting, critics would not make the mistake of identifying the meaning of a literary text with the sum of its significations. For the question, 'Are you trying to say something?' asked of a statement in words, may appear to be different from the same question when it is asked in regard to an event or action, but it is not so really. Thus, my wife lays the screwdriver and the new plug on the arm of my chair. 'Are you trying to say something?' I ask. The physical placing of the articles on the chair arm is the *content* of the action (as I have just defined content above); the idea that I should put the plug on the new pop-up toaster is the *meaning* of the action. This structure can be applied to verbal acts as well as physical ones. In this case we must handle the 'Are you trying to say something?' formula with more care. Because action and commentary (statements of meaning) are in the same medium, language, we tend to lose sight of the structural interrelations. If my wife now says, 'Isn't it cold in here?' the visitor – and even I myself at first – might understand her meaning at its face value, as a description of a state of affairs as regards temperature. I, however, 'when the penny drops', know that her innocent-sounding observation *means* something else: it means that the draught coming in under the door, which should have been attended to by myself long since, remains unattended to. So the 'Are-you-trying-to-say-something?' formula can apply equally well to linguistic as to physical actions. This is not quite the same as the code ('Isn't you-know-who touchy tonight?'), or the conventionalised de-neutralisation of a given expression ('When I say "box", run!'). *It is the understanding of an utterance*. My contention is that the formula applies as well to poems and that poems are as dumb in their eloquence as paintings and symphonies. They also are acts, 'trying to say something', something sometimes other than the overt denotational content – the significations – of their words. Some thinkers hold that all language is of this order, that daily discourse, for example, is a table beneath which we kick or caress each other. Some literary theorists, as we shall see, hold in particular that all poems say something other than their surface meaning. But this is a matter of interpretation in a different sense and I want to leave that until later.

For the time being, I want to underline the intentionality of this argument. Myth, as Barthes describes it, is a way of determining meaning. We have to grasp what 'meaning' is proffered through or by means of the overt designata of the work's signs: the poet means what he means to mean – neither more nor less. The intentions have to be *realised* as intension, in Leavis's important phrase. They are to be understood neither as otherwise expressed determination nor as pure signification.

The poet's words are not just semantic units arranged in patterns which arbitrarily assume significance because of the way in which they are ordered. They are signals to us: the poet signals his intentions. Sometimes he does this in the title – something which both is and is not part of the work. When Paul Klee calls a trembling linear portrait 'Long-haired soulful' he is doing more than giving his picture a label for the catalogue. He is doing less, though, than interpreting it for us: we can only accept that title and drawing are part of the same thing, and that the artist is telling us how to look at it. Similarly, when Cézanne calls a painting of a house 'La maison du pendu', nothing can prevent us from reading his picture in a particular way 'in the light' of the title. The same is true of Géricault's series of 'mad' portraits. Alternatively, modern painters tell us how to look at their pictures by calling them 'Painting' or 'Composition'.

This matter of the title, however, is a mere point of entry for a

whole theory of scansion, interpretation and intention. I should
wish to argue that not only must the title be construed as a signal
or directive from the author, but that every element, every sign
within the work itself, must be *read as* signal. It is at this point
that we must be sure of our grasp on our fundamental conception of the art-object. The danger is to 'identify' or recognise
types of signal within the poem, and to allow ourselves to prise
them apart from a 'thing' which they allegedly illluminate. We
must be quite sure on this point: the poet's signals are not, as
perhaps the instance of the title suggests they are, extraneous
from the work – they *are* the work: what we prise apart in so
doing is the poem from itself. Thus, our philosophically sharpened distinction between form and content can again stand us
in good stead. We can grant that the content of a poem is what
can be discussed, identified, talked about in the critical meta-
language. This still leaves the form intact, merely pointed at, or
at best recognised. The signals of the poem are not mere tokens,
substitutes for some hidden reality: they *are* that reality. But they
constitute that reality not as the meaningless coloured particles
constitute the factitious symmetries of the kaleidoscope, nor as
the intrinsically meaningful elements of the significant-form
theorists make up the aesthetic diagram, nor yet quite as the
logician's p's and q's and hooks and v's form the functions
which ordinary language can fill with its variables. The forms of
the poem differ from these various linguistic codes not merely in
the amount of connotation they proffer: this way of distinguishing art-language from discursive language is, as we have seen,
only half-adequate. It fails to account both for the degree of
overtone, nuance and sheer gesture in so-called ordinary speech
(especially as that verges upon oratory), and at the same time for
the degree of precision and definiteness in the language of the
poem. Meaning in poetry is not, *pace* Barthes in *S/Z*, a gold dust
(moonshine?) sprinkled on the inert body of the poem: that body
itself constitutes its meaning; there is no extrinsic denotation
upon which the lovable waywardness of poetic intuition or
imagination casts its fecund, distracting and disruptive density,
secondary meaning or connotation. Meaning in poetry orig-
inates in the first instance – or must be characterised in the first
instance – as signal: the signs signal how they themselves are to
be read, and they are like objects only in so far as we *get* them,
much as we must get a joke. I see no reason for not extending the
parallel and insisting that 'taste; or capacity to respond varies

neither more nor less than a sense of humour. 'Yes, I understand', says Margo, in *The Good Life*, 'but why is it a joke?'

Getting the poem, it goes without saying, means something
more complicated than getting a joke, but it is, I submit, in
crucial respects, similar. One of these respects concerns intention:
there is a crucial difference between the accidental 'joke' – the
slip-of-the-tongue conflation of contexts or identities that seems
funny, of which the type is the spoonerism – and the real joke,
where part of our amusement derives from the feeling of having
got in tune with the wit's 'meaning'. A great deal of literary
criticism consists in conferring 'meaning' upon texts – that is, of
turning something neutral into an 'accidental' joke, sometimes
on the understanding that in literature there are no slips of the
tongue. I shall come to this question later. Here I wish to deal
with the nature of the getting. Getting the poem means, in fact,
viewing it along the right lines of longitude. This brings back the
matter of contexts. Not all the possible contexts (socio-historical
circumstances, ideologies, *Zeitgeist*) can be assumed in a poem: it
is an error of much literary criticism that it assumes that they
can be. Voloshinov's context itself, we remember, includes and
excludes too much to be useful without further definition or
delimitation. It is not merely the context in the sense of the
surrounding history of the situation which determines, or
informs, the utterance; it is the speaker's conscious, half-
conscious and even 'unconscious' exploitation, acknowledgement or admission of this context. If, for instance, a speaker is
ignorant of what has been going on recently – ignorant, for
instance, of things he 'ought' to be conscious of – the class-
struggle, say – then we cannot say that the context informs what
he says. Context in this sense could enter only in the form of
irony.

It is just such contextualisation-within-the-text which
Aristotle institutionalised as dramatic irony. I should wish to distinguish sharply between irony of this sort, which is structurally
and textually demonstrable, and that irony which is so common,
even today, among academic critics. In academic irony, it is the
text itself which is ironised by contextualisation. Whether the
writer (or indeed the text) likes it or not, whatever is said in it
can be gainsaid, cancelled, controverted or ignored by the
superimposition of the critic's contexts as irony. Let us say, for
instance, that the critic dislikes James Joyce's 'aestheticism' –
the heroic commitment of author and persona in *A Portrait of the*

Artist as a Young Man to the pursuit of art and its transcendental values; at the same time he recognises the power and achievement of the book. What he does is to fill the gap between what he himself thinks is important and possible and what Joyce appears to commit himself to in the text, with irony: this gap we can call ironic differential, and it is perhaps the most pervasive and mischievous form of contextualisation known to us.[11]

In the case of Joyce's book, the context is, roughly, that complex tradition of artist-as-hero deriving in the end from Dante's hero-worship of Vergil, but in the more immediate background coming from the great Romantics – Byron, Wordsworth and Ibsen, in particular. To understand Joyce's novel, we have to be in tune with this tradition: we have to get inside its lines. The same is true of Mallarmé's poetry as a whole, and indeed that of T. S. Eliot, W. B. Yeats and most of their major contemporaries. Take, for instance, Mallarmé's sonnet, 'Le vierge, le vivace et le bel aujourd'hui'. We cannot be said to have understood this poem at all unless we 'see' that the swan with its beak soldered fast in the ice of a mountain lake is a symbol of the poet, with his exquisite impotence, his fear of fulfilment, his tragic yet farcical inability to take off. On the broadest interpretation, we can see the swan as a symbol of the human soul, of human aspiration. At any rate, the poem 'means' nothing unless its symbolism is understood: it is certainly not about birds. These 'two' interpretations, moreover, are not in conflict; they are merely narrower and broader, more and less precisely articulated versions of the same myth: it is this myth which shines through the proferred image, as its meaning. The meaning is the realisation of the intention through the content.

Not all contexts, therefore, are political or economic, though some critics would want to interpret the symbolist impasse politically. The point is that the poet has to be able to count on his reader's picking up the meaning, getting the point, intuiting the right lines of longitude through which his poem makes the section.

The textualist critic, who possibly has a Cambridge History degree behind him, finds it easy enough to pretend that his informed reading of the poem is just a particularly sensitive response to the words on the page, so that no extra-textual help is required. But in fact he is not responding to a series of semantic counters whose structural interrelations elicit a particular response, like the formula in Eliot's objective-correlative theory. He is responding to and with a whole system of selected conventions signalled to him by the poet *often above the poem's head*, as it were, and rapidly marshalled by him into the 'informed' response. This means that the reader has to *assent to* the poem before it can work for, or on, him. He has to choose to eliminate certain unwanted associations of the verbal counters and structures the poet uses. The poem does not play on us like light on a sensitised plate producing a photographic image. It works on us, but works on us only in so far as we agree to co-operate or collaborate with it. This does not mean that we are free to create or re-create the poem according to our whim or ideology – though this in fact is what many literary critics nowadays think they are entitled, or even obliged, to do. On the contrary, it means that we are obliged to pay more and more rigorous attention to the interpretation of the poet's signals in order to honour the intention within them. For the various signs that make up a poem are not equivalent each to each, or fair game for the critic-hunter with his elephant gun: they constitute structures.

Jan Mukarovsky acknowledged this in his concept of the dominant. According to Mukarovsky, the poet deliberately 'foregrounds' certain elements in the poem; these foregrounded elements constitute its poeticness, foregrounding consisting in deviation from ordinary usage. The critic's role is therefore to identify or recognise the infrastructure of foregrounded elements within the ordinary language the poet necessarily avails himself of in the interests of communication: 'The dominant thus creates the unity of the work in poetry. It is, of course, a unity of its own kind, the nature of which in aesthetics is usually designated as "unity in variety", a dynamic unity in which we at the same time perceive harmony and disharmony, convergence and divergence.'[12] We recognise without difficulty the usual hallmarks of stylisticist or formalist method: the proffering of the value-judgement as if it could be used objectively as an infallible instrument for detecting precisely what it has assumed! But this is par for the course. Stylistics has come a long way since Mukarovsky wrote these words, but only in the direction of increased dogmaticism. No mainstream literary critic would be surprised, much less offended, at Mukarovsky's pronouncement, though he might be both surprised and offended at the assumption of prophetic authority with which it was uttered. I have all along suggested that what the critic habitually does is to describe the significant structures within the physical facts (words, notes, stone, marble) of the total work, for, as Rudolf Arnheim observes, 'the representation offers a structural equivalent to the experience that gave rise to it'.[13] This is obviously the case, for instance, with the new and revolutionary work. An example might be the elucidation of the structural principles of a late string quartet of Beethoven, or the indication of the basic series and transmutations of a mature Webern work. But this is not always the case. Accepted classics may benefit. An early proto-structuralist analysis, L. C. Knights's *How Many Children had Lady Macbeth?*, directed the reader's attention away from old-fashioned biographical concerns to the play's organic imagery and the shapes enacted in it. Thus, our interest may be redirected from a moral to a more relevant standpoint.

At any rate, the concern, in Arnheim, Knights and Mukarovsky, is to locate or recognise the work's 'significant' structure – its literariness. This infrastructure is not a dead thing, the purely semiotic or formal convergence of elements. It is an expression of what I shall call directive impulse – the author's realised intention to eliminate such-and-such associations and to affirm others. It is the refusal to grant the existence of the directive impulse that vitiates much of Barthes's *S/Z*. In the interests of *Liberté, égalité et fraternité*, Barthes wishes to deny the text and the author the right to dictate to us the way it is read: 'we must renounce structuring this text in large masses, as was done by classical rhetoric and by secondary-school explication: no *construction* of the text: everything signifies ceaselessly and several times, but without being delegated to a great final ensemble, to an ultimate structure.'[14] All signs are equal, and none are more equal than others! This is surely a recipe for nonsense. Barthes vacillates throughout the book in his attitude toward the 'classical' *lisible* text, as we shall have cause to note again. Certainly, the difference between nineteenth-century realist texts and experimental modernist ones is effectively broken if we deny the classical text its right to dictate how it is to be read. Hence, presumably, the half-sarcastic tone Barthes adopts towards Balzac throughout the book: Barthes's kind of modernist criticism habitually turns the strengths of realism against realism, and treats it as, at best, failed modernism.

'Classical' texts – to adopt for a moment Barthes's somewhat archaic terminology – gather their resonances precisely through their dictated infrastructures: directive impulse assures the signs of the text both their interrelations and their capacity to function as signals. Certainly, the signs have their meanings in the codes they represent. This is to equate codes with conventional content; on this level *S/Z* is an example of the type of criticism inaugurated by Empson in *Seven Types of Ambiguity* and *The Structure of Complex Words*. Indeed, Barthes himself provides a sound paraphrase of Empsonian methodology, with its intention of 'working back along the threads of meanings'.[15] Where Barthes is wrong is in ignoring the semantic and functional hierarchies of the text and reducing it to an egalopolis of equivalent signs. This produces not multivalence but on the contrary, a uniformity of function which effectively inhibits meaning. (It is perhaps a consequence of misreading Freud: Freud's concept of displacement in dreams allows switches of role between major and minor symbols, so that insignificant objects are craftily made to bear the load of meaning. But this merely makes the matter of getting at the work/dream's hierarchy a little more difficult: some things still remain functionally more important than others, only they are often in disguise.)[16]

Again, we are reminded of the fact that we are concerned here also with a theory of utterance as well as of poetry. We could never read or understand a single sentence, let alone a poem or story, if Barthes were right, and we were not constantly obliged to eliminate unwanted associations and to refrain from following threads of meaning where they might appear to lead without direction from the author. Wool-gathering is an apt metaphor for this sort of criticism, which not only reduces the text by expanding its frontiers, but in fact cancels the need for it: why not take for our 'text' the *Oxford English Dictionary* or the typesetter's box? There, too, we find an infinity of digressions. The differences between the typesetter's box, the *O.E.D.*, a bad poem and a good one are, in part at least, to be explained by the digressions we are not permitted to make, by the wool we are not allowed to gather. The weakness of de-textualisation – as of Barthes himself in this instance – is that it fails to observe both that the limits of digression are in fact ordained by the limitations of the text, by the import of the utterance, and that the import of the utterance is created by the effect of the writer's signalising his intentions by his choice of word, gesture, tone.

The deliberate self-limitation of the text is its passport to meaning. We need not accept the kind of view of 'specific and determinate meanings' of the absolute kind opposed by Stanley Fish.[17] There is no 'absolute' meaning, in the sense of actual inert properties lying around like elements and matter in the external world. Meaning is not like that because language is not like that. Language is not a natural, externally existing thing, like matter or space; it is conventional, and its statements reflect the basic linguistic prerequisites which I shall offer below: they assume (*a*) the existence of a 'world' outside language itself, (*b*) the will and need to communicate, and (*c*) the willingness and ability of other like minds to understand the communication. Thus all *langue* is *parole: pace* Saussure, what is tabulated under *langue* is not language but the logical properties of language, the rules and conditions without which we could not have language in the first place. Now if anyone suggests that meaning is out there, like a substance, then he is simply wrong. But if, on the other hand, someone else suggests that this means that there are no possible definite meanings, then he too is wrong: he doesn't know the rules of the game. Any proposition can be understood: to understand means to pick up the intention behind the utterance. In Fish's example, 'Is there a text in this class?', the student who made this statement (it is not really a question, since the girl expected no answer) knew that the professor to whom it was addressed would get it wrong. She knew he would mistake the intended context: thus her question, which was really about theories of interpretation, could seem to refer to classroom procedure. A third possibility given by Fish is the same question asked by a student who had used the same classroom previously and might have left a textbook there. A fourth is the de-neutralised, trigger example, where the utterance of these words is meant by pre-arrangement to act as a code for another person to act, leave the room or make a disturbance. But Fish's conclusion, that the student's question contained no 'meaning' that was not put there by the listener and that understanding consists of fitting context to statement, is far from satisfactory. There may well be examples – in archaeology, in ancient history, for example, even in a police enquiry – when we don't have any set of contexts or frameworks to make sense of a statement. We must recognise the set of marks as a statement in the first place. Having done so, we may well have to find out what it means;

this *in turn* means creating a context for it. But we can only do so when we have understood it. And our understanding is severely restricted by the elements and structure of the given statement. The order of the words, the grammatical rules of the sentence, the literal meanings of the words and all the other shadings of convention and argot we bring to our language – all these are part of meaning. And the most important element is the one disregarded by Fish: intentionality. His student *meant* to be misunderstood and was, and therefore, in her success, was testifying precisely to that definiteness of meaning Fish thinks his example discredits.

We can extend the example to literary texts: few examples of literary ambiguity fit Empson's seventh type: full ambiguity, in which the poem can be read exactly in two different ways. This kind of writing (certain Shakespeare sonnets being favourite examples) is like those *trompe-l'oeil* paintings Dali used to toy with in the 1930s: it might be a staircase leading up into a mysterious castle, with a seashore in the background: it *is*; but on a second look it turns out to be a portrait of a woman. This was a favourite type of example in phenomenology: the Maltese Cross that can be a white cross on a black ground, or a black cross on a white. Such signs, to be sure, have no one meaning: they are simply ambiguous, a white cross on a black ground or a black cross on a white. But, like the Dali picture and the Shakespeare sonnet, this example is only an extreme way of pointing up a certain feature of language. It is extremely rarely that we can find such examples of absolute ambiguity: and we might hazard the suggestion that if all language, all signs, were similarly ambiguous, language itself would be useless: it would not, indeed, have come into existence. In the vast majority of cases, the ambiguous meanings that accrue in a poetic text accrue precisely because of the text's self-commitment to *a* meaning, and the reader's ability to pick up this meaning. If there are two ways in which a text or statement can be read, neither of which relates to the other and neither of which yields to the other, then we do have a text or statement which says either of two things. But this doesn't mean that any cock-eyed observation we can find meagre grounds for making about any statement or poem is equally justified, and therefore that there is no definite and determinate meaning. The primary fallacy here is to assume that meaning must be like physical matter, independent of being

picked up. Fish's counter-fallacy is to ignore the fact of intentionality altogether, even though the example he chooses is precisely
a clever exploitation of intentionality.

'Come to the meet!' It is not so much context as conscious
exploitation of context which will alone make sense of this call,
and prevent the listener exploring homonyms to convert the
utterance into an invitation to a feast. Intention in this sense is
always at work in the literary text, as in the daily utterance, and
the reality of the poem consists in the inner direction the poet
incites us to read his signs along. I say 'inner' direction, because
the effect of admitting the notion of intention in utterance is in
fact to make 'meaning' strictly inaccessible to analysis. I should
wish to argue in fact that meaning is always inward, unstructured and undisclosed. It is always withheld. In this it is like the
past. In history the past must always be treated as *evidence*, as
clues to be interpreted. We fool ourselves if we believe that it *is*
the past. Thus, the propositional function, the logical form (syl-
logism or symbolic equation) is really without meaning: like the
Theory of Descriptions, it is a capacity for meaning, and lays
down the possibilities for utterance. Meaning itself can only be
predicated of actual utterances. Thus, the dictionary itself does
not give us meanings, but only definitions, rules for use.

When, therefore, I say 'Come to the meet!' the interlocutor
who later refuses to admit that I invited him or informed him of
anything because of the ambiguities of interpretation possible, or
who says, 'Wait a minute while I find out what you mean', and
who then refuses to let me help him by repeating, varying, or
paraphrasing what I said before, on the grounds that what I
have spoken I have spoken, and must now be tested for its
'meaning' – such an interlocutor (he is not unlike certain literary
critics) must be ruled out of order. Similarly, meaning in the
poem is not to be arrived at solely by analysing the vocables for
import, or following out (irrespective of the author's directives)
any thread that might suggest itself or by accident happen to be
there: it is to be negotiated only by identifying, deep-reading or
intuiting the direction of the poem's codes and selecting the
decisions the poem's super-code (or dominant, in Mukarovsky's
term) asks us to make before its codes can be made sense of and
ordered. We have to assent to the poem, but we can assent to it
only after we have agreed to play.

There are many ways of expressing a refusal to play. One is

Plato's way – pretending that poems have the same purposes as moral or practical statements, and therefore finding poets guilty of misrepresentation. Another is the ideological way, testing the ideas or doctrines of poems against those held by the critic to be true. This can be frankly political – the 'vulgar' Marxist condemnation of Dante or Shakespeare as lackeys of imperialism, or of Dickens for not adopting the 'correct' attitude towards the class-struggle. A third is the 'common-sense way – indicting the poet for transgressions against known fact. One can easily imagine a time when Ibsen's *Ghosts* would be unperformed because it is based on a medical fallacy, Dante unread because God doesn't exist, and *Antigone* ignored because people's souls don't suffer eternal torture if a handful of earth is not thrown on their corpses at death.

These examples are extreme and meant to parody existing procedures. My point is simply to emphasise the fact that reading poems is not to be reduced to an externalised analysis of import or content, but must always involve the critic-reader in the effort to intuit or deep-read the poem's meanings, which are always inward ones. From this point of view, however, there is nothing mystical about intuition: it is as teachable and as learnable a faculty as the more easily grasped methodologies favoured by stylistics. The critical act is always an act of deep-reading: and as readers we are all critics, as critics no more than readers. This throws a different light on the so-called value-judgement criticism of F. R. Leavis. For too long, critics of a formalist bias have enjoyed a false superiority over critics like Leavis who adhere to the idea that literary criticism is the art of knowing what's good and what's bad. Certainly, Leavis narrowed his range unnecessarily and occasionally came close to self-parody in his mania for establishing that one work – acknowledged to be good – was less good than another also allowed to be good. But this was largely due to accidents of temperament and to the circumstances in which Leavis carried out his criticism. Essentially, there is nothing narrowing or subjectivist in his emphasis upon the 'sincerity' of the poem: every authentic act of criticism is implicitly a quest for the poem's sincerity in the sense that no mere recounting of the poem's formal elements is ever enough to elicit the value-judgement or constitute an interpretation. For the value-judgement is the response not so much to the poem's effectiveness as to its nature. Value-judgement criticism – what we have raised to the highest degree in the work of Leavis – is nothing more or less than a more finely tuned formalism. The 'form' of the poem exists along longitudinous lines of intersection, which have to be apprehended before the poem can be seen. Thus Leavis's moral seriousness is not extraneous to criticism, a boringly puritanical intrusion into the proper business of literary criticism, but one of a number of authenticating ways of deep-reading not only for the value of literary texts but for their structure. The value-judgement is a necessary element of every authentic critical act, because without it we are left with mere words, signs without codes, codes without direction, configurations without particularity; to say or to feel (to *know*) how a poem works is implicitly to praise it, but it is by the same token to identify it.

(iii) TELLER AND TALE

Mention of Leavis brings us to a major problem, however. 'Who' or 'what' means? Leavis's insistence on form in the novel indicates that he regarded the novel as being created according to internal laws. He rarely talks of the social influences on a novel and never refers to the solution of ethical problems in the manner of a real moralistic criticism. We see this, for instance, in the essay where – with the utmost tenderness – he takes Lawrence to task for moralistically re-writing *Anna Karenina*.[18] It is probably a crude distinction between formalistic (or intrinsic) criticism on the one hand and a moralistic (or extrinsic) criticism on the other (as if such formulae could do justice to the complexity of the acts involved in appreciating works of art) which has given rise to the idea of Leavis as primarily a moralist. In fact he is concerned with the strength of a book's texture, the consistency of its impulses and the truth with which a sentence consorts with the impulse begetting it. Such a methodology assumes, naturally, that the sentence in the text bears relations to other things than mere aesthetic titillation on the one hand or merely 'other words' on the other. The assumption indeed is that the work takes place in a field, and that this field is important to us as human beings, not merely as fossickers among signs. Leavis, we can say, was a moralist because he was a critic, not vice versa. Indeed, his moral fervour and his critical fineness are one and the same. This is especially true in his distrust of the late Romantic author-cult, his steady adherence to the tale rather than the teller, to the text rather than the author. Yet, of course, he was too acute not to know that in this context the terms *text* and *author* are to be treated as interchangeable. Michel Foucault's efforts to free texts from their authors by trying to show that 'author' is some kind of 'ideological product' that 'impedes the free circulation . . . of fiction'[19] are really so much wasted energy, though expended in a time-honoured tradition. (He really adds nothing of theoretical importance to the old New Criticism in this respect.) When D. H. Lawrence warned us 'Never trust the teller, trust the tale', he was putting us more surely on the right track. It is only logical to assume a relationship of congruency between what the natural man thought and believed *qua* natural man and what appears in the pages of his book. But the natural, and still more the social, man is a complex and often dislikable character, whose human prejudices lead him to write a lot of nonsense along with the small percentage of good work he is capable of. Learn to spot this, Lawrence tells us, and ignore the propaganda – the rest that is 'littérature', in Verlaine's scathing phrase.

It is this ore or radium in the mud that we learn to pick up when we learn to read. And it is this precious matter which is ignored or re-buried in the ponderous researches of so much literary criticism. This is why we are always in need of the value-judgement; in a sense, the value in the text is like a mute gesture, or, to change the metaphoric base, a twinge from the unconscious saying, 'Look, I'm over here!' These examples make it clear that right from the start we have to acknowledge the existence of a problem that in a sense sets at nought every attempt to produce a theory of literature or a tidy theory of artistic meaning: works of art are often of unequal value. They are not at all elegantly coherent organisms which we can safely examine for their 'meanings', as if one clue will lead us to another, until we have the whole thing accounted for. This is not merely because we as critics are limited and incapable of explaining it all, but also because texts themselves, as human products, are often confused, partial amalgams of inferior and superior matter – of *musique* and *littérature*, of poetry and propaganda. The criticism of F. R. Leavis is really based upon the need for the critic to be a sleuth, ignoring the proclamations of the author-as-propagandist or natural man and, as Lawrence suggested, to learn to pick up the trail of the *real* meaning sunk inside the dross. Many a great work seems to have been born in spite of its creator. But this merely changes the ground of the act of intending to the unconscious, or race-mind, for example.

This is an insuperable obstacle to any fully coherent critical theory, and I don't intend to try to explain it away. Besides, its very existence is from one point of view heartening: it means that literary texts – real literary texts – can't be got up by academics who know all the answers and possess all the blueprints. More importantly, the example of Leavis's criticism forces us to look more closely at the question of the text's intentionality: what is it *really* trying to say? Because of the way society and culture in the West have evolved over the past two hundred years, it is no longer possible to regard art-works as performances on given themes. The whole question of what a text is becomes itself a radical part of the critic's work. Within the confusion of styles, influence of past achievement, the serious art-work evolves, frequently at odds with itself. Leavis's criticism becomes more, not less, important the farther we proceed into the territory of our own future. To say when and where a writer succeeds might well prove to be the most important of all interpretative tasks, since it may well seem identical with identifying its intentional form. But this brings us to the matter of interpretation proper – the relationship of the larger movements and meanings within texts to our own philosophies and world-views.

(iv) CONCLUSION

Before we ever get to the question of 'the' interpretation of the poem, therefore, we are obliged to recognise the act of reading for a less simple matter than is sometimes thought: it is not a matter of registering, nor of simple understanding. Reading a poem has much in common with understanding an emotional situation (as in Voloshinov's example). It is in important respects different from understanding a logical argument in which a translatable, definable 'import' is establishable. It veers off in the direction of understanding a political speech, but goes on past that, since none of its statements is allowed to be paraphrased. Import is compromised right from the start by intention:

we have to *get* the poem, and understanding its words is often closer to getting a joke than evaluating military intelligence. In sum, we might well wish to say that reading was in essence interpretative.

This, however, is misleading. At best we might permit ourselves to call this *interpretation* $_1$. This first thing we have to do is to decide whether any given theory is a theory of scansion or of interpretation. In Stanley Fish's case, as I have indicated above, we are offered a theory of scansion, which is offered as if it were a theory of interpretation: 'What I have been saying', Fish concludes at the end of an attempt to answer the question 'What makes an interpretation acceptable?', 'is that whatever they do, it will only be an interpretation in another guise because, like it or not, interpretation is the only game in town.'[20] 'They' are the traditionalist critics (M. H. Abrams and E. D. Hirsch in particular) who think they are merely describing texts when they are in fact interpreting them. So far we agree with Fish: we are 'in a situation with' language from the start. But Fish's victory banners have to be pulled in again when we understand that establishing the interpretative nature of the reading-act – whether in relation to speech-act theory or to Voloshinov's sociological intonations – gets us nowhere in the larger matter of establishing a 'correct' reading of a text. We have merely rephrased the definition of reading and re-marked the territory to be interpreted. For this is undoubtedly the major battlefield for criticism now. What is criticism's function? Is it merely describing, recognising and pointing to the internal dimensions, the structural skeleton, the inscape or the 'significant' shape within the text's empirically given form (rhymed couplets, strophe, sonnet)? Or is it reading these forms *as* something else? It is in this latter sense that interpretation requires to be analysed itself, and for this purpose a scansion-theory like Fish's is inadequate. Phenomenological analysis, likewise, provides a de-textualist theory of scansion while masquerading as interpretation. For this reason, the debates in the late seventies between Abrams and Hirsch and the Yale de-constructionists leave the major issues untouched.[21] We could accept that reading is interpretative (I have tried to show that it must be seen as such) without accepting that interpretation is of one sort or another. We shall examine next the claims of an 'empiricist' theory and of a contrary hermeneuticist theory.

8 Interpretation

The standpoint of the present book is that of empiricism. Fundamentally, an empiricist criticism insists that the role of the critic is to show the text for what it is. This assumes, among other things, that the text *is*. But this need not commit the empiricist to a pure textualism, as in fact Abrams and Hirsch tend to imply. Pure textualism is a scansion-theory that refuses to acknowledge the problem of interpretation. In fact many apparently textualist theories have been soundly based in interpretive principles. The New Criticism in general and the criticism of F. R. Leavis in particular spring to mind. Recent critics have stressed this 'anomalous' reliance upon smuggled-in standards. But in fact any useful critical theory or practice must mingle scansion and interpretation, much as it must slide from description to evaluation. Interpretation-theories depend upon visions of life, philosophies, ideologies (to use the loaded Marxist term). There is no need for this set of assumptions and visions to be clearly articulated: in fact, one must suspect the critic who is able to do so. Critical praxis is far too complex and subtle to allow of very clear articulation: it is really the mind of a civilisation that speaks in the work of a Lukács or a Leavis. Thus, demands for a 'value-system' or interpretation-theory are likely to be more or less disingenuous. We 'know where we are' in reading Leavis or Lukács (ideologically opposed empiricists).

Thus, an empiricist criticism can be genuinely interpretative and can insist on the need for understanding the text's historical or psychological provenance. It can, that is to say, accept a scansion-theory that combines de-textualist and contextualist factors easily enough: it can accept, for instance, a modified phenomenology (indeed its best examples do). It is unfortunate, in fact, that so much dust has been raised by the barnstorming tactics of in fact quite orthodox scansion-theorists, whose basic principles leave the matter of the text's interpretation untouched. All that an empiricism must demand is the primacy of the text as statement: it insists on the level of the aesthetic.

In this chapter I shall be concerned with the counter-claims of various anti-empiricist schools to have discredited such an attitude towards literary criticism. The debates about explanation and interpretation as they were carried on in the 1960s will not be considered here, since the main issues have already been discussed under scansion-theory. What we are concerned with here is the opposition between a straight empiricism (the text must be respected for what it is, because it can only be apprehended *as* it is) and various hermeneuticist modes (the text cannot be isolated cleanly and its meanings, if any, lie deeper).

(i) MACHEREY AND DE-CONSTRUCTION

Pierre Macherey rejects both empiricist and hermeneuticist modes, the first merely reproducing the text, the second destroying it by placing it up against a hidden meaning or assumed norm. Since he raises many issues later discussed by more nihilistic hermeneuticists, Macherey will make a convenient starting-point. He rejects empiricism on two related grounds. First, it seems to impose a posterior and parasitic role upon the critic. Secondly, it rests upon an unacceptable epistemology. It is with this second point that we must begin. Macherey's view of empiricism as a whole is, we must say, characteristically French: for him, as for Piaget and Lévi-Strauss, empiricism consists of a primal logging of 'facts' with no awareness of the influence of other factors upon this painstaking logging. According to Macherey, the empiricist believes that 'The truth is instantaneous, merely an accurate glance over the order of things'.[1] The empiricist also believes that 'The real object is a kind of pillar on which the truth is to be displayed'.[2] Against this supposed epistemology, Macherey argues the conceptualism of Foucault: the facts tabulated in a science form their own knowledge, a knowledge related only tenuously to the real world. It is this world of knowledge, an elaborate system of forms and methods, which confronts us in any discipline, be it medicine, criminology or literary criticism. Thus, the literary critic's world is stocked not with shaggy textual objects (pillars with the Truth displayed on them), but with 'Forms of Knowledge' made up by the critic and by the complex system of terms and procedures into which he inserts himself. Thus knowledge, according to Macherey, is 'an addition to the reality from which it begins'.[3] This disposes at once of 'the text' and therefore of the empiricist critic's slavish reverence for it. Discursive practice having thus established its autonomy, the critic can proceed blithely, ignoring the text's demands for attention. The error of empiricism, then, lies in failing to see that in cognising an object we re-constitute it as a 'Form of Knowledge'. Empiricist critics wish to stock literary criticism with shaggy textual objects and see their function as to 'discover' these objects, and 'be united in the discovery of their truth'.[4] This abject slavishness is rejected haughtily in favour of some more important, more mysterious function, which, unfortunately, Macherey is unable to define. In both respects – the abandonment of an empiricist doctrine of actual texts and the postulation of a more important though obscure role for the critic – Macherey anticipates de-constructionist critics.

As far as the practice, as opposed to the theory, of literary criticism is concerned, Macherey believes that the critic should be intent on bringing out 'a difference within the work by demonstrating that it is other than it is'.[5] Some such view is clearly forced upon Macherey by his refusal to acknowledge the status, even the actual existence, of the shaggy textual object. Since the text is only a form of knowledge, created out of our own intellection and our own system of categorisation and discursive practice, we can hardly be said to study it: what we are to study, therefore, is the origination of this form of knowledge. Thus Macherey reaches something like Lucien Goldmann's position, concerning himself with the text's relations to its provenance, except that history in this case is not that solid stuff out there, but the more intangible variety enwrought in our language and understanding. It is easy now to see why Macherey should have wished to produce a theory of the *production* of the text: the text is 'produced', not in the palaeo-Marxist sense of determination by economico-political forces, but in the Foucault-ish sense of realisation out of discursive practice. Thus, the literary critic cannot be concerned with the 'text', since this has been discredited, but with 'the principles by which a text becomes "an object of knowledge"'.[6] The ground of literary criticism has been shifted, therefore, from the positive structure and inscape of the text to the fuzzier borderland between the 'text' and our construction of the text as knowledge. For 'the question of structure is not the delayed materialisation, the late incarnation, of a pre-existing meaning, it is the real condition of its very possibility'.[7]

It is easy to see how such principles, if accepted – and they have been, widely – may appear to lead to the disintegration first of literary criticism, then of literature itself. Certainly, the sceptic will want to see the critic back the theory up with practice, and will inevitably be disappointed (or relieved) by the relative harmlessness of what Macherey actually says about particular texts. It is one thing to enjoin the study of the text's 'production', the principles by which it 'becomes an object of knowledge'. It is quite another to put this into practice. From this point of view, Macherey is a paper tiger, like many of the de-constructionist critics he in part anticipates. But since the theoretical principles and methods Macherey uses have been fairly widely influential, it is worthwhile looking at them a little more closely. Machereyan principles can make life difficult for the unwary empiricist, to put it no more strongly. What then is the basis of his attack upon a hypothetical empiricism?

In the first place, unfortunately, we must note that the image of empiricism Macherey invokes as the enemy is so crude that it can play no serious role in an intellectual debate. Every thinker to some extent caricatures the doctrines he is attacking, but there is a limit to the degree of caricature: it must be recognisable within its distortions. Macherey's empiricism can, perhaps, faintly be recognised in the crudities of Boyle. As far as mainstream empiricist philosophy and philosophy of science are concerned, there is no point of contact between Macherey's caricature and the reality. No empiricist has ever believed that, 'truth is instantaneous' or that 'the real object is a kind of pillar on which the truth is displayed'. No empiricist, either, has ever believed that the *idea* of a natural object or process or event was not in a different modality from that object or process or event itself – that knowledge was not, in Macherey's words, 'an addition to the reality from which it begins'.[8] It has been necessary a number of times to insist upon this fact, and it will be again: an explanation would not be an explanation if it were not in a different order of reality from what it purported to explain. Modern philosophy of science, modern science itself, stems from the basic methodology and attitude of empiricism. This does not mean that it is not aware of the fact that its own working methods, its language of inferences and postulations, themselves constitute their own universe with internally coherent and consistent laws; or that adjustment and revision of 'world-view' does not take place also on the level of this theoretical and self-consistent universe of discourse. The difference between an empiricist philosophy and a rationalistic view such as that expressed variously by Foucault, Piaget and Macherey, is that empiricism accepts the need for constant and consistent calibration between theoretical discourse on the one hand and 'reality' on the other. It holds, that is to say, that theory and discursive practice bear constant obligation to observable reality: thought and conception are not autonomous, nor can they go merrily on their way in complete disregard of the world of facts which generated them in the first place. An empiricism asserts basically that science and language are related in certain ways to those phenomena and processes which brought them into being, and that these ways impose upon the philosopher and the scientist alike a certain burden of responsibility. This burden is apt to assume two different forms: one is logical self-consistency, which can apparently proceed in disregard of the actual world; the other is accountability *to* this world. In fact, these two practices are not independent or distinct. A basic logicality in things will be seen to underlie the requirement of logicality in discourse. And the apparent difference between empiricist attitudes towards accountability and pre-empiricist attitudes is to be explained purely in terms of world-view, of belief about the nature of reality. Neither in the sixteenth nor in the seventeenth centuries did sane men deem it possible to prosecute 'thought' without regard to the nature of reality.

This whole series of considerations can be applied to literary criticism. Literary criticism, like other modes of enquiry, has its own rules and characteristics, and thus constitutes its own order of discourse. But this does not mean that it completely re-constitutes the shaggy textual object into a 'certain form of knowledge', which requires itself in turn to be analysed in terms of another 'certain form of knowledge' which the analysis re-constitutes. It is clear that this way of thinking leads to an infinite regress, such that we would never get ever to the 'certain form of knowledge' itself. This would lead to a world overstocked with logical entities: forms of knowledge would crowd out not merely the shaggy objects of which they are forms, but each other. We could never in fact say anything about anything, but would have to talk continuously about the certain forms of knowledge which our talk itself was constituting. Although he never faces this theoretical difficulty, Foucault effectively confines enquiry to the particular area dictated by his rationalism: the real subject of *The Archaeology of Knowledge* is not knowledge, but theories of knowledge. Foucault compares certain aspects of discursive practive, the language of eighteenth-century botanists or criminologists, for instance, with that of their nineteenth-century counterparts. This is its own field, certainly, but it should not be taken as a brief for dispensing with the primary level of knowledge altogether. Knowledge may be divided for convenience along the lines I have suggested, between the object of knowledge and the various practices and methods by which we register our awareness of this object. The only obligation we have is to remember the correspondence between the two. The 'certain form of knowledge' which is the literary text, for instance, as it is allegedly 'produced' by literary criticism, is only different from the 'given' textual object in a manner of speaking. In this, it is no different from natural objects. The electron whose behaviour is recorded or predicted by the physicist may be represented as a figment of the physicist's techniques, merely an element in his discourse, a 'certain form of knowledge' produced by his methodology. This does not prevent him from adjusting his view of its 'nature', of its structure and behaviour according to the results of observation and experiment. Physicists discuss the ultimate constituents of matter or holes in space in terms not ultimately different from those in which gardeners discuss fertiliser or zoologists animals, and it is a mischievous delusion to suppose that physicists, gardeners or zoologists are merely using discourse, or carrying out purely linguistic operations, or referring to purely fictitious entities created by their discourse.

If an empiricism insists on no more than this, it insists on no less than that the persistent existence of these objects outside the scope of our language exerts constant steady pressure upon that language and upon our use of it. A criticism or philosophy which loses sight of this basic fact about the condition of language and thought loses contact also with its own nature. Literary criticism is important in our kind of society, as I have suggested above. But it does not have a mysterious, autonomous existence and function: it is parasitic on shaggy textual objects, and subject to their constant steady pressure. Reading a poem is in some respects like watching the Cup Final. We can go to Wembley and 'be there', or we can watch it either on the BBC or ITV. A mystical de-textualist like Macherey is like a man who says that watching the Cup Final on one channel is so different from watching on the other that we cannot speak of 'the' Cup Final at all. The ball is off the field; Ardiles is receiving attention from the coach. The BBC shows a close-up of Ardiles' face in agony; ITV shows the face of the Manchester City player who tackled him. A spectator at the game is looking at one of the turrets above the stand, another is lighting a cigarette. Can we say, from all these different experiences, that there is 'no' Cup Final? Or that the ITV coverage is Cup Final[a], the BBC's Cup Final[b], the spectators' Cup Final[c], and so on?

It is clear that the kind of reference facilitated by language is not, and does not have to be, of this nature. To speak of 'the Cup Final' is to allow that 'it' was experienced in so many different ways, without dissolving into non-being. So it is with literary texts. They have their being and their being is their meaning. Macherey's work is a monument to the spectre of 'meaning': since meaning is only conceived as an entity (meaning$_1$ in its fluid-receptable version), we must dispense with it altogether, and speak evasively of absence, of gap, of silence. The meaning of a sentence depends upon the meanings of the words in it and the syntactical relations they are made to hold. Because these words and syntactical rules depend for their capacity to formulate meanings upon the entire linguistic system of which they are part, we cannot therefore deduce that we cannot study the meaning of the sentence, but must concern ourselves only with the 'real condition of its very possibility'.

What is true of ordinary propositions applies also to literary texts: we can speak of their having meaning, or of their being specifically meaningful, without committing ourselves to the fallacy that they are self-enclosed ideolects, mysterious and self-sufficient. The resources of the relevant culture, or linguistic system, create the capacity for meaning: they do not create the meaning itself, for meaning is a function of assertion.

Now we have here evidence of a profound schism in contemporary criticism. For Macherey, it is not enough for the critic to describe the work: he must have a more important role. Accepting an empiricist, descriptive role is demeaning: 'Dependent entirely upon its object, the critical judgement is required only to reproduce and imitate it by tracing its obvious outline.'[9] Now if we replace Macherey's contemptuous 'obvious outline' with, say, Arnheim's 'particular configuration of forces', or my own 'internal dimension' or 'real form', we can see that Macherey has given a reasonable definition of a certain form of criticism – one which we might happily call empiricist. There is no reason for such a criticism to bow its head in shame: the outline isn't always obvious, and it is an important, difficult and subtle function the critic has proposed himself, one which is, in our kind of society, vitally important. Why then does Macherey despise it? It can only be because he really despises also the literary texts which the empiricist critic takes it upon himself to describe. For the only 'displacement' the book can accomplish (by displacement we must take it that Macherey means 'effect') is, he says, 'to be consumed, to move out from the provisional container of the book into the minds of possible readers, minds in diverse states of clarity and readiness'. 'Why not?' we might ask. The work exists, Macherey says of the literary text as conceived by empiricism, 'only to be received'! Why not? Why else should it eixst but to be read, to be 'consumed', to have an effect upon people?

A mature empiricism is made up of at least two interdependent beliefs. The first is that, in our society, this act of reading is by no means automatic, like the reception on the retina of an image, so that criticism (explication, interpretation) is a necessary part of literary culture. The second is the belief that the critical performance is a complex process, involving (a) the critic's initial 'understanding' of the text, (b) his description of its configuration of forces, internal dimension, inner form, or value, (c) the reader's reception of this description, and (d) his *re-*experience of the text under the influence of this description. It is this last element, (d), I suggest, which is principally absent from the work of those critics who see criticism as autotelic discourse. According to (d), the critic does not add anything to the text: he merely alters (and enriches) the reader's experience of the text. But this view in turn depends upon (b), that the critic's 'version' of the text is neither an alternative replacement of the original nor a mere repetition of its elements. It was the fault, as we saw, of stylistics and formalism, that they believed that mere transcription of elements would yield interpretation. It does not; the criticism must diverge from the text to be of any use. But the critic's useful divergence from the text cannot take the form of a substitute for it, because it is in the meta-language, not the object-language. This divergence, moreover, takes place in a different dimension, that of value and 'pertinence' (in Todorov's term). The critic's statement therefore of the text's internal dimension or real form (= its literariness) neither offers an alternative experience to the text nor a distortion of it. Because the critic uses the meta-language, the variety of things he can say is theoretically unlimited. The critical performance is only completed when the reader who experiences it returns to the text to *re*-experience *that*. It is vitally important to remember that criticism assumes an effect upon a possible reader, an effect only possible if the reader has first experienced the text and then later re-experiences it. This is to say, of course, that the critic's performance is essentially dialectical. And it is this element of the dialectic which is missing from all those modern critical modes which assume an autotelic, self-sufficient function for criticism. Criticism is part of social behaviour, and if it is prosecuted in a self-involved way it becomes aberrant, anti-social behaviour. The question we must ask of a critical text is not 'is it true?' but 'is it useful?'

All this is part of the meaning of an empiricist criticism. And all of it rests upon one major assumption: that what happens when a literary text is 'received' in the mind of reader is quite simply important – important morally, spiritually and socially. The inescapable conclusion to be drawn from those critics who try to give criticism its own end and autonomy is that for them literature has simply ceased to be important: the texts, and the experiences they offer, are not considered to be in themselves of sufficient value and significance. The empiricist critic respects his own function primarily because he respects the texts upon which it is practised. The qualities felt to lie in texts give them a status: collectively these exalted texts constitute the literary tradition, a body of especially privileged works distinguished by their quality and set up as standards. Obviously an empiricist criticism such as I have just outlined will tend to support the idea of such a tradition. In fact, the question of tradition which has exercised critics in America so much recently,[10] is dependent upon the question of the textual object: the real issue is not whether we support the idea of a tradition or not, but whether we respect the idea of the text – the work of art, the aesthetic object. To de-textualise or contextualise the aesthetic object is necessarily to reject it as an independent source of value. The central issue here then is that of the status of the aesthetic object in criticism. The view I am presenting as that of an enlightened empiricism rests upon the fundamental conviction that the literary text, like all other art-works, exists at the level of the aesthetic, and that this aesthetic existence is the source of its value.

It is just such a conviction which has come under attack. In Pierre Macherey this results in insoluble contradictions, resulting, in turn, in equivocation: the text is 'autonomous' but not 'independent', it is not 'created' but 'produced', it is not 'illusion' but 'fiction', it is not 'ideology' but '(transforms) our relations to ideology'; most slippery of all, it is not 'determined' in the crude old Marxist sense, but is 'the intersection of several lines of determination'. At the end of all this, it is hardly surprising to be told that the work of art is really nothing at all, a mere negative photograph of certain ideological absences. Pierre Macherey is a Marxist and his criticism is designed honestly to discredit 'bourgeois' culture, that is, the culture of the West as we have it now. He has nothing to put in its place. But that is not really the issue. The question is whether we accept the fact that the subject-matter (or the object-language) of criticism is the text – the aesthetic object – or whether we follow one of the de-constructive modes available, and de-textualise the work, leaving unaddressed the question, what is the nature of the experience offered by the text?

It is in the light of such questions that we must consider the matter of interpretation. An empiricist model of interpretation insists that the 'meaning' of the text lies in the words the text uses. A hermeneuticist theory of interpretation, on the other hand, insists upon what (at first sight anyway) looks like the exact opposite: the surface meaning of the text (what an empiricism might be able to establish) is never the important one, we must look elsewhere. Or perhaps we should say else*wise* , for it is really the nature of the act of reading that is, again, in question. A mature empiricism allows 'reading' to take place in the traditionally understood way: we read by perusing a surface and understanding its import. However complicated this might be in neurological or psycho-physiological terms, it is always a more or less straightforward matter. An extreme or sceptical hermeneutics insists upon the reverse – that whatever reading is, it is never simple and never perhaps what we think it is. Over the past ten years or so, a complex tradition of sceptical hermeneutics has grown up which scorns the possibility of an empiricist criticism because it rejects the presuppositions upon which it is based. Do these new modes of interpretation enable us to dispense with the level of the aesthetic altogether, and thus with the 'text' as traditionally understood?

(ii) BLOOM AND THE INTERTEXT

The inadequacies of a too simple-minded formalism or structuralism have long been apparent even to critics whose main work is in establishing the text's features in an empiricist spirit: something seems left out of account. To handle this sense of inadequacy, Jonathan Culler distinguished between structural poetics and a structuralist criticism. Structural poetics has as its task to establish the text in all its linguistic complexity. Structuralist criticism, on the other hand, has the task of reading the text so established *towards* some deeper meaning:

> A structuralist criticism . . . as opposed to a structuralist poetics, which does not aim at an interpretation, tends to use as models of significance notions of language, of literature itself, and of the sign.[11]

This shares the philosophical aridity characteristic of structuralism, an aridity which emerges still more depressingly in what follows: 'The successful critical act will show what the poem implies about the status of the sign and the poetic act itself.'[12] It is characteristic of structuralist and semioticist criticism to send us from text to semiotic commentary and back to text without anything significant having happened. Culler merely expresses a sense of the need for some rationale beyond the poetics: 'There is no way to escape from such models altogether, for the simple reason that one must have a sense, however undefined, of what one is reading towards.'[13] What sort of thing this might be Culler does not say: it is a mere desideratum.

What does Culler mean by 'reading towards'? In what way is this different from 'mere' reading? Is there such a thing as 'mere' reading? Clearly, a method which divides the critical process into two parts (structural poetics and structuralist criticism), as if these represented two different experiences, is incapable of doing justice to the complexity either of texts or of the act of reading them. Hermeneuticist modes claim to be rectifying precisely this fault by showing that neither text nor reading is as the empiricist believes them to be.

The gauntlet was thrown down by Harold Bloom, who claimed that the act of reading, far from being the absorption of a given textual surface, is and 'must be transgressive'; literary texts are like the Torah in Gershon Scholem's description which 'consists, in the last analysis, of interpretations or definitions of what is hidden'. Thus, we must accept either that no text is to be read at its face value (or merely described, even in the enlightened way I have outlined above), or resign ourselves to a facile ignorance, under the tutelage of Matthew Arnold, 'greatest of School Inspectors'.[15] There are two aspects to Bloom's position – a scansion-theory and an interpretation-theory – which don't always cohere. Bloom embraces a de-textualist scansion-theory which he calls intertextuality. This notion is not unlike the concepts of tradition variously proffered by T. S. Eliot and F. R. Leavis; but where both Eliot and Leavis insist on the aesthetic independence of the texts within this tradition so that the tradition is modified by the texts, for Bloom the texts are modified by the tradition: 'What we call "literature" is inescapably connected to education by a continuity of twenty-five hundred years.'[16] Writing is like living, in that it is caught up from the outset in a mesh of influences; it is 'ravaged by otherness', because the writer's literary language, like his personality, was not given him entire, absolute and independent, but only something he discovered too late, when it was already created for him. Bloom dismisses outright the idea of the absolutely original poem (as Eliot had fifty years earlier): 'What happens if one tries to write, or to teach, or to think, or even to read without the sense of tradition? – Why, nothing at all happens, just nothing. You cannot write or teach or think or even read without imitation, and what you imitate is what another person has done, that person's writing or teaching or thinking or reading.'[17] Tradition, therefore, is re-defined as the intertext – that is, the interacting sum of all the texts that have ever been written and read. Thus there are, properly speaking, no texts at all, only commentaries on all the other texts: creation becomes interpretation.

This is the scansion-theory that props up, or is propped up by, Bloom's hermeneutic theory. Bloom's intertextuality severs poetic and literary language from those enclosed 'meanings' and

referents beloved of the empiricist critic: it is not the overt desig-
nations of texts we are concerned with; these merely mask the
real content. A valid criticism, we remember, 'consists, in the last
analysis, of interpretations or definitions of what is hidden'.
Bloom's thesis is a confusion of hard- and soft-core modernisms.
It is a matter of empirical fact that the great wealth of the
English literary tradition has led to an *Angst*-ridden situation for
the writer. The great classical masters confronted the primal
situation of mankind bravely and effectually: modern writers
(such as Thomas Pynchon) are reduced to 'sado-masochistic
parody' of the tradition. This is soft-core, but strictly speaking,
Bloom's theory applies to all writing, of whatever period, and
his main contention that all reading is mis-reading, and all texts
shadowy reincarnations of one great master-text (*'Text itself'*), is
hard-core, and effectively does away with any concrete analysis
of what the surfaces of texts say. It is the nihilistic implications of
such a position which Bloom tried to scotch with his postulation
of a Freudian master-plot in literature. De-constructionism has
shown no interest in any such master-plot of literature, and has
been happy to follow Bloom's dangerous implications to their
logically illogical conclusion: if all texts are re-doings of past
texts, then they are reduced to language, interpretations of other
interpretations; literature never has had a 'content', it is put into
motion by language itself. Bloom strongly dissociates himself
from this 'serene linguistic nihilism', rooted in the fallacy 'that
language by itself writes the poems and thinks'. Yet he himself is
condemned to despair, because of his belief in the essentially
interpretative nature of all texts: 'Words refer *only* to other
words, to the end of it.'[18] The battle lines, then, have to be
re-drawn. We began with a simple opposition between an
empiricist criticism, content to do justice to the text in all its
complexity on the one hand, and a hermeneutic criticism insisting upon *reading towards* deeper content on the other. Now we see
that the scene of confrontation has shifted. Bloom insists upon
analysing 'what is hidden'; de-constructionism accepts the invitation to disregard the surface meanings of the text, but denies
that there is anything hidden: it follows Foucault in believing
that for modern man 'Things and words were . . . separated
from one another'.[19] Thus, de-constructionism concurs in
Bloom's rejection of the empiricist meanings in literary texts, but
rejects in turn his primal family romance, his deep Freudian

content, wishing to concern itself only with linguistic traces, the play of discourse.

(iii) NEO-FREUDIANISM

Yet the common Freudian orignation of Bloom's criticism and that of mildly de-constructionist critics such as Geoffrey Hartman and Hillis Miller suggests not only the fundamental kinship of apparently opposed schools, but a certain ambiguity within de-constructionism itself. To analyse this ambiguity we must ask ourselves why it is that Freud has made such a spectacular return to literary criticism. Freudian criticism had always been the butt of the sophisticated *littérateur*: if Ernest Jones's *Hamlet* and Freud's own *Leonardo* were the best one could expect, what hope was there of a continuance in that direction? A wise Rip van Winkle put to sleep in 1945, say, could certainly never have predicted that in 1970, when he awoke, he would find a critical *avant garde* largely dominated by the methodology of Freud. What is the explanation of this puzzling phenomenon? Geoffrey Hartman, an eminent neo-Freudian, dismisses the old Freudianism contemptuously: 'We read them now', he says, 'only to know the worst.' Their exercises are 'tactless, crude and reductionist'.[20] Yet Freud now provides method for whole schools of *avant garde* criticism. Why?

The explanation is not difficult to find. If Freud had earlier provided his disciple-critics with material with which to fill art-works (Shakespeare's plays with Oedipus complexes, Leonardo's pictures with ghost-birds), he now provides them with techniques for emptying them. *The Interpretation of Dreams* — probably the most influential single work of Freud's in the current scene — is now used to provide a hermeneutic methodology, not an inventory of symbolic equivalences. Freud is important, that is to say, not because he taught us what meanings to find in dream-images, but because he imparted a systematic way of subverting the apparent and overt. He has thus become a paradigm of the hermeneutic critic, remorselessly sceptical of surface meaning.

It is at this point, however, that the doubts arise. For we see in the exploitation of Freud's methodology only one of a number of nihilistic symptoms in contemporary criticism, the result if not the aim of which is nothing less than the systematic discrediting of Western culture and Western society as a whole. It is notable that two other great Jewish thinkers – Marx and Einstein – have also provided weapons for this campaign. The twentieth century has been at the same time the worst age in the history of ages of Jewish persecution, and perhaps the greatest age of Jewish thought. Marx taught us to interpret the forms of culture as superstructure. Marxist superstructure and ideology are the political equivalents of Freudian defence-mechanism: ideology and the overt images of dream are the lies of society and the conscious mind respectively. Marxism disregards the overt values of literary texts (its fine thoughts, beautiful images, universal Truth) and characteristically attempts to discredit its 'appeal' to its readers by suggesting that both writer and reader are unified in delusion. It is the means of production and the class-struggle that are the real dictating forces behind literature, not the writer's declared intention of analysing motivation, celebrating Nature or exploring the 'human condition'. The soul, God and the human condition are all analysed away as ideological constructs designed by power-groups to perpetuate the *status quo*.

There is a natural transition from such sceptical modes of analysis, according to which none of the values of so-called 'bourgeois culture' must be allowed to remain intact, to psychoanalytical disintegration, according to which none of the claims made by the bully father-ego – a liar with his paid-up factor in the underworld (the preconscious) – can be accepted at their face value, so that nothing remains of utterance but accidental hints unwittingly divulging the real truth. Sartre was perhaps the first thinker historically who saw the possibilities in a Freud–Marx axis. The power of such disintegrative modes of analysis is augmented still further when it is allied, vaguely and tendentiously, to a rationale of relativity and indeterminacy picked up from popularised accounts of the work of Einstein and Heisenberg. Like Freud and Marx, Einstein has also had the effect primarily of loosening Western man's sense of his own certainties. Relativity and indeterminacy are still coins with a certain amount of value in criticism, and the critic seeking to discredit received cultural ideology is still likely to turn to them when in need of ammunition. Suffice it to say that these concepts are so little understood by laymen that their use by a literary critic or political philosophy is likely to betray only a symptom of a certain disingenuousness in the critic. The general theory of relativity certainly does not justify the critic in saying that 'everything is relative', nor does Heisenberg's principle of indeterminacy apply to anything outside the specific theoretical situations framed in its terms: it is not a licence for a general cultural free-for-all.

Such caveats are particularly important in the case of the new Freudianism. Freud himself strove hard to reinforce the ego and – by implication – the civilisation which is the ego's image, by alerting it to the attacks of the id, and also by trying to uncover the source of the ego's lying habits. He was essentially a lord and master, a sexist husband and generally a pillar of the establishment. Was he nevertheless the founder of a new order which is disorder, glorying in the opportunities for revision, disruption, misreading, the 'Freudian slip' – the psychopathology that is 'of' everyday life in precisely that double sense Geoffrey Hartman exploits, that is, as both proceeding from it and glossing on it? What inspires the new Freudianism is the hope of answering these questions affirmatively: it seeks to show that Freud's analyses of consciousness and of everyday language can be applied to all forms of utterance, so that the 'institution' which Freud hoped to establish in place of the old discredited order (which was after all partly based upon authorised lies) itself becomes vulnerable to its own hermeneutics.

Clearly to effect such a programme it is necessary first to debunk the primacy of those famous contents – the sexual and familial crises and situations which were the fodder of the old Freudians. Freud must be exploited for his disintegrative hermeneutics, not for his positivistic uncovering of other Truths. The new literary Freudians wish to exploit Freud's sceptical hermeneutics without saddling themselves with the meanings revealed by this hermeneutics. This is the difference between Bloom, for instance, and a de-constructionist like Hartman. Bloom wishes to undermine empiricist criticism because he thinks it is superficial and ignorant; he wants to replace the overt content of literature with a deeper underlying one. Hartman wishes to undermine meaning itself, not just the particular meanings of given texts (or dreams) but any meaning – meaning itself. Thus, he must discredit not only the conscious lies revealed in Freud's patient analyses, but the generally accepted contents discovered to lie beneath them. Speaking of *The Inter-*

pretation of Dreams, therefore, Hartman observes: 'Freud does not reduce dreams to sexual messages but insists rather that infantile sexual experience structures what is dreamed.'[21] We are not to say, therefore, that Freud his discredited one content (the conscious mind's overt lies) to replace it with another (the sexual obsessions beneath them). We are to say that the sexual experience provides mere structure. If accepted, this will conveniently dispose of those embarrassing meanings divulged by Freudian fossicking. It is significant, too, that Hartman's statement comes in an essay supporting Jacques Derrida's plea for a 'hermeneutics of indeterminacy'. Here is a conjunction of the modish disintegrators.

In fact, however, Hartman is quite wrong to say that 'Freud does not reduce dreams to sexual messages'. (His use of 'messages' is odd and we will come to it in due course.) On the contrary, Freud insisted, against the cogently urged reasonings of Jung, Adler and others, that dreaming had a more or less exclusively sexual function: it was not the mere material of dreaming, but its goal that expressed 'sexual desire'.

Freud obviously experienced a good deal of embarrassment on this head, in fact. He was prepared at one point to stand behind Otto Rank, who had asserted that 'On the basis and with the help of repressed infantile sexual material, dreams regularly represent present-day, and also as a rule erotic, wishes as fulfilled, in a veiled and symbolically disguised shape.'[22] To the footnote in which he quotes Rank's observation, added to the text of *The Interpretation of Dreams* in 1911, Freud later, in 1925, added a further and longer note in which he defended himself first against the possible charge of plagiarising Rank, and then against the general 'bourgeois' charge of saying that 'all dreams have a sexual content'. He adduces the evidence of his own analyses of childish and superficial dreams in which the wish-fulfilment process takes the form of satisfying simple desires such as eating and drinking and urinating. He then hesitantly concedes the activity of the sexual function in a watered-down form as 'erotic', in his own broader sense of libidinal and instinctual forces as opposed to destructive ones. This is still fairly defensive. Later in the book, however, Freud is more overt: 'The more one is concerned with the solution of dreams, the more one is driven to recognise that the majority of dreams of adults deal with sexual material and give expression to erotic wishes.'[23] But of course these are only general, summary statements: what is really important is the constant concern, throughout *The Interpretation of Dreams* to establish the wish-fulfilment function of dreaming, even in apparently contradictory cases such as anxiety dreams. Anxiety in dreams, we are told, 'may originate from psychosexual excitations'.[24] Anxiety stands revealed as oblique exploitation of sexual energy which is frustrated or unused in conscious activity. Again and again, moreover, Freud stresses that the most innocent-seeming dreams reveal, under analysis, a solid sexual function: they are innocent only through the crafty machinations of the censor in the pre-conscious, who fools the conscious with a smoke-screen of trivialities. 'It is fair to say', Freud summarises, 'that there is no group of ideas that is incapable of representing sexual facts and wishes.'[25]

The basic purpose of Freud's investigation was threefold: to establish the fact that (a) dreams are wish-fulfilment, all contrary evidence notwithstanding, (b) they come from reservoirs of infantile experience and memory, and (c) they are functional. The dream he defines specifically as 'a (disguised) fulfilment of a (suppressed or repressed) wish',[26] and the wish that is *'represented in a dream must be an infantile one'*.[27] All we need to add to these well-known facts is the significance of Freud's emphasis upon the particular functionality of dreams: the content of the dream (imagery, instigation, and so on) is one thing; the function served by the exploitation of this content quite another. The function served, Freud leaves us in no possible doubt, is nearly always sexual.

It is, therefore, not true to say that Freud regarded the dream as merely being 'structured' by infantile sexual experience. There is not a page in *The Interpretation of Dreams* which leaves us in any doubt that it is the goal of dreaming, its function, which is sexual, not the structure. It is, of course, wrong to call a dream a message: it is not, it is the functional act of satisfaction. No recipient of the message is required; the dreamer need satisfy only himself: the ritual that he is performing is not like speech – it is not like communication at all. It is more like a primitive purification rite, in which the performer requires no audience, no congregation, rather as a believer crosses himself on entering a church. The dream is an act, not a message. Hartman's use of a linguistic model for dreaming here is surely significant. For his kind of Freudianism can appear to problematicise the literary text only because of an acceptance of that peculiar mode of Freudian thinking associated with Jacques Lacan. Lacan effectively reduced the unconscious to language: 'The unconscious is neither primodial nor instinctual; what it knows about the elementary is no more than the elements of the signifier.'[28] This motif reappears in Hartman: 'language can be said to characterise the very structure of the psyche.'[29]

This would certainly have been news to Freud, as indeed would Lacan's translation of *condensation* and *displacement* (the primary modes of symbolisation in the dream-work) into Saussurean terminology. In the models of the mind given in *The Interpretation of Dreams*, the principal elements are sensory perception (the input-end of the mechanism), mnemonic processes, and motor action (the output-end of the mechanism). In these models, and throughout *The Interpretation of Dreams*, there is no suggestion that language has any privileged position. It is essentially an instrument at the service of an inchoate set of drives and obsessions that are satisfied more with *visual images* than with the names that language enables the dreamer later to apply to these images. It is characteristic of de-constructionism, or more broadly the movement I shall later call logomania,[30] to concern itself so exclusively with language as to eliminate from existence the drives and realities which language merely gestures towards. This complex matter I shall deal with in more detail in the next chapter. Here, suffice it to say that the obsession with language in much recent thinking constitutes a gross over-simplification both of the nature of the human condition and of the problems that condition poses. The de-constructionist version of Freud is a case in point: it overlooks the fact that the processes uncovered in Freud's analyses (a) took place largely in terms of visual imagery by no means to be exhausted in their linguistic identities, and (b) that the analyses, like the dreams they operate on, presuppose actual experiences and emotions outside the scope of the dreamer's language. The 'content' of Freud's analyses, in other words, was not language but extra-linguistic experience.

A genuine Freudian hermeneutics must recognise this fact. What the neo-Freudian wishes to do is to preserve the disintegrative effect of Freudian hermeneutics (showing everything to be what it is not), without standing by the consequences of this attitude and committing himself to a psychotherapy to be confirmed or falsified and *fixing substantival ceiling to the critic's theoretical scope*. It is this 'invidious' substantivism which de-constructionism wishes to avoid. What de-constructionism is committed to discrediting is a language-theory of 'closure' (in Derrida's term) – that is, determinate meanings in specific situations. An empiricism, as we have seen, is committed to the opposite view: that whatever else its ultimate purposes might be, the text is to be understood in its given terms: it has meaning, is meaningful. Thus, de-constructionism represents an extreme (and, I shall try to show) an illicit stage of hermeneuticism: the surfaces of texts must be disregarded not in the interest of a deeper meaning, but because meaning itself is a sham, a mere relativity of 'discourse'.

As an illustration to the general case, I give Jacques Lacan's 'interpretation' of Edgar Allan Poe's story 'The Purloined Letter', together with Jacques Derrida's attack on Lacan's article.[31] I do so out of no admiration for the Poe story, Lacan's 'analysis' or Derrida's critique of this analysis. The story is second-rate, the analysis pedestrian where meaningful, silly where not; the critique run-of-the-mill (though perhaps exceptionally sensible for Derrida). I do so simply because it illustrates neatly the relationship of palaeo- and neo-Freudian criticism. Basically, Lacan's analysis divides into two parts: the pedestrian part is palaeo-Freudian, and consists in interpreting the story in terms of penis-envy; Poe disguises female penis-envy in the garb of a 'harmless' detective story about a lost letter. So far, so good: this is routine Freudian interpretation, no sillier than many. Indeed, less: for the story *is* trivial unless we attend to a hidden something, something which calls to us through its presentation of certain narrative relations: the movement from table to mantlepiece, for instance, the juxtaposition of protuberance and vacuity. Lacan's analysis is something Freud could be imagined producing, let us say, if the teller of the story were a patient under analysis.

But of course this is just what Lacan cannot stomach: this is palaeo-Freudian substantivism – the story is being given a definite meaning. Stage two – the identifyingly neo-Freudian stage – is the translation of *this* allegory (that of penis-envy) into another: the 'allegory of the signifier', in which Saussurean linguistics provides labels which are tied around the neck of those embarrassingly 'real' things (letters, queens, mantelpieces, and so on) in order to gut them of any reality. The story is really saying, Lacan asserts, something about language, about signs. Now this second reading is made on the strength of the fact that Poe doesn't tell us what was *in* the letter which the queen so badly wanted re-claimed. We don't know what the letter says, we only know that the queen wants it back. Because it therefore lacks a meaning, the letter is like the signifier in semiology. It was able to produce its effects *within* the story – on the actors in the tale, including the narrator, as well as *outside* the story, on us, the readers, and also on its author – without anyone's ever bothering to worry about what it *meant*.'[32]

This device is sufficient to redeem Lacan's analysis from its dangerously palaeo-Freudian substantivism: we are not to think that Lacan has located definite meaning in the text; on the contrary he has shown us that *Poe* has shown us that meanings are not predictable: signifiers lack signifieds. It is difficult to think of a more transparent sleight-of-hand: Lacan's allegory of the signifier is purchased at the expense of every shred of credibility. It is a mere rhetorical device that Poe refrains from telling us what was in the letter to bother the queen – the kind of astuteness which made him withhold the description of the horrible creature awaiting the victim of the Inquisition in *The Pit and the Pendulum*. More, we don't *need* to know: it is enough that the queen and the blackmailer know. The letter has an added power of meaning for us, the readers, precisely because we don't actually know its contents; contents which are in effect over-determined by the intensity of interest with which all the actors in the tale pursue it. It is, therefore, sheer nonsense to say that the letter produces its effects because it has no meaning: on the contrary, it produces its effects because it does have meaning. The fact that it is not important that *we* know this specific meaning is neither here nor there: that is a matter of aesthetic economy. As a matter of fact, we know as much as we need to know: it obviously concerns some indiscretion of the queen's, some affair or other. All that matters is that the actors in the little drama know the letter's contents, and therefore its meaning. Dupin, like ourselves, needs only to know of the letter's importance: its 'meaning' for him is, therefore, 'information-leading-to-scandal-which-must-be-avoided-at-all-costs . . .'.

As de-constructionist, Derrida finds this absurd semiological allegory insufficient compensation for Lacan's substantivist reading. He accuses Lucan of converting Poe's 'literature' into a pre-given psychoanalytic content: 'The displacement of the signifier is analysed as a signified, as the recounted object in a short story.'[33] Barbara Johnson summarises Derrida's very orthodox criticisms by saying that Derrida accuses Lacan of treating Poe's story 'as "a real drama," a story like the stories a psychoanalyst hears every day from his patients'.[34] In other words, Derrida accuses Lacan of the fault almost every psycho-analytic critic has been accused of – importing his own contents willy nilly into what he reads, and reducing the literary meaning of the text to psychoanalysis: Lacan gives the letter purloined as definite and concrete a 'meaning' as the palaeo-Freudian critic gave to phallic protuberances and uterine vacuities; he also ignores the story's 'literary' qualities. (These are threadbare in Derrida's account, consisting largely of its 'frames' – that is, its relations to other Poe stories.)

Now there is nothing particularly important in Derrida's hav-ing chosen to play angel's advocate here: no man is incapable of common sense, and what he says is neither original nor espe-cially acute. The whole episode nevertheless makes clear two things. First, that any psychoanalytic reading of a text must base itself upon the specific contents suggested by Freud: Oedipus situation, repression, trauma, unconscious drives. To commit oneself to psychoanalysis at any level is necessarily to accept that these terms refer to processes and experiences daily suffered by living people and that the sheer importance of these processes and experiences is what, in turn, makes the literary text matter to us. These terms can be structuralised, of course: we can pre-tend that the linguistic expressions used to refer to them have no meaning outside themselves; we can dice them up, shred them, disperse them into strata, spheres, formation, according to what-ever geometrical or archaeological model we choose. But beyond that there is the world transcribed in that knowledge – the world which Husserl, for instance, constantly held steadily in view when suggesting the process of bracketing-out meaning in order to find out something about the way we experience. A psychoanalytic criticism has to confine itself to locating in liter-ary texts traces of those psychic events and processes regularly undergone by actual human beings. As such, it is neither more nor less valid than many other modes of enquiry. But it certainly cannot be offered as a final untying of the hermeneutical knot.

It is not possible, I submit, to have a psychoanalytic criticism which does not treat the residual content of Freudian analysis as operative and substantival in the work of art. In order to substantiate a psychoanalytic reading of a text, some such deposit, trace, shadow, ghost or structural analogue of some recognisable Freudian content must be present. It is no use relying upon Freud's general resourcefulness as a provider of translation-mechanisms to redeem or rescue a text from its overt or empirically testable meaning: *this is only to push the frontiers of interpretation back one stage*. If it is prosecuted in good faith, a Freudian hermeneutics establishes 'meanings' as definite as those of empiricism: like those of empiricism, its findings can be confirmed or falsified – in theory at any rate. Lacan implicitly recognised this by arranging an escape-hatch for the 'deep' Freudian content of the Poe story by means of the implausible signifier-allegory. Sooner or later, the rap must be faced as the interpreter runs out of appeal courts. This means in fact that Lacan's interpretation is only a pseudo-interpretation, or rather perhaps, a sturdy interpretation dressed up as non-interpretation (sheep in wolf's clothing, or lamb-as-mutton, it's some kind of drag).

The vast majority of neo-Freudian de-constructionism is either pseudo-interpretation or conventional interpretation disguised as a new radicalism: hermeneutically speaking, we end up behind the line we started from.

Paradoxically, the particular 'closures' entailed by psychoanalytic reading – the deep interpretation that underlies not only the surface of the text but the de-constructionist's negative pretensions – may well be justified. In so far as a psychoanalytic reading is the 'correct' one, the de-constructionist case is *de*-confirmed; it appears that these texts-without-signification have their signification all right, but it lies under the surface, as in Freud. Such a view, as Macherey points out, is dubious, since it implies a 'theoretical distinction between realities and appearance' and therefore has 'no theoretical value'.[35] I should nevertheless be prepared to go along with such a distinction in this case, just as I am prepared to accept Freud's psychic topography of id–ego–superego because of the phenomena it helps to explain. We must insist, however, that Freud would have regarded as criminal nonsense the notion that interpretation can be abandoned in favour of a so-called hermeneutics of indeterminacy. The result of Freudian interpretation is not to disintegrate a text, but on the contrary to strengthen it from below.[36]

(iv) HERMENEUTICISM

What is the upshot of all this? Where does a Freudian methodology of paranomasia take us in our search for interpretation? It takes us, paradoxically, back to where we started. There is nothing in Freud to suggest, much less justify, an abandonment of what I should call an empirical or experiential mode of interpretation. That is to say, a mode which assumes a certain condition to which literature refers, and in reference to which its products are to be analysed. Freudian analysis does not dissolve the bases of utterance, it merely changes the foci of the interpretation of utterance. Thus, what is at issue is the proper description of these foci, and this in turn means asking, again, what *is* the nature of Man? Merely to bring forth examples of ambiguity hoping that this will disqualify any 'closure' of meaning is sheer folly, an intellectual irresponsibility equalled in its fecklessness only by its methodological confusion. There is certainly nothing in Freud to justify such a stance. Neither is there in Nietzsche – also exploited by de-constructionists as a founder of disintegration. Nietzsche's 'deep-reading' of Greek tragedy in terms of the Appollonian-Dionysiac drives outraged Greek scholars because it seemed to ignore the textual facts.[37] Yet it does not, any more than Freud's analyses.

This controversy can be found in every age. Jean Picard attacked Roland Barthes's *Racine* on largely the same grounds. And this might seem to be at the root of the matter of interpretation: honour the text, or ignore it and go through to other meanings. Harold Bloom has pointed out that the controversy itself is as old as Hellenistic criticism with its 'crucial clash between two schools of interpretation, the Aristotelian-influenced school of Alexandria and the Stoic-influenced school of Pergamon.[38] 'The school of Alexandria championed the mode of *analogy*, while the rival school of Pergamon espoused the mode of *anomaly*.' Thus, the analogists regarded the text as a unity with one fixed meaning, the anomalists regarded it as 'an interplay of differences and had meanings that rose out of those differences'.[39] We could surely extend Bloom's observations backwards and sideways: have we not here that fundamental dualism exemplified in the philosophies of Aristotle and Plato? Aristotle the empiricist, always testing assertion by reason (as his modern successors would by experiment), in order to give a description of the world, Plato using the given only as a shadow cast by the ulterior, anterior and superior World (the Ideas are all these in Plato). This is not to 'reduce' Plato to a theorist of articulation: it is on the contrary to raise a theory of articulation to the level of a philosophy. Properly speaking, there can be no theory of meaning without a philosophy of life. This can be dressed up one way or another to sound less embarrassing, but it is as well to come out in the open. What we have in theories of utterance or articulation is theories of life expressed at a linguistic level.

This emerges even more clearly in another historical illustration of this basic hermeneutic dualism: the mediaeval need to explain and justify poetry by showing that even in its pagan form it was always doing something *other than* (and of course *better* than) it appeared to be doing on the surface. The mode of analysis chosen – the allegorical – had been laid down by the Stoics who habitually interpreted the ancient myths and legends in terms of moral properties: the myths might seem foolish and fanciful – in fact they were stern moral allegories, illustrating virtues and vices. It needed only a greater sophistication and deepening for this to emerge as early Christian Bible interpretation in terms of the literal, typical and the moral levels. Dante added to these three levels of meaning a fourth, the anagogical, or mystical. This in general became the accepted Christian way of explaining or justifying what otherwise appeared shamefully irresponsible or wicked writing: poetry was not destructive or licentious, but deeply moral.

This suggests perhaps a rather superficial kind of interpretation, reducing literature to illustration of ethical premises and Christian doctrine. In fact, though, there is nothing superficial in mediaeval Christian interpretation: as the example of Dante suggests, an allegorical hermeneutics can go right to the heart of the literary enterprise. It suggests that there is a realm of Truth which we can only approach through images or allegories, and this, I should argue, remains as a *sine qua non* of any serious literary criticism.

Such a view depends, again, on a philosophy of life: our epistemologies like our hermeneutics depend upon our ontologies and teleologies. We have seen this in the case of psychoanalytic criticism. We see it also in Nietzsche's interpretation of Greek tragedy and Kierkegaard's deep-reading of the Abraham and Isaac myth.

These and other examples suggest that, against a crude empiricism, we must accept the existence of an ancient tradition of interpretative or deep-reading criticism. The idea that this is somehow irrelevant to serious literary criticism (which is what one encounters in certain extreme empiricist critical views) is itself a parochial absurdity. But by the same token we must also reject the idea that the existence of ambiguity at the textual level, or of dual readings of the same text, somehow forces us to accept that the text had no 'meaning', or that it does not exist, that there is no *King Lear* or Book of Genesis. This is as great an absurdity as the extreme empiricist delusion. In the first place we must underline what we have seen emerge already – that deep-readings of texts themselves reinforce the text from below; that is to say, they enunciate a world-view, or theory of being, as emphatically as that view *may be set forth in the text's surface*. Thus, psychoanalytic readings of a text do not free the text of its surface meaning, they merely show that surface meaning to be *other than* it might *at first* appear. Or rather – and here we approach the real crux of the matter – they show that the surface affects us the way it does because of what it *is*: it *is* an allegory of penis-envy, or a paean for the lost father, or whatever. That is why it gets at us. This is very different from saying that the surface text is irrelevant, or a lie, or dispensable, or meaningless. What the psychoanalytic interpretation has shown is that the truths the writer wished to divulge could not be divulged except through imagery and allegory. It does not show that the surface text has no meaning; on the contrary, it shows that it has a richer meaning: change the surface text, and you change the 'deep' text. The text is specified by its deep-readings as much as by its overt meaning.

(v) 'THE CORRECT INTERPRETATION OF THE TEXT IS THE TEXT'

Now this completely alters the landscape. We can allow the possibility of psychoanalytic readings, for instance, without sacrificing a specifying theory of hermeneutics, since psychoanalytic readings do not dispose of the surface text, they merely anchor it more securely in the psyche. Thus, a picture of interpretation begins to emerge which is totally different from the one so frequently proffered by contemporary critics. We begin to see that the gap between an empiricist criticism and a hermeneuticist criticism is perhaps less great than has been imagined: perhaps, indeed, that there is no gap at all. For the interpretation of the hermeneutical critic appears simply as a truer or deeper description. No one has ever supposed, except perhaps the rawest stylistician, that literary texts can *just* be photographed in the analyst's techniques, with *no* deeper readings of the elements tabulated: the difficulty with all textualist analysis has always been precisely that if you don't know what the words 'mean' you can't analyse their function in a poem. And knowing what they mean means a lot more than knowing how they are currently used: it might be necessary to call on a deeep reservoir of historical awareness, as is the case with Jakobson's criticism of Shakespeare. Where does the critic cut off this extra-textual awareness (which might take the form of knowing that Constantinople had just fallen, or that there had been a plague scare, or whatever) from a 'pure' linguistic competence? This is too obvious an objection to a textualist criticism to seem worth repeating. Yet it must be repeated. Jakobson's insistence that the critic must know the language he is analysing fails to answer this objection: it emerges that it is not possible to say that the words on the page have a 'pure' identity. The result of having to accept this fact is at first paradoxical, yet if it does appear paradoxical it is only because of the nature of some of our presuppositions. For the truth is that the text is *not* other than it appears: on the contrary, its disarming danger is that it does indeed declare its meanings; they are worn on the surface – that surface the analyst appears to disregard in his hermeneutic fossicking. It is a naïve delusion to imagine that the surface (that is, the plot, imagery, argument, 'form') of a text can be irrelevant to its 'meaning': the surface carries the signs that the analyst analyses. There is nothing he analyses which is not the poem. Therefore, all he is doing is listening to the poem more carefully – reading it indeed more deeply, but reading it none the less. Consider: how does a critic arrive at a psychoanalytic reading of a story or poem? By seeing in certain elements of the text certain significances. But what does 'significances' mean here? It means only that the elements play a certain role in a certain structure. The structure – which is, ideally, *the whole text* – is the sum of these signs, together with the statement or 'form' they help constitute. There is, as I have said above, no separating any formal skeleton from other dead matter in the work: to speak of formal skeleton is simply a way of describing the work done by the elements of the text: it is not to isolate some of them at the expense of the rest. Now this is exactly what Derrida accused Lacan of doing in the case of the Poe story. This is the error of isolable symbols: Lacan ignores the text, by looking through it to certain pre-existing structures (neuroses, mental patterns, whatever) with which the text happens to have some coincidence. When Derrida accuses Lacan of ignoring the literariness and the frames of Poe's story, he was doing much more than saying he was leaving some of it out of account: he was saying that Lacan was misreading the story's purpose (its intention). He was regarding the psychic 'facts' referred to in Poe's story (penis-envy, castration-complex) as existing through the story, on the other side of it: his own reading therefore was 'parallel' to Poe's reading of these facts and, therefore, in the same linguistic mode, whereas in fact such a 'reading' is in the meta-language, and incapable of commenting on the writer's material in this way.

The formal skeleton of the text, then, is not a pre-existing structure isolable by the critic, but simply a way of describing the way the text works. To the description of this skeleton (stress-pattern, emphasis, internal dimension, real form, or whatever) the lineaments of the text are necessary and important: they are not mere ciphers, symbols of an absent reality: they *are* that reality, only they need more attentive reading than sometimes appears necessary at first.

This allows us to say, I think, that the 'problem' of interpretation is to a large extent a pseudo-problem: any interpretation (deep-reading of an allegorical, Bloomian, or psychoanalytical kind) is perforce a description in so far as it is a valid interpretation; any description (Aristotelian, Leavisite, New Critical, enlightened *explication de texte*) is necessarily an interpretation. The surface of the allegory *is* the allegory, in so far as we require it to be what it is in order for the 'meaning' to be what *it* is. Unless we translate the allegory into something we already know, and thereby bypass the text in favour of our own prior knowledge, we must admit that its 'meaning' is indecipherable from itself. The Lacan–Derrida debate over the Poe story highlights a much older kind of controversy: ultimately, to 'translate' a poem, story or play into an allegorical symbolism is to translate it out of itself. We are not, after all, forbidden to observe the letter of the textual law, ignoring its spirit (which is really what Bloom and others accuse Arnoldian realists of doing). On the contrary, the law of the text *is* to be expounded, it *is* to be sermonised on.

Thus, we are able to reaffirm an empiricist and Aristotelian stance: the letter of the text is to be interpreted, but it remains the letter of the text. The sin against the Holy Ghost is not to dare to interpret the letter of the text: it is to disregard the letter of the text, and substitute for it the unrelated contents of one's own consciousness or of another knowledge. For the 'letter of the text' we can read 'structure': the structure of the text determines its significance, and if the structure is altered, the significance is altered in the same degree. But constituent elements determine structure just as structure determines significance. The error of formalism is to imagine that the elements of structure can be read just as form, as appearance: as we have seen, reading must be interpretative because elements *mean* something, and the structure made up out of the conflict of constituents must be read, just as the constituents themselves are. But the constituents could not engage in conflict, and therefore the structure could not be born, unless they had identities – meanings. Thus, the whole idea of an unlimited, unstructured hermeneutics is inherently absurd. There may be many different readings of a particular text, but they must, at the very least, be structurally compatible.

(vi) REDUCTION TERMS

The existence of many readings of a particular text is often contingent, in fact, upon the acknowledgement of separate levels of interpretation: I do not mean separate levels in the text, but in the critical language. It is at this point perhaps that it is most appropriate to refer to R. S. Crane's discussion of the critic's 'reduction terms': 'preferred general distinctions such as will enable us to formulate and unify the complex oppositions and resolutions of themes in which, as embodied concretely in the patterns of words, images, characters or actions, we must suppose that their total meanings consist.'[40] Unfortunately, as Crane points out, critics tend to draw upon a vast reservoir of received wisdom – 'such familiar and all-embracing dichotomies as life and death (or positive and negative values), harmony and strife, order and disorder, eternity and time, reality and appearance, truth and falsity, certainty and doubt, true insight and false opinion, imagination and intellect' – and so on. And, as Crane then remarks, 'it requires no great insight to find an inner dialectic of order and disorder or a struggle of good and evil forces in any serious plot . . .'.[41] The critic's task, Crane concludes, is not to impose such reduction terms arbitrarily on any work, but only where structurally appropriate: 'The structure of meaning we are concerned to exhibit is one that we must suppose to be objectively in the poem by virtue of the poet's act of expression.'[42] Crane's summary of 'recent' criticism (the lectures his book largely reproduces were given at Toronto in 1952) is masterly, and to a large extent could be reproduced above to supplement my own differentiation of descriptive and interpretative criticism. Finally – and inevitably – his own positive recommendations fail to break out of the circle he has described: to locate a poem's 'subsuming form for the materials' and hence its central or mastering form is impossible except by employing the means of criticism Crane has already discussed. But it is also a regression to the old essentialist aesthetics: it presents a creative world of forms 'sufficiently coherent and intelligible', which exist 'in (the) mind'.[43] Crane's affiliation to the rationalistic criticism represented by Yvor Winters is apparent: logicality and coherence require to be supplemented by so many more of the considerations Crane has somewhat sarcastically summarised earlier as to be useless as methodology.

Crane's insight into the inadequacy of much of the more extreme hermeneuticist criticism, however, is enduringly valuable: it requires common sense to see when and where the 'reduction terms' may be applied in any given case. There is more to it than this, however, and Crane's rationalistic good sense which carries us so far will carry us no farther. What we are confronted by in the multiplicity of reduction terms or points of reference in criticism is something comparable to the relationship of object-language to meta-language referred to above. We found, it will be remembered, that the meta-language (literary criticism in this case) has greater scope than the object-language but less power. It is a kind of set-theory relationship: the class of four-legged animals contains four-legged animals: the class of classes of vertebrates contains the class of four-legged

animals *and* and the class of two-legged animals, but *not*, as it
were, the four-legged or two-legged animals, safe within the
classes that contain them. So, the meta-language of criticism can
refer to the contents of literary texts, but not the 'things' (objects,
processes, emotions) which are referred to in those forms. Transferring this to the realm of interpretation we find the following:
the greater the scope (that is, universality or applicability) of a
theme outside the given text, the less is its power of interpretation of that text. The central point is the same one as Crane
makes ironically that 'it requires no great insight to find an inner
dialectic of order and disorder . . . in any serious plot'. Crane
himself approaches to an answer to the general problem with his
concept of the poem's 'central meaning':[44] the good interpretation is that which explains most of the poem's elements, without
ignoring what doesn't fit the theory, as Lacan ignored Poe's
literary frames, in Derrida's accusation. But to speak of a poem's
'central meaning' is really to beg all the questions that matter.
To answer this question fully we need a theory of literary theme
or content, and I shall give one in due course. In the meantime
let us pursue the idea of decreasing power of interpretation
accompanying increased scope of application.

This idea means that we can allow different interpretations of
the same work providing they are on different levels of scope. For
instance, a vast number of works will be describable as being
'about' life and death, or struggles of good and evil. This is at the
most basic, or to reverse the metaphor, the most general level of
interpretation. Fewer works will be found to exemplify interpretations at a higher or less general level – that, for instance, a
story exemplifies the Oedipus situation, or a castration-complex;
or, to turn to a different source of interpretation, the struggle of
winter and spring.

At a higher level still, fewer works will be found to illustrate
the conflict of mercantilist and capitalist economies. Fewer still
the jealousy of a man for his wife's lover. Only one, the jealousy
of Leontes for Polixenes.

This, certainly, is to equate meaning with content in a way
that may seem unacceptable. Yet a great deal of hermeneuticist
criticism consists of the simple postulation of particular contents
in particular works. And is not the series of increasingly relevant
(which is to say hermeneutically cogent) propositions directly
parallel to the increasingly differentiated statements by which

we bring ourselves to the point of reproducing the actual words of a poem when asked finally to describe its contents? And does not this finally bring us, by a circuitous route, to the empiricist view that the correct interpretation of the text is the text?

For it is now seen that interpretative criticism is subject to the same rule as descriptive criticism, of having to add to its descriptive statements a weighting value-judgement: the hermeneuticist must assert not simply that such-and-such structures or contents in a text are structurally compatible with certain archetypes or external patterns; he must also insist that the consequence of encountering them in the text produces a particular effect. Maud Bodkin herself joyously welcomed the necessity of such an attestation: something in us, she observed, 'leaps in response to the effective presentation in poetry of an ancient theme'.[45] The word 'effective' testifies to her acceptance of the critical recognition. Bodkin rightly emphasises the functional nature of the archetypes, and the dependence of literature upon such functionalities. We could add to this what should already have been apparent: that psychoanalytical criticism likewise presupposes such a functioning, that the mere picking out of structurally compatible analogies (to use Crane's word) does not of itself constitute an interpretation. The apparent existence of numbers of different interpretations of a given text, in other words, is not to be taken on trust: it does not disprove the existence of particular specifiable meaning any more than the existence of verbal ambiguity disproves the possibility of definite meaning in utterance and lucid communication. In fact, we could say that most of the 'interpretations' put forward by critics are not interpretations at all, any more than the retailing of different definitions for a word amounts to an interpretation of the meaning of a sentence. The whole bundle of compatible structures – Freudian, Jungian, Marxist, Frazerian – itself constitutes nothing but a grammar: mere possible structures awaiting utterance before they can assume meaning. Merely to point out the presence in a text of a structure compatible with such-and-such a psychoanalytical complex (castration-fear, Oedipus fixation or whatever) does not in itself constitute an interpretation. The critic has then to relate the structure to everything else in the work, and therefore to establish its *effectiveness*. Once again we are obliged to acknowledge the role of recognition in the critical act: to be an interpretation, a critical description has to insist that the complex outlined in the text is *uttered* by the text, not merely accidentally there. It does not matter that the writer's conscious mind was unaware of the utterance: this is an old argument. We can accept that the ego that signs the poem is subsumed or embedded in a greater psychic whole, and that this greater psychic whole is embedded in a societal or race-historical psyche or whatever. It does not (in the present context anyway) matter what or who utters the poem, just so we admit that it is uttered, and that unless it is, it is no poem. It does not matter whether we postulate some unseen agency in the utterance: Foucault's mythical exteriority of discourse, for instance, reduces utterance to an impersonal 'Anyone who speaks', but anyone speaks from nowhere because it 'is necessarily caught up in the play of an exteriority.'[46] E. E. Cummings himself never thought up anything so mischievously mysterious as that! Only think how much agonising man could have spared himself if he had only known that 'he' did nothing – it 'was done', and done from 'nowhere'. Certainly it gets capitalism off the hook. We should be grateful. If, however, we wish to preserve some measure of actuality and pragmatism in our dealings, we must surely pursue the lines suggested by Freud and Jung that our dreams and our poems are similarly dynamic – functional, in the psychoanalytical sense. For the very thing we cannot combine with an adoption of psychoanalytical procedure is an idea of the inertia of language: language – *parole*, at least – is uttered, and utterance is functional. So that we need to fix only the functionality of the poem: it is a mistake, I think, to try to establish the level of its origination too firmly. Whether it proceeds from conscious will, the drives and instincts of Freudian analysis, from the race-memory or from the discursive formations of a culture (I would suggest it proceeds from all of them) is, at the level of criticism, or interpretation at least, immaterial.

Such a view has important repercussions. The meaning of a text is not to be identified with its contents: we can distinguish, as Freud does, between the material describable in the text-dream (its content, in our philosophically sharpened sense) and the import of the whole text-dream as the contents are activated by intention. Isolable contents (political ideology, psychoanalytic complexes and blockages) are like the words in the dictionary or the letters in the typesetter's box: possibilities rather than meanings. Meaning is acquired only as enterprises are embarked upon: the text is an enterprise, and the name of the enterprise is utterance. Thus, the content of a work can be summarised in the meta-language, within the limits suggested above. But the *meaning* of the work is no less than the effect or import of the whole. The meaning of a poem is neither its purified signs, as in structuralism, nor in the associations of these signs, as in inferential criticism. Until the associations of words are directed in assertion, we cannot properly speak of meaning at all, only of meaning-potential.

From this derives the essentially dynamic nature of poetry: assertion in the poet and perception of assertion in the reader are essential before the metaphysical act of communication is embarked upon. And the metaphysical act of communication must be embarked upon before meaning accrues.

Such a view is in conflict with a considerable number of significant modern critics, with those in particular who wish to discredit traditional critical interpretation by discrediting the ability of language and its constructions to hold 'meaning'. It is with this question we must now be concerned.

9 The Roots of De-Construction

(i) PROPOSITIONALITY

According to the view of meaning outlined in previous chapters, an art-work is a particular organisation of formal elements, elements bearing 'contents' which are uttered, and thereby brought into meaningful statement. To say that a work *means* something is to say that it has both import and intention: its meaning is the myth it proffers through its content. This way of seeing things is apparently threatened by the modern tendency to inundate the channels of communication with what seem to be conflicting interpretations of literary texts. If the text does not disappear under the deluge, it does at least seem over-interpreted to the point where it can seem to mean almost anything, and therefore to seem to 'mean' nothing. But, as I have suggested, most so-called interpretations are not real interpretations at all: they are mere constatations of possibilities – analogies between elements in the text and phenomena outside it, either in other literature or in general discourse or in 'reality'. Whether such constatations become real interpretations depends upon their capacity to explain what is felt to be the assertion – the meaning of the work.

Again, however, this argument depends upon the acceptance of the notion of a 'real' meaning. The general position articulated in the present book is that we are justified in speaking of a 'real' meaning, and that texts refuse to be dissolved into the critic's discourse or to vanish into their own ambiguities. Indeed, the presence of ambiguity in a work, far from weakening the sense of 'a' meaning, tends to strengthen it. Ambiguity may be defined as the structural determination of different meanings within a given text. Such meanings are brought together by the work's frame: they may be resolved in harmony, as in so-called 'classical' texts, or co-exist in meaningful inter-commentary, as in so-called modernist texts. In this sense, to speak of 'a' meaning resolves into the assertion that the work proffers itself meaningfully, and that its elements do not fray off into inarticulacy or irrelevance. And if there is a degree of tautology in this, it is only in the nature of critical language that it should be so: here, as always, the critic is really shouting 'Look! It works!'

It is the failure to differentiate these structurally determinate meanings from merely free 'readings' (text from meta-text), that lies at the root of extreme de-textualist criticism. The conception of meaning – meaning as intrinsic to text, not superadded by reader – does not, then, amount to a denial of ambiguity or of irony. To speak of *the* meaning of a text is perfectly compatible with speaking of the text's multiple or even self-contradictory meanings. The de-constructionist who tries to show that a text is in contradiction with itself and thus, in some way, demonstrating the necessary failure of discourse to achieve 'closure' or definite meaning,[1] is likely to be forgetting that no matter what meanings the text juxtaposes, aligns or harmonises, they constitute a whole which requires interpretation, and which is, in a serious sense, as incapable of contradicting itself as of referring to itself. In the case of much modern art, we are forced to accept images and themes which are broken off and discordant. But to grasp or 'get' the meaning of these incompatibilities and ambiguities, we must first appreciate them as specificities. We must, in other words, appreciate the work's self-commitment to *a* meaning, even if we see that meaning as ambiguous or multiplex. The secondary meanings, richnesses, overtones and multivalences, of which William Empson pioneered the conscious analysis, accrue only through the reader's dedication to what the work declares readable. I have described this above in terms of the work's intentionality: it is in tune with, or in line with, the lines of longitude of which the visible work is the section.

We shall understand the whole process better if we abandon the purely semantic or semiotic approach to criticism. Literary texts cannot be treated purely as signs having import. They are intentional, and their signs need to be read. It was the fault of excessively pure textualist criticism that it treated texts as being complicated signs needing only to be described structurally. There is a great danger in separating the intentional from the intensional aspects of meaning. Those texts which can be shown to have such intricate meanings, when meaning is defined in terms of structure or formal interrelation, can suddenly appear to mean anything. The two sorts of meaning, in fact, face in different directions: intentional meaning faces outwards, intensional meaning is turned inwards upon its own semantic and semiotic possibilities. It is precisely when we don't feel that we have to try and find out what the text or author means in the outward-turning sense, that we begin to feel doubts about the propriety of saying that it 'means' anything: why not just say 'it *is*'?

In actual fact, as I have tried to show, a literary text like any other art-work is held in tension between the two sorts of meaning. And it is the outwardly turned meaning (the intentional one) that really dictates that it has *a* meaning, a meaning that belongs to it, and which we must honour. When its meaning is to be inspected on its surface, among its signs which can mean anything we can find them to mean, in disregard of the author's or the text's signals that such-and-such possibilities are to be ignored, then indeed we feel entitled to, and even obliged to, take the text away from its author and throw it on the mercy of its critics. 'The poem', Wimsatt and Beardsley intoned at the height of the ironist era, 'belongs to the public'.[2] The concept of the Intentional Fallacy embodies, we have seen, much that is itself fallacious: it assumes that poems are to be inspected as 'any statement in linguistics or the general science of psychology'[3] is to be inspected. In fact, we have seen that they require to be interpreted, and that much of the understanding derives from reading between the lines, picking up signals, 'getting' tone and line of longitude. The reading of poems, that is to say, properly speaking assumes much that is closer to the older idea (what Wimsatt and Beardsley called the intentional or Romantic view) of seeing what the poet *wants* to say: only by seeing what he wants to say do we see what he does say. It is the same as in the ordinary life situations which Voloshinov describes: all the man says is 'Well'. An outsider, ignorant of the recent history and therefore oblivious to the imports of the vocable, as well as insensitive to the raised eyebrow and the dropped wrist which accompanied its pronunciation, couldn't be said to have understood it, even though he knew Russian (or English or whatever) as well as the two men involved in the situation.

Now this general view itself depends upon a very important supposition: the supposition that the statements of poetry are uttered. The question that arises is, can this utterance be regarded as a 'real' utterance, like my utterance when I in fact ask my wife the time, or refuse her invitation to have tea? This question has exercised many critics' minds recently, and it bears closely upon the matters I wish to discuss in this chapter and the next: primarily, the matter of the reality, and the reference to reality, of literary texts. It can, in the first instance, be divided into two aspects: one formal, the other philosophical. Formally, we must insist that if to understand a poem we have to know what the writer meant or wanted to say, then we are accepting that what appears in the poem is to be treated as a serious statement, as serious at least as the deposition in the court of law, or the statement under oath. Now it was, apparently, precisely this seriousness of utterance which was destroyed with the Romantic and post-Romantic separation of the language of poetry from the language of reason or logic or everyday discourse. The problem thus created has been called the problem of propositionality, and it has been exhaustively discussed by Gerald Graff in two books.[4] In these books Graff tries to show first that literature is in essence propositional, in that its sentences and statements can be shown to be no less capable of meaning than those of ordinary language; and then, that a literature which refuses to accept its own propositionality is bound to be working 'against itself'.

Now there is no doubt that a sentence in language – an order of words conforming to the rules of the language in which it is written, and otherwise making sense – is propositional, whether it is uttered playfully, seriously, written down under oath or thought in the silence of one's own head. There is no need to demonstrate this fact: it is condition of our use of the words 'meaning' and 'language' and 'propositional'. It makes no difference, from the linguistic point of view, whether the sentence 'Balbus jumped over the wall' is spoken aloud, in rage, read out of a Latin grammar or inserted into a poem; its meaning is not altered by the circumstances of its utterance. Neither is it altered by the psychological attitude the speaker might hold towards it. Nor, even, is it altered by the fact that there is no such person as Balbus. Linguistically, the sentence is defined by its consonance with the grammatical rules of the language it is written in. This applies to literary sentences: any sentence from a poem or a play is just as propositional as a sentence from a treatise of geometry or a deposition in a court of law.

From this point of view, the propositional controversy is otiose: it is not up to critics or poets or philosophers to decide whether the statements of poetry are propositional or not, but up to the language itself. What is much more interesting and important, of course, is the more philosophical assertion that the statements of poetry are in some sense to be defined by their quality of being 'fictions'. This view is in fact as old as literature itself. In its modern form, it derives from the Romantic philosophers, from Schiller with his concept of a *Spieltrieb* in man, and from Kant with his notion of *Zweckmässigkeit ohne Zweck* (pointfulness without point). In the twentieth century this notion of the 'art-drive' as being essentially related to the sense of play has been repeated by the modernist critics, Ortega y Gasset and I. A. Richards. Richards's idea that the statements of literature are pseudo-statements is usually held to inaugurate modern critical theory in this area. A bald recent formulation is that of Barbara Herrnstein-Smith, who argues quite simply that the defining quality of poetry (literary texts) is that they are fictive, that is, not meant to be reacted to or believed in as we would react to or believe in the equivalent statements made outside the realm of the text.[5] In Herrnstein-Smith, we have a formulation essentially derived from J. L. Austin, who simply bracketed literary statements out of his discussion of speech-acts by calling them void.[6] This view has been questioned by Wolfgang Iser,[7] but without a great deal of purpose, in my view. Austin wasn't playing down the importance of literature; he wasn't concerned with literary values at all. And, in fact, the correctness of his procedure in excluding literary matters from his discussion has been attested by the enormous effect he has had upon literary criticism. Austin's exclusion of literary statements was simply methodological: he didn't want to be saddled with awkward questions such as, but what about the rhetorical question in a poem? The fact is that Austin's descriptions of speech-acts apply indiscriminately to literature and to discursive speech: literary statements are 'void' only in so far as their operativeness in ordinary language situations is concerned. Otherwise, they follow the same formal rules as all speech.

Thus, no theory of literature as fiction, or literary statements as parasitic on ordinary-language statements, can offer us any enlightenment as to the real nature of literature. Of course, the statement of the narrator in a novel that he was in such-and-such a place at such-and-such a time is different from the same kind of statement if made under oath, or under the milder, but no less morally binding, oath of writing his autobiography or telling a friend a story from last year's holiday. Of course, the actor who mouths 'I love you' in the play doesn't actually *mean* that he loves the girl who happens to be playing the female lead; of course, the poet who says he loves Chloe cannot be called a liar (supposing that we had some supernal lie-detector and could call back the dead to stand trial) if it can be shown that he loved Clorinda, or another girl, or a boy, or nobody at all but himself. In these respects, literary statements are no different from idle wool-gathering ('The-cat-sat-on-the-mat' chanted satirically, for instance, to bring out the stupefying boredom of an afternoon of rain, with nothing else to do), or from merely verbalising, or from using an everyday sentence as an instance in a philosophy class or a Latin grammar book. In a vast number of cases, sentences are spoken which cannot be cross-examined for their truth or their falsehood. It might be worth emphasising, incidentally, that a sentence can be perfectly meaningful which is neither true nor false: 'The cat sat on the mat.' Which cat? When? All we require is a general consonance with the rules of grammar and a coherence with ordinary reference: 'The cat sat on the adverb' is the same sentence grammatically as 'The cat sat on the mat'. But it doesn't 'make sense', and we must remember both that this requirement must always accompany the requirement of grammatical correctness, and that the capacity to make sense is not the same as truthfulness.

A statement, for instance, may be understood, even if it is understood to refer to nothing, to be uttered playfully, or for no reason. There is a great difference between the pointless remark and the remark that, failing to 'make sense', cannot really be said to be a remark at all. 'Balbus jumped over the wall' makes sense, whatever the conditions of its utterance. I know there is no such person as Balbus; I know that the speaker who makes the observation is 'just talking'. But I am still called on to understand the remark. I am still called on to see that it is a remark different in kind from 'X an da po gayy naggy doo'.

Propositionality, in other words – by which we must mean simply the sense-making qualities of complete syntactic units – is not decided by any correspondence between statement and state-of-affairs. Neither is it decided by the correspondence between statement and *possible* states of affairs. The belief that it is, motivated the efforts of logical positivists and linguistic analysts to define the meaningfulness of statements entirely in terms of the verifiability of their constituents. The truth is that the verification-principle applies only to a small region of human activity. It is adamantly not an account of meaning nor of meaningfulness. In a curious way, the error of verification-theory dovetails with that of the pseudo-statement in art. Even in the most sober philosophy of science, a great many statements in philosophy have no truth-value – are neither true nor false, not because they are nonsensical, but because they are different sorts of statement. Hypotheticals, for instance, such as 'If I went there, I would see her', have neither truth nor falsehood: they are uninterpreted functions. Which is to say that they are formal. Once again, we are driven to conclude that to make sense is not the same as truthfulness.

Language has a vast number of possible uses, and we make a serious error if we suppose that we can divide all discourse into just two varieties – true, discursive talk on the one hand, and non-discursive literary talk on the other. There is a vast number of intermediate sorts. Relatively few *kinds* of statement need to be checked for their truth. 'Cats sit on mats' makes different demands upon verification from those that 'The cat is sitting on the mat' makes; both are different from 'The cat sat on the mat', when this sentence is not supposed to be checked up on. What determines whether the statement is meant to be checked up on is not some mysterious property akin to truth, but simply the context of utterance. If it is the defining error of empiricism to assume that only statements meant to be checked up on deserve serious attention, it is the defining error of the new French rationalism (Foucault, Piaget, Barthes, Derrida and others) to assume that because some statements cannot be verified, no statements can, and hence that all statements fail to refer, leaving us with discourse – language without anchorage in time, psyche or history. It is the error of Anglo-American modernism, on the other hand, to have accepted too readily the tempting art–science dichotomy, yielding the etiolating doctrine of the pseudo-statement, at best gingered up by a health and efficiency psychology of aesthetic response.

The tendency of these doctrines (French rationalism and Anglo-American modernism) has been to isolate literature from the serious concerns of man: literature is jacked-up out of history, it has neither past nor future, it is 'itself', sheer discourse – fiction. A purely linguistic analysis of literature must inevitably lead to such self-defeating conclusions. What we must do is to reconsider the function and purpose of all art. A purely linguistic analysis of literary texts will tell us nothing about their function and status as literature. Thus, it is fatuous to assert (as Barthes did)[8] that literary texts cannot reflect or reproduce 'reality'. Of course they can: they do it as mimesis. The question we must ask is, what use do they make of their bits of mimesis? The significance of the realist novel or the Dutch genre painting is not exhausted by its designata – by the identity and recognisability of the scenes and objects it paints; but whatever significance accrues over the artist's transformation of these things is structurally and intrinsically *related to* these identities. To say that the literary text, when it mentions people, things, places, weathers; when it strives, moreover, to imitate their surfaces and behaviour, somehow miraculously fails to 'refer' to them is sheer metaphysics – linguisitc nonsense. If I use the word 'bus' I cannot claim *not* to have mentioned a bus, because it is part of the language game I am playing that the use of nouns of this sort *is* a mention, and involves me in reference. The mistake of much recent theorising is to detach literary statements from the object-continuum upon whose existence they are in fact contingent. This makes for a doctrine of literary magic far more fantastic than anything the Romantics ever dreamed up. Literary statements are, in this, as in certain other important respects, not dissimilar from ordinary language statements: certainly they are not above the laws of language.

Suppose a film director goes to Budapest to make a film: he requires footage of Hungarian trams and streets to fit into the film he is going to shoot largely in Pinewood, and takes shots of trams, ladies, policemen, houses. If he shows them to us in private, we say we watch film images *of* Budapest life: trams, ladies, policemen, trees, houses. When later we see the entire film, we recognise the shots and sequences we have already seen in the private show: we do not then think that these shots and sequences have ceased to be images *of* trams and streets and houses. We don't say, the tram in that shot is not a real tram, it's only an image in a film. The fact that the director has used the footage in a fictional narrative doesn't alter the ontological status of image or tram: the tram doesn't stop being a tram merely because the director has put it into a film. The point is, what is the arrangement of the shot in the film narrative *trying to tell us*? That is the question for the interpreter. In a realist narrative, the same rules apply. A story about a man getting into debt, losing his wife and eventually hanging himself, is still a story 'about' a man getting into debt, losing his wife and eventually hanging himself. The newspaper story upon which Flaubert based *Madame Bovary* is the same story as the one Flaubert tells. The belief that such events and fragments of mimesis suddenly cease to refer to what they imitate or reproduce simply because they are placed inside the art-context is one of the superstitions of modernist criticism. It is the same with art as with dreams: we dream in images drawn from the dream-day (the day before we dream). These images are put at the service of the unconscious mind. They are thereby robbed of their overt signification, and made to play a different part in the dream. This doesn't mean they aren't images of men, towers, bottles or whatever; or that we can disregard these identities to get at the meaning of the dream: exactly the reverse in fact: we can only get at the meaning of the dream through the identity of the contents. So it is with literary texts.

The mischief has been caused by the acceptance of a too-simple distinction between 'real' statements that can be checked for their truth-value, and the rest that can't. Art-statements belong to the latter; they must be saved from non-meaning: hence the numerous doctrines of linguistic magic that have proliferated in recent literary criticism. In fact, we have seen that there are many ways of using language other than those of true/false statements as matters of fact on the one hand, and nonsense on the other. In the first place, we must accept that even the statements of logic and most philosophical discourse aren't capable of verification in the crude empiricist way. When the philosopher reasons and discusses he does so largely by entertaining hypotheses and illustrations, possibilities and probabilities. We don't accuse him of using pseudo-statements when he is in the middle of making some elaborate point about universals or counter-factuals. More to the point, we don't accuse ourselves of uttering nonsense or pseudo-statements when we give examples, illustrate points, crack jokes in everyday life. Obviously, the poet's statement that his heart aches and a drowsy numbness pains his sense is not to be responded to as a cry for help, a disguised phone-call to Lifeline. To this extent, of course, we separate the needs of the man from the utterances of the poet. But this doesn't mean that we can treat these utterances as if they had nothing to do with pain or life or purpose in general. The reason why we don't (or shouldn't) dial for the psychiatrist when we read a poem (let's say it is one by Sylvia Plath) is not that the poem is nothing to do with real things like suffering and pain, but that the purpose of writing the poem was not to get help, but to do something else. And this means that what the poem both reveals to us and offers to us is of greater value and greater import than any solace or numbing balm medicine might afford. The poem makes us feel that we don't *want* to be put at rest, if being put at rest means quenching the sorts of emotion the poem both fosters and expresses: the pain is a vehicle for something else.

It is – we might plausibly suggest – this 'something else' that the doctrine of the pseudo-statement was supposed to protect. But the consequence of the doctrine has been to destroy the 'something else' (the poem's value, simply) by cutting off the vital links between it and the human emotions that brought it into existence. A poet is, so far as the reader is concerned, like an actor whose repertoire needs to be fed by experience of the emotions and acts it reproduces: he cannot move, please or instruct his audience unless he knows the states he is imitating. At the same time, his imitations not only move his listeners, they tell them something they did not know about the emotions they respond to in recognising them. Now, the role of this actor-poet is complex, and of course deeply, inextricably intertwined with the historical circumstances in which he is performing. I shall turn to this historical factor later. Here I wish to emphasise the interdependence of the audience's emotional history and the actor's: they are at one in this, at least. We have art because we can recognise our emotions externalised in this way; but also quite simply because we are capable of sympathy with each other. At bottom, all art *is* mirror-like, as the vast profusion of mimetic theories of art attests. But this does not by any means confine the significance of art to its capacity for reflection, or remove modernist abstract arts from the general reflectional law of art. Our dreams, our reveries, our fantasies, our reflections, and our meditations all take us beyond the limits of verification; but they do not remove us from our human situation.

Now this analogy, between the poet and the actor, must be handled with care: it *is* an analogy, and the essence of an analogy is the fundamental separateness of the things compared. If they were the same, there would be no analogy; there would be identity. To say that in certain respects the poet is *like* an actor is not to deny that in others he is not: in other respects he is like a dreamer, in others like a shaman or sooth-sayer, a medium. In others, like an ordinary man ordinarily suffering or exulting. I exploit the analogy with the actor to point up one particular quality of poetry and all art: to some extent, no matter how intense and honest we feel the writing to be, the poet is distinguished by an ability to stand aside from what he is writing, to direct its course and shape its development in order to satisfy certain laws of presentation. This, however, does not mean that he is a hypocrite, or that he doesn't feel the emotions in his poems; still less that there are no such emotions there. On the contrary, art will always be distinguished by its capacity to 'give form to' our own recognisable emotions and thoughts. There is no isolable 'art-emotion'; but neither is art to be reduced to self-expression. There may be no quantifiable difference between, say, Tchaikowsky's expression of his unhappiness in his letters or in reported conversations, and their expression in his music. It is merely affected to deny that his sixth symphony is 'about' personal suffering. But it is still, in the sense suggested above, a performance of that suffering, well tailored, dramatically staged, craftily managed. Thus, there is no conflict between the view of the poet as actor and the so often expressed vision of the artist as sayer of deep truths: in appropriating his own thoughts, the poet creates them for others. That is the name of the game.

(ii) SIGN AND SIGNIFIER

'Between the author and the man that suffers', thundered F. R. Leavis, 'there can be no divorce.'[9] There is no conflict, I have said, between Leavis's moralism and his aesthetics: he habitually inferred the participation of the poet's deepest self from the *quality* of the text's surface, consistently testing the text for its authenticity. This reliance upon the value-judgement, I have said above, does not take Leavis out of the realm of literary criticism into that of moralism: on the contrary, it is simply a particularly severe application of the fundamental principle of all literary criticism – the critic's witness of the text's literariness. In registering so sensitively the pressures, vibrations and shock-waves set up by the work, Leavis enhanced its value. Consistent with his own methodological consistency, Leavis later became an increasingly forthright advocate of a cultural philosophy associated with continuity and traditionalism, as opposed to change and revolution. Remaining a textualist, he gave increasing attention to the broader social and cultural implications of the 'positive values' he found in texts.

In this, too, Leavis was merely more honest and coherent than those modernist textualists who have cut off the pseudo-statement of literary discourse from the embarrassing hinterland it in fact drags along with it. The alternative to a Leavisian culture philosophy, or indeed to the Lukácsian Marxist alternative, was to continue along the path of textual autotelism towards the cul-de-sac of sheer discourse, 'Words, words, words' – what Harold Bloom has called a 'serene linguistic nihilism'. The statement that is not *meant*, that is not uttered, can indeed be examined for its interrelations: it dictates no reading, since it does not dictate at all. Structuralism – essentially a product of the same economic, social and intellectual forces as produced the earlier critical revolutions in England and America – sought to put the textualism of the revolution on a scientific basis. But it had from the start an intrinsic politicality, bourgeois, but directed against the bourgeoisie itself, and deliberately using the tenets of a textualist critical philosophy against the culture that had spawned it. From the time of Lévi-Strauss's *Structural Anthropology*, with its attack on European ethnocentricity, structuralism has been coloured by a more or less overtly leftist political philosophy. It has not only shown no desire to uphold the best of the old tradition; it has, to the contrary, sought to undermine the bases of tradition, privilege and leisure, by weakening belief in the very nature of Western discourse itself. The end-product of this tendency is that post-structuralist phenomenon, de-constructionism, which, ending with language, seeks to destroy language itself.

At first sight, there is a definite fracture between structuralism and de-constructionism. Structuralism, as its name implies, seems to be a philosophy of order and clarity; de-constructionism an essentially negative philosophy bent on destroying first the myth of analytical objectivity that had seemed to be the real goal of structuralism, and then the general myth of language and discourse itself. If structuralism is essentially a textualist philosophy (*the* textualist philosophy), de-constructionism appears as essentially de-textualist. The antithetical relation between the two movements is well captured in Roland Barthes's description of his own slide from structuralism to post-structuralism: 'It is not a question of revealing the (latent) meanings of an utterance, of a trait, or a narrative, but of fissuring the very representation of meaning; not to change or purefy the symbols but to challenge the symbolic itself.'[10] Elsewhere, Barthes insists that structuralism should seek 'less to assign completed meanings to the objects it discovers than to know how meaning is possible.'[11] Structuralism, Barthes implies, is appropriate to the analysis of an earlier kind of writing – the literature of the 'classique', or of what he calls 'works', as opposed to 'texts'. 'Works' are those classical or traditional writings which bully and marshal the reader's responses; 'texts' those modernist writings which do not marshal symbols into patterns, and thus coerce the reader's responses, but constitute a methodological 'field'. This field is the occasion of innumerable adventures of the reader's, and obliges him to acknowledge no structural determination within the field itself. The text can mean whatever the picaresque hero-reader happens to make it mean by letting himself be waylaid by recognitions of other texts, or 'accidental' denotations touched off in the field of the text itself.

Now it is easy to pull this farrago of imprecise metaphors to pieces and show that Barthes has really simply assumed a vague historicist scenario (the same one as is described in *Writing Degree Zero*, dividing literature up around the year 1848) and then just advocated a 'new' way of reading (loose, associative, random). He gives no criterion whatever for identifying a 'work', except the historical one, nor any indication of any serious ways in which literature written after 1848 differs from that written before. Yet his somewhat cavalier espousal of an essentially de-constructional mode of reading does serve to underline the difference between classical structuralism and its later mutations. An initial view of structuralism seems to corroborate this. There would seem to be little common ground between such a philosophy and the de-textualism just defined by the later

Barthes, and indeed the de-constructionist principle in general, with its professed aim of fissuring the sign and thus undermining belief in the capacity of language to refer.

Yet de-constructionism is really a predictable development of classical structuralism. In the first place, we recall that Lévi-Strauss himself repudiated the formalism of the Prague school on the ground that it regarded form and content as separate, and form alone as intelligible, thus reducing content to a residual layer, 'deprived of any significant value'.[12] Structuralism, Lévi-Strauss claimed, put form and content on the same footing, 'susceptible of the same analysis'. Now it is precisely the nature of this analysis which we must inspect to see how easily structuralism accomplished its own self-destruction. For Lévi-Strauss's work reveals a profound set towards a determinism of forms: structuralism, as he practised it, became strictly a contextualist method, in that it sought not to show the *meaning* of the works with which it dealt, but the coherence between the structural patterns of works and certain pre-existing laws of structure. Lévi-Strauss was adamant that no descriptive positivism could unravel the 'meanings' of social structures. The laws that govern and constitute so-called reality remain beyond apprehension: they can be inferred but not perceived. Like Locke's 'underlying somewhat', Kant's noumena and Hegel's *Ding an sich*, reality itself, therefore, remains beyond probe.

This fundamental denial of the philosophy of experience (that is, empiricism and the general critical philosophy of science to which it gave rise) is a fundamental element of all structuralism. Structuralism is a rationalist methodology, and in general it tends to assume the dualism that has been endemic to rationalism since Descartes and the occasionalists. Such a tendency is particularly French. It receives a typically polemical statement by Jean Piaget who should, one would think, know what pragmatic research was. There is, Piaget proclaims, a 'steady agreement between physical reality and the mathematical theories employed in its description'.[13] Piaget professes to find this 'amazing'. Now one would have thought it distinctly *un*amazing that a man's description of an object should agree with the object in general structure and configuration. One would have reckoned without the French mind: 'This harmony between mathematics and physical reality cannot, in positivist fashion, be written off simply as the correspondence of a language with the object it designates . . . rather it is a correspondence of human operations with those of object-operators, a harmony then, between this particular operator – the human being as body and mind – and the innumerable operators in nature – physical objects at their several levels.'[14] We could not hope to find more naïvely and unconsciously expressed that ineradicable cartesianism that separates the French not merely from the English but from all other intellectual traditions. The French mind would rather posit some miraculous harmony of systems (parallel clocks – mind and body, for instance, wound up, set and synchronised in the pineal gland) than acknowledge that mathematics and physics 'correspond' to reality because the men that created their languages made damned sure they did.

Now this rationalistic substructure of Lévi-Straussian structuralism is neither accidental nor unimportant, but of its very essence. There is a profound difference between strict formalism (or such *un*strict formalisms as the New Criticism) which purports to establish the 'meaning' of a text on the evidence of its signs alone, and structuralism, which postulates laws outside the text which the text – perhaps – instantiates. The tendency of an interpretative theory like structuralism is in effect to *deny* the autonomous meaning of signs, without ever assigning actual meanings to them. My formulation at this point, to be sure, assumes a certain meaning to the notion of 'actual meaning'. By actual meaning I intend some anchorage of the given sign or sign-set in empirical reality: it is this anchorage which structuralism characteristically denies.

To show how it does so, we must introduce the methodological tool which is, in a sense, the most important single element in structuralism: the Saussurean analysis of the sign. Saussure's general theory of the sign, as is well known, is borrowed from Locke's *Essay Concerning Human Understanding*: the *Cours de linguistique générale* is important, among other things, for its having introduced empiricist language critique into the French tradition.[15] Saussure accepts unchanged from Locke the general conception of the sign's basic properties: signs are (1) comprised of 'sounds as signs of internal conceptions', and (2) arbitrary: 'they signify only men's peculiar ideas, and that by a *perfect* arbitrary imposition'.[16] Saussure modified Locke only once. Instead of following Locke in using the general word 'sign' to refer to words and other general ways of referring to ideas, Saussure re-introduced the ancient distinction of signifier–signified. The

Stoics had distinguished between three elements of language: (1) the sign or sound itself, (2) the objected denoted by the sign, and (3) the conjuncture, or coming together, of the two in meaning. Now, this is plainly a description not of the sign itself but of the general condition in which signs and signification function, and it is the third element in the Stoics' description which has given bother to modern theorists, such as Foucault. Foucault attributes the crisis in modern language to the simplification of this ternary arrangement of signs to a binary arrangement, in which signs are related to the things they mean, with no third element necessary. This seventeenth-century development, of which Locke gave the most decisive account, clearly corresponds to a change of world-view, a disbelief in the religious and metaphysical ideas which had coloured man's earlier vision of the world. It was Locke who saw that the important feature of the sign which had been hitherto neglected was precisely its sign-ness – the plain fact that we learn to associate particular sounds with particular events more or less arbitrarily, not because of some God-given property or existent analogy between sign and object. Our world begins here.

So far Saussure follows Locke. Where he deviates from Locke is in introducing the old Stoic structure of sign and object (minus the conjunction) into the structure of the sign itself. This is a revolutionary move indeed, and one fraught with all manner of disastrous consequences. It is one thing to say that signs function because they are understood to refer to agreed-upon things. It is quite another to say that the identity of the agreed-upon object *is part of the sign itself.* This is quite unlike the logic of the Stoics. Of course, signs could not work – language could not exist – if words did not refer, in the end, to things. That is the basic prerequisite of language. It is obvious that a sign signifies: obvious, in other words, that a word is only a sign by virtue of the fact that it stands for something, and that if there isn't something that it stands for, then it isn't a sign. What, then, is the purpose of introducing the notion of the 'signifier'? When is a sign not a signifier? When, conversely, is anything a sign that lacks a signified – something referred-to or meant? Saussure's distinction does not help us understand what is meant by a sign, since it is precisely the existence of the relationship between a word (sound, written mark or whatever) and an idea, that is understood by the expression *sign* in the first place.

The signifier–signified distinction suggests a quite spurious linguistic model: it makes it seem as if *some* signs towed invisible referents along as part of their meaning, while others did not. But this is not so. All signs are alike in their capacity to *act as* signs. All that changes is the way in which signs are understood to be used in particular circumstances. Nothing is gained, either, by introducing the idea of concepts into the theory of the sign. Locke, to be sure, had spoken of words as being 'signs of internal conceptions', in order to distinguish the vocal sounds of men from those of parrots. But this means that language presupposes a general situation of consciousness before it comes into existence. It does not mean that we must speak of a sign as *signifying* the concept: the sign signifies the thing (table, mountain, God, idea of civil obedience, whatever), not the concept of the thing. Otherwise, we should be involved in an infinite regress, with signs standing for concepts standing for concepts standing for concepts and so on.

The signified cannot be *in* the sign, or part of it, in the way that the signifier *is* the sign. The reality of the signified is not part of the sign, but a condition of the application of the sign. All that philosophy should do is specify the conditions in which signs can function. If we accustom ourselves to the idea that our concern is with the function of signs, not their metaphysical essence, we shall be in a position to avoid the anomalies of semiology, according to which 'the sign is a compound of a signifier and a signified'.[17] It may be useful for linguistics to describe its objects of study in this way. On the plane of philosophical enquiry and ordinary usage, the distinction is not only otiose, it is dangerous. It is dangerous because it suggests the possibility that a language could exist in which mere signifiers floated about miraculously divested of something they used to possess: signifieds. If we have to content ourselves with the simple description of the behaviour of signs, their use and conditions, this 'difficulty' disappears: we have to accept simply that some signs behave in this way, others in that.

Now the essence of the linguistic sign is that it can be used in the absence of what it generally stands for. Language constitutes an arsenal of available signs (symbols) which can be used in the absence of any referent: that is what a sign is. The word 'lion' can be used without the user referring to, or thinking of, any actual beast. There is the marginal case of the sign that doesn't stand for any actual thing – unicorn or golden mountain: the empiricists came to regard words like 'necessary connection' and 'innate ideas' as such terms, empty signs. However we handle this problem, it is hard to see how introducing the subdivision of the sign into signifier and signified could help clarify matters. Some signs – unicorn, for example – we can agree always lack *referents*. There is no real difference between saying that 'unicorn' is a sign that can never refer to anything real, and saying that it is a signifier which has a signified (that is, the concept 'unicorn'), but no referent. In this sense, no sign can lack a signified; hence the term is at best superfluous, helping us to clarify nothing. There are, moreover, in language many other kinds of sign – particles, prepositions, connectives – which cannot possibly be said to have signifieds: here too we are better off simply calling them signs, understanding that language needs many sorts of sign, and that not all of them refer to things as nouns do. The mystique of the signifier in linguistics is not unlike that of the sensum in philosophy. Philosophy, still in its infant naming stage, separated the things that we see from the objects which we thought we saw, gave the new things a new name (sensum), and called the whole thing epistemology. Linguistics, in its infant naming stage, separated the sign from what it was alleged to be a sign of, gave it a new name (signifier) and called the whole thing semiology.

In semiology itself, and in the literary criticism influenced by it, the effect of Saussure's subdivision has been to facilitate the in fact quite illicit divorce of literature and language in general from those matters and states of affairs they were alleged to express. The signifier assumes a lift of its own: 'We are promised', Dan Sperber wrote of Lévi-Strauss, 'an exploration of the sign, that is unions of signifiers and signifieds. Yet if the reader begins looking for the signifieds he soon realises that the underlying code relates signifiers to other signifiers: there are no signifieds. Everything is meaningful, nothing is meant.'[18] In general, semiologists and structuralists have been able to conceive of a realm of signifiers divorced from reference, and bearing relationship only to each other, only because of Saussure's obliging manoeuvre. Without it, writers would have been obliged to describe the behaviour of signs, always needing to justify the assertions about reference and non-reference by referring to the particular state of affairs concerned. With the signifier to hand, they can pretend that they have somehow mislaid or lost the signifieds, or that Western culture has: so the signifier runs riot through the pages of Barthes, and Lévi-Strauss and, latterly, of Colin MacCabe and others, like a bacillus in a fantasy of H. G. Wells, or an influenza virus, manufacturing millions of unwanted copies of itself.

Semiotics, the harder-minded empiricist version of semiology, derived from the writings of C. S. Peirce and Charles Morris and wholly consistent with linguistic analysis, has faced the same sort of crisis as semiology: if we are to handle 'meaning' purely in terms of the interrelationships of signs, what truck have we with what they stand for? This problem has been confronted by a number of anthropologists and semioticians who are fully aware of the dangers of a pure semiosis. There is, in fact, a semiosis of every subject. That is, any subject can be handled purely semiotically, without reference to what the signs stand for in reality. However, a mature concensus among anthropologists seems to maintain that 'there is little support for a reduction of anthropology to semiotics'.[19] More radically, Umberto Eco has shown that there must be a division between the semiosis of a subject and the underlying or referred-to matter itself – the material in virtue of which the study exists, so that a purely semiotic analysis can make no contact with this realm.[20] If we had not been committed to the mystique of the signifier, such caution need not have been given. We should have to say, for instance, whether such-and-such a sign could be correlated with such-and-such facts; in other words, we should have to describe the behaviour of signs fully, paying due attention to their verifiable status. It is easy to see how dangerously easy the Saussurean distinction of signifier and signified makes it for writers to apply themselves only to the form of the code rather than take account of the essentially dialectical interaction between code and our experience of those matters codified.

Literary criticism is persisting, in the face of an embarrassing weight of evidence, in regarding literature as if it could be handled in purely semiotic terms. This natural bias in semiology has reinforced the tendency already described in Coleridge, Mallarmé, Bergson, Richards and others to claim special status for literary language. If, in Richards's formulation, literary statements are only pseudo-statements, we must cease to look for the meaning of literature in the correlations we can make between literary texts and 'life'. It is easy, again, to see how

Saussure's dichotomy aided and abetted this tendency: given that they were only pseudo-statements, not uttered but abandoned, literary sentences can be regarded as signifiers incapable of finding signifieds. Since they are not 'meant', they can refer to nothing.

Yet this is, as we have seen, a confused view both of literature and of language. The question we have to ask is, what kind of things are people doing when they use language in the literary way? We have seen that a sign need not be used to refer to any particular thing; but it does not therefore lose its capacity to refer to what it is generally taken to refer to. The whole question of literary language therefore needs to be looked at more carefully. It may be true that literary texts do not refer to actual situations as statements of historical fact do: the poet who says he loves Chloe cannot be called a liar if it is shown that there is no such person as Chloe, or that he was in fact having an affair with another girl at the time he wrote the poem. (He *can* be called a liar, but only by the literary critic who means that the poet is insincere in the poem, and has therefore written a bad poem). This has been established belief since Aristotle first distinguished between poetry and history. What is new about certain currents of modernist theory is the critic's tendency to behave as if he believed that literary language is in some mysterious way separated from what would normally have been conceived as its reference – human life, love, pain, death. Not any *one* man's love, life and death, we note – that would be history, in Aristotle's term; but love, life and death in general, upon which the poet, like the actor and the dreamer, discourses wisely and effectually. It is the denial of this essential functionality of literature which is so striking in the new poetics.

Following my own earlier practice, I shall distinguish a hard-and soft-core variety of the tendency. Matters are often complicated by an unconscious regression from the hard to the soft position, or vice versa. Soft-core de-constructionism allies the old Richards–Bergson preference for a special category for literary language (the pseudo-statement, poetry as fiction) to a Saussurean terminology. Thus, Paul de Man claims himself an adherent of semiology, 'the science or study of signs as signifiers; it does not ask what words mean, but how they mean.'[21] Now this, of course, is no news to the linguistic analyst or ordinary language philosopher; it would have been no news to David

Hume. Structuralism, de Man goes on, enables us to 'bracket' the 'question of meaning, thus freeing critical discourse from the debilitating burden of paraphrase'.[22] This Proustian hebetude adequately characterises the soft-core de-constructionist, who usually rests content with uncovering ambiguities and ironies like the older Empsonian New Critic and then using these as evidence that the text is divided against itself.

The hard-core variety extends the territory of the soft-core variety. Instead of saying that only poems and novels don't refer to actual situations, because after all they are fictions, in Herrnstein-Smith's term, it maintains that all language consists of signifiers without signifieds. Now this, of course, breaks with Saussure as well as with Locke. Meaning has traditionally depended upon a consistent correlation between signifiers and signifieds, or if we prefer not to assume the distinction, upon a consistent reference-capacity in language. We note, by the way, that the 'linguistic nihilism' which holds that signifiers can have no signifieds is easy to articulate by means of Saussure's dichotomy, almost impossible without it. The very distinction almost begs to have its terms set asunder. In fact we could almost say that the degradation of meaning is an inevitable con-comitant of structuralist thinking, which bases itself on the Saus-surean distinction of signifier and signified and, rapidly losing interest in the signified, avails itself of the opportunity to do away with it altogether and turns itself into a 'pure' semiotics. In literary criticism, this degradation of meaning has been accom-plished largely through the prestige of one man, Jacques Derrida.

10 Logocentrism and Logomania

(i) DERRIDA AND 'PRESENCE'

In a series of books published between 1967 and 1970, Derrida tried to do what Barthes suggested in his essay 'Changer l'objet lui-même' – challenge the basis of the symbolic itself, discredit representation, undermine the authority of the sign and render final and irrevocable the severance of *signifiant* from *signifié*. Now this is plainly, on the surface at least, more radical than anything attempted by Lévi-Strauss, and indeed contrary to the spirit of Lévi-Strauss. At the same time, as we have seen, it is really in the spirit of structuralism, with its insistence on distinguishing a realm of signifiers – of signs, that is, that may well turn out not to stand for anything. The clearest statement of Derrida's views is to be found in the interviews with Michel Glazer published in 1972 as *Positions*.[1] But the most important and the most seminal of his works is without doubt *La Voix et le Phénomène*, a straight philosophical critique of Husserl's meaning-theory, published in 1967.[2] Much of Derrida's later work has presented itself as more or less straightforward literary criticism.[3] As such it is comparatively uninteresting, a somewhat fussy, over-methodologised series of disquisitions on aspects of texts which do little to modify our views of the texts in question or the major theoretical questions underlying our interpretation of them. It is the theories presented in *La Voix et le Phénomène* which have had the decisive influence, and it is these which require to be examined and evaluated.

In his book *Logical Investigations*,[4] Husserl distinguishes between two aspects of statements: expression (*Ausdrück*) and indication (*Anzeigen*). These bear respectively a kind of inner psychological character and an outer, directive one. Now this dichotomy of Husserl's is a version of an earlier one put forward by Frege:[5] Frege's *Sinn* is Husserl's *Ausdrück*, his *Bedeutung* Husserl's *Anzeigen*. Husserl had begun his philosophical career with a work which attempted a psychology of arithmetic.[6] It was Frege's criticisms which in part induced Husserl to give up this wrong-headed attempt. It is hard not to see Husserl's analysis of meaning in the *Investigations* as a parallel attempt to psychologise meaning. Frege's distinction had been introduced to get round certain difficulties in logic raised by the fact that two phrases can refer to the same thing but have different meanings. The phrase 'the evening star' has the same referent as the phrase 'the morning star'. But an ignorant man might 'know' the meaning of one phrase without knowing also that what it referred to was the same thing as was referred to in the other phrase. So that linguistically, the two phrases do not mean the same thing, though they refer to the same thing. They have, in Frege's terms, the same reference but different meanings. Further complications raised by the existence of non-existent entities, such as the unicorn and the golden mountain, which were pushed into prominence by Adolph Meinong, led Bertrand Russell, at about the same time as Husserl was writing his *Investigations*, to elaborate the theory of descriptions.[7] According to Russell, existence was not a property, and therefore could not be predicated of things; nouns are merely shorthand descriptions of things, existence merely a function of assertion. Thus, to assert that a thing exists is to say that the statement there is an *x* fulfilling such-and-such descriptive conditions (being white, feathered, yellow-billed) is true. If there is no *x* fulfilling these conditions we simply say that the existential assertion is false and there the matter ends. (Existence itself has no substantival force; much confusion would be avoided if it were understood that these arguments apply also to Heidegger's 'being'.)

Husserl too is troubled that a statement can have meaning ('The golden mountain is round') yet lack a referent. According to Husserl what statements require to be meaningful is two elements: they must be *meant*, as it were in the private world of the speaker's consciousness, and they must refer to something objectively present. There is, therefore, a subjective expressive element and an objective denotational element in every act of meaning: 'Ideally speaking, each subjective expression is replaceable by an objective expression which will preserve the identity of each momentary meaning (*Bedeutung*).'[8] For Husserl, in other words, the meaning of statements depends upon the establishable presence and correlation of objective situation and subjective expression. The difficulty is that such an establishment turns out to be impossible in actual fact: it is 'impracticable' and 'cannot in the vast majority of cases be carried out at all'.[9]

The purpose of Derrida's critique of Husserl is twofold: to undermine the possibility of any such relation, thus to show that Husserl's distinction of expression and indication if untenable. The conclusion to be drawn is that no proper theory of meaning can be sustained on these lines because Husserl assumes precisely what he has set out to prove: the concepts of sense and objectivity are smuggled in from the start. In this, Husserl is only typical of Western logic from Aristotle onwards: thus Derrida can announce the 'closure' of Western metaphysics, if not 'the end of history'.[10] This set of reasonings is taken from Heidegger, to whose general position Derrida adds only his own critique of Husserl's logic. This is the programme. How is it achieved?

Derrida undermines Husserl's logic by seizing on Husserl's doubts of the practicability of making a satisfactory analysis of the correlation of expression and indication. Derrida tries first to show that Husserl's logic is based upon an implicit and unacknowledged logic of presence, a logic which rests upon the assumption of 'an initial limitation of sense to knowledge, of logos to objectivity, of language to reason'.[11] That is to say, Husserl's metaphysics (and implicitly the metaphysics of the Western tradition as a whole) is based on a 'common matrix' which Derrida calls 'presence: the absolute proximity of self-identity, the being-in-front of the object available for repetition, the maintenance of the temporal present, whose ideal form is the self-presence of transcendental *life*, whose ideal identity allows *idealiter* of infinite repetition'.[12] Derrida's role as high priest of de-constructionism is based upon the arguments put forward in this critique of Husserl's logic and in particular on this analysis of 'presence'.

The essence of this analysis is that 'presence' – understood in Husserlian terms as the ideal union of subjective expression and objective indication – can only properly be reflected in speech as opposed to writing. Speech has been privileged by philosophers and linguists from Plato to Saussure because it takes place in the presence of the objects or situations referred to, and at the same time literally in the speaker's own head: it is the quality of hearing-oneself-speak which Derrida holds up as the European ideal of language. I hear myself speak: I can lie, but I know I lie; I am not otherwise betrayed by the medium. But in writing, my marks are a pale reflection of this immediacy of speech, and can be interpreted in various ways, thus destroying the ideal unity of meaning. If we undermine this prestige of speech, we can undermine the whole tradition of Western metaphysics and logic. Writing has always been regarded, Derrida points out, as 'supplementary' to speech precisely because it lacks the convincing *thereness* of speech. What Derrida tries to do is to show that the 'logic of the supplement' reveals an unnoticed lack in what it is held to supplement. If, therefore, writing is thought to supplement speech, speech itself must be deficient in some way hitherto unacknowledged. This 'logic of the supplement' is one of Derrida's most influential weapons: he uses it, for instance, to weaken the 'perfection' of sexual love, by exploiting the supplementary nature of masturbation. Rousseau had described masturbation as a supplement to nature. But since you can only supplement what can be supplemented (that is, what is incomplete), the existence of such supplementarity effectively demonstrates the inadequacy of sexual love, as the existence of writing shows the inadequacy of speech and the existence of a supplement the incompleteness of Webster's Dictionary.[13]

To these arguments we must add one more important element – Derrida's notion of *différence/différance*. This is an untranslatable play upon the French words for difference and deference. The idea is similarly untranslatable. In so far as it can be articulated to anyone outside the traditions of the French language, the idea of *différance* (the word did not exist in French before Derrida) refers to Saussure's view that an important quality of signs is their interrelatedness. We do not have, in language, a random set of discrete sounds arbitrarily associated with ideas or things, but a set or system of signs which we are able to understand because they are different from each other. This means, according to Saussure, that there are no absolute terms. This admission is triumphantly seized upon by Derrida to show that not only are there no absolute and fixed terms (every sign carrying meaning only in virtue of its *relations with* other signs), but that terms and signs mean only because they are *different*. Difference, in the best traditions of French metaphysics, is then made a substantival

element in Derrida's system. Ignoring the fact that signs according to Saussure's reasoning also signify because they are *similar*
to each other, Derrida elaborates an intricate theory of meaning
in which terms *defer* to each other in *differing* from each
other: yielding us his amalgam of difference and deference or
différance.

All these ideas – slight and indulgent as some of them appear
to anyone outside the French tradition – are basically derived
from Derrida's critique of Husserl's theory of meaning and in
particular from Husserl's admission that he was unable to provide a satisfactory analysis of 'presence'. Derrida, following his
logic of supplementarity, tries to show that the conditions for
successful utterance can never be fulfilled because there can
never be any genuinely objective present moment. Husserl cannot account for the grammatically correct but non-referring
expression ('The present king of France is bald', for instance),
except by calling them nonsense (*unsinnvoll*), and this can only be
done by assuming a theory of meaning (one based upon objectivity) which was what he was supposed to be proving. And it is
this underlying assumption, an assumption common to Western
metaphysics since the Greeks, that Derrida wants to unmask.
The whole of Western metaphysics, according to Derrida, is
based upon 'the systematic interdependence of the concepts of
sense, ideality, objectivity, truth, intuition, perception and
expression'.[14] It bases itself, therefore, upon a logic of objectivity,
which cannot be sustained because the 'presence' upon which it
itself in turn is based can never, on Husserl's own admission, be
demonstrated. 'Presence' therefore is the common denominator
and villain not only of this piece, but of the whole of Western
metaphysics. It is the critique of this concept which we must
ourselves criticise if we are to place Derrida's peculiar role in
current literature and philosophy.

(It is a critique which bears relations to another problem of
logic, which we must mention first before passing on to the major
issue. This is the problem of simples, as it was faced by Russell
and Wittgenstein in the first two decades of the century. The
theory of logical atomism was designed to lay down the basic
features of simples – atomic expressions which were incapable
themselves of being defined. These must refer to sense-
impressions because they alone are reliable. Everything else is
built up of these basic logical bricks. Russell reduced everything

to three atoms: *here*, *this* and *now*.[15] Wittgenstein conceived of 'objects' as colourless things which made 'real' objects by entering into configurations. It is these configurations which we refer to in language. Thus, 'Objects are what is unalterable and subsistent; their configuration is what is changing and unstable'.)[16]

(ii) PHILOSOPHIES OF TIME AND CHANGE

Derrida's analysis of presence, then, stems from Husserl's admission that he was unable satisfactorily to give an account of the way in which subjective *Ausdrück* was to be translated into objective *Anzeigen*: there is no genuinely present moment, and therefore no genuinely present objective situation. Everything can be known 'in itself', Husserl concedes, but what is objectively definite should permit us to give it objective determination, and 'we are infinitely removed from this ideal . . .'. We should be able to 'describe any subjective experience in unambiguous, objective, fixed fashion'. But such 'an attempt is always plainly vain'.[17] The reason for this despairing admission is the fact that experience takes place in time, and time, by definition, changes, so that there is no present moment fixable.

Now Husserl's treatment on these matters is by no means original. Still less is Derrida's. It is similar to analyses of language and experience carried out at various moments in the history of philosophy. Most relevant to Derrida, perhaps, are certain of the pre-Socratics (notably Zeno and Heraclitus); Hegel; Heidegger; Whitehead and Henri Bergson. Heidegger and Bergson certainly had influence upon Derrida, Whitehead probably not, but he must be mentioned in this context because of his own direct influence on certain Americans (Charles Olson, Joseph Riddel) whose views approximate closely to Derrida's.

Husserl, as we have seen, had opened up the way to Derrida's position by admitting that time confounds all our attempts to arrive at a satisfactory analysis of meaning: there can be no 'present moment', in which meaning takes place as in 'the blink of an eye'. Everything is mired with what Husserl called 'protention' and 'retention' – anticipations of the future and traces of the past. There is no present moment, then, and no pure consciousness of the present moment. The movement of time is a 'phasing', which includes both present and past. This idea is used by Derrida to support his 'de-construction' of the fiction of 'presence'. All the philosophies which anticipate or influence Husserl and Derrida in respect of their analyses of meaning and the present are philosophies of time.

Zeno's paradox of the arrow which can never get to its destination because it is a series of arrows, none of which can properly be said to move, has in a sense been given a form of validification by the movie camera, which shows us that the apparently unbroken flight is made up of an infinite series of moments of arrest. Philosophers have usually been irritated by Zeno, as Aristotle was, and the paradoxes can in fact be broken down by philosophical analysis to reveal their spurious trickiness.[18] Yet Zeno set a kind of problem which philosophers and logicians will probably always be worried by from time to time. Derrida is an instance.

Derrida's indebtedness to Hegel is more substantial, however. Hegel's analysis of Kant is cited by Derrida at a crucial stage of his own critique of Husserl; this critique itself, indeed, does little more than echo Hegel's. It is from Hegel that Derrida (and, I think, Husserl himself) takes the idea of a totality – a great whole incorporating everything, of which all human perceptions and descriptions are necessarily fragmented parts. (Bloom's 'intertext' is born here too.) In the Absolute Idea, according to Hegel, all contradictions are resolved. Anything falling short of the Absolute Idea – which is to say, anything at all – is broken and self-contradictory. According to Hegel, the nature of a thing is constituted by the relations it holds to all the other things synchronically and diachronically related to it. Since nothing exists alone, independently of space and time and the other phenomena that make space and time, nothing can be known that is not partial and, therefore, to some extent in contradiction with itself. From this, Hegel derives the essential incompleteness of all ideas and of all things. Indeed, there *are* no things, in the sense of independent, isolable entities, there are only parts of one massive All. Thus, also, we can never really be said to know anything, since to know something we should have to know everything about it, which – given the scenario just sketched – is not possible. Hegel's critique of Kant, as Derrida says, can also be applied against Husserl.

Although he lacks Hegel's transcendental confidence, Derrida takes much of the spirit of Hegel's semelfacture. For him, too, the 'closure' required by an adequate theory of meaning is denied by the essentially time-bound, indefinable nature of the present moment, and the impossibility of defining isolable facts as knowledge. So it is when we turn to the later philosophers whose work either anticipates or influences Derrida – Heidegger, Whitehead and Bergson. All are philosophers of flux and time; all have been widely influential. Bergson's influence in particular has been noted more than once above. He was a key influence not only on creative writers such as Proust and T. S. Eliot, but on critics and philosophers such as T. E. Hulme, I. A. Richards and Susanne Langer. It is no doubt Bergson's eloquent descriptions of the nature of remembering in *Matière et Mémoire* that lie behind Derrida's critique of Husserl and, perhaps, behind Husserl's own account of time and 'Internal time-consciousness'. Nothing, Bergson tells us,[19] is experienced free of earlier memory-traces, so that nothing is really experienced at all in the way that the sensitised plate receives light or the Lockean *tabula rasa* its first impressions. From this insight into the nature of experiencing in time, Bergson moved to his own critique of language, with its weakness at describing reality. Reality is essentially a flux, as it is in the pre-Socratics. Bergson supposes language incapable of any objective truth, first because language seems to posit fixed identities where nothing in fact is so fixed, being in a constant state of transition from one temporal state to the next; and second, because it appears to enable us to give a direct account of experiences which are in fact only experienced through the mediation of memory and acquired personality. The verbal and mental image, therefore, became for Bergson the falsifying agent; language is the mask of the lie, and the ideal of objectivity the *fata morgana* of the empiricists.

A similar philosophy of flux and change led A. N. Whitehead to discard the representative capacities of language. Bergson's flux becomes Whitehead's 'process', 'One all-pervasive fact, inherent in the very character of what is real is the transition of things, the passage one to another'.[20] This essentially pre-Socratic picture of reality leads Whitehead to a de-constructive articulation-theory: 'However we fix a determinate entity, there is always a narrower determination of something which is presupposed in our first choice. . . . These unities, which I call events, are the emergence into actuality of something.'[21] This seems to allow us to replace the old static 'thing' with the post-

Einsteinian 'event'. But even this Whitehead will not let us get away with. Here too our language would let us down: 'This abstract word (events) cannot be sufficient to characterise what the fact of the reality of an event is in itself.'[22] No idea, Whitehead therefore concludes, 'can in itself be sufficient. For every idea which finds its significance in each event must represent something which attributes to what realisation is in itself.'[23]

From these bases, Whitehead tries to derive a language of 'prehensions' (= the old perceptions) and 'events' (= the old things) which will not distort our perception of reality. This ideal has inspired not only the aesthetics of the Black Mountain school in America, but also, in a transformed way, the 'serene linguistic nihilism' of de-constructionism itself. For if one way of meeting Whitehead's challenge is to try to create a kind of degeneralised, phenomenalist language which does not distort reality as Western discourse based on separative logic of fixed general identities does, another is to accept the incapacities of language serenely and revel in the new freedom of sheer discourse – language without reference, signifiers without signifieds. Thus, American literature, according to Joseph Riddel, 'rejects (or at least puts in question) representation, humanism and history.'[24] Man is, in Riddel's Bloomianised version of Charles Olson, always 'a secondary condition, prefigured as the wanderer who has always repeated the primordial "First Murder". The world – space was actually in the beginning random, distribution, space as difference.'[25] Man, feeling himself as an outsider, tries to make himself central: 'his belated discovery of himself, or insinuation of himself, of his centrality, therefore, which Olson identifies with humanism, becomes evident in the very invention of metaphysics and radiates through the literature of the West, particularly in its preoccupation with epic or narrative.'[26] Having thus disposed of human culture at a sweep, Olson and Riddel move on, with a hubris that would be monstrous if it were not fatuous, to prescribe the 'new writing', 'a nonphonetic writing, in what preceded logocentrism.'[27]

This lurid cocktail of a theory is typical of a great deal of the critical thinking of the period in which de-constructionism emerged. In its pristine form it is already there in the metaphysics of Bergson, Heidegger and Whitehead: all that Olson has added is a vague, Frazerian-Freudian mythology of ancient father-worship and sacrifice. The upshot is the anti-humanism

which was pioneered by T. E. Hulme[28] and is dominant also in
the thought of Michel Foucault. Olson's attempt to refute Western metaphysics because it discriminated what can't be discriminated, parallels Whitehead's critique of an image-fixing
language and Bergson's rejection of intellection based on crystal-
lisation of what can't be crystallised. According to all these
views, language lies – falsifies – in so far as we think of it as a
reproducer of reality: it lies, in other words, so long as we try to
relate our signifiers (words and concepts) to the signifieds we
suppose to lie behind them: things and events only seem to be
still and separate; they are in fact in a constant state of change
and interrelationship. The Black Mountain writers try to prescribe a new language – one which is, in effect, essentially non-
linguistic, a 'script' that has the quality of the Mayan indices
and one which would indeed enable us to live without thinking.
Mainstream structuralists follow Lévi-Strauss into elegant
silence. De-constructionism elects for a lively play – sheer
discourse, which turns out, alas, to be composed mainly of literary
criticism.

All these alternatives share the same property of being dependent on the rejection of a particular view of language and of
reality. Once we accept the Whiteheadian-Bergsonian view of
reality as flux, and add to it a theory of language as reproducer of
reality, it becomes impossible to accept a language as traditionally conceived and practised by those linguistic realists known as
empiricists. This kind of linguistic realism – realism which
accepts the adequacy of language to perform its functions – is
referred to by Olson and by de-constructionists as logocentrism:
the belief in the power of language adequately to reflect reality.
Logocentrism, according to de-constructionist thinking, asserts
the empire of truth, a realm of fixed values and positive verities
which words successfully evoke and refer to, and novels and
poems efficiently mirror. Against this logocentrism, Bergson and
Whitehead and Heidegger declare that language always and
necessarily fails of adequate representation: it distorts and lies.
In this, the philosophers follow the poets:

> How shall the heart express itself?
> How shall another comprehend?
> Shall he know by what things you live?
> The thought expressed is a lie.[29]

From this position, it is not hard – indeed it is necessary – to reach the apparent linguistic nihilism of Derrida and other contemporary writers. Paradoxically, the essence of this view is that logocentrism's real error is that it is not logocentric enough: logocentrism believes that words refer to things (that signifiers have signifieds), that reality is a kind of content of language. The truth, they argue, is that language failing (for the reasons given above) adequately to represent or refer to reality, we are left with nothing but language: we are condemned to discourse. This of course leads literary criticism along the same path as literature itself, for 'If, as Derrida puts it, linguistic signs refer themselves only to other linguistic signs, if the linguistic reference of words is words, if texts refer to nothing but other texts, then, in Foucault's words, "If interpretation can never accomplish itself, it is simply because there is nothing to interpret." There is nothing to interpret, for each sign is in itself not the thing that offers itself to interpretation but interpretation of other signs.'[30]

Language, Derrida had said in his critique of Husserl, never presents reality, it always *re*-presents it – presents again, that is to say, the residue-logged, trace-laden, already interpreted signifiers of our own and humanity's past discourse. So we reach the diametrical opposite of logocentrism: paradoxically, the rejection of logocentrism leads directly to the total confinement of thought within language itself – logomania, the superstitious belief in the power and absoluteness of language without the belief in the effectiveness of language to make contact with, refer to or denote reality.

(iii) THE BASES OF LANGUAGE

The nature and the root of logomania (which has been with us since Bergson and the symbolists) was accurately diagnosed by Ernst Cassirer. Paradoxically, it starts from precisely that naïve view of linguistic realism it claims to supplant. Beginning with the fact that, in Cassirer's words, 'measured by the naked "truth" of an object, idealisation is nothing but subjective misconception and falsification', logomania concludes that the error lies in regarding language as bearing any relations to anything outside itself: 'All that "denotation" to which the spoken word lays claim is really nothing more than mere suggestion; a suggestion which, in face of the concrete variegation and totality of actual experience, must always appear a poor and empty shell.'[31] It is a short step from this disillusionment, as Cassirer summarises, to the conclusion that 'modern sceptics of language have drawn: the complete dissolution of any alleged truth content of language, and the realisation that this content is nothing but a sort of phantasmagoria of the spirit.'[32] If we substitute for 'phantasmagoria of the spirit' the word 'discourse', or the army of signifiers, we have in Cassirer's words an exact description of de-constructionism, and indeed of structuralism, and all those late offshoots of symbolism which have engulfed French thought. It is precisely because Lévi-Strauss and Barthes, Derrida and Lacan, accept *au fond* a naïve denotational view of language that they have been driven to conclude in despair that language and literature can have no 'content', and thus no meanings, in the sense in which empiricism uses the word.

The answer to this dilemma is not to battle away at a more and more watertight theory of denotation and reference, as if to make a water-bag that won't leak, but to re-cast the questions underlying the whole quest. What is 'truth'? What is the nature and purpose of language? What conditions must language fulfil? What conditions does language require to be able to function and come into existence? And, underneath all these, the two prime questions, what is the nature of the relationship between language and reality? and, what is reality really like?

Bergson and Whitehead, as we have seen, answer the last question first, and then proceed to answer the earlier questions rather pessimistically: reality is fluxy and subject to the constant work of time; language falsifies because it represents what is changing and fluxy in images which are static and unchanging, the relationship of language to reality is as mirror to object, and its purpose is somehow to do full justice to the nature of reality, and in so doing present us with truth. If human communication depended upon the absolutist claims made for language which Bergson and Whitehead – and to some extent Hegel – claim to be refuting, then these various de-constructions of human knowledge would be justified (though in this case, we would have a tricky task trying to describe just what people had been doing the past five thousand years). What we are concerned with then is the nature of these underlying claims and suppositions understood to be made in language and, then, the question, what sorts

of thing need to be taking place when we say that we are referring to something ('something' here being not another sign, but
something 'real')?

To start with, we must point out the important difference
between theories of reality and theories of expression. The Elea-
tic paradoxes cleverly exploit gaps in language, in particular the
gap opened up by the fact of time. We can't dip our hand into
the same river twice; what we see when we watch the flight of an
arrow is, in fact, an infinite series of static arrows, none of which
can reach its destination. Now it is clear that this observation is
about words, not arrows. No one would stand in the way of an
arrow armed only with Zeno's paradox. So it is with Heraclitus's
river into which we cannot dip our hand twice. This theory is a
matter of what we mean by 'water' and 'hand' and 'dip'. In the
case of the arrow, the alleged difficulties could, for instance, be
handled by giving each static arrow a different number, or tying
a piece of string to the arrow. Then we could say, 'If you want to
talk about the arrow, tell us whether you mean the one that
comes back when I tug it in after it has landed – the real one that
hurts – or those other paradoxical ones which all have different
numbers, but are really the same.' The difference, of course, is
not between arrows but between types of discourse.

Hegel's immensely ambitious account of the universe, to be
sure, certainly seems to be about 'reality'. But many of its arguments are in fact about words, not things or experience. His
conception of the limitations of knowing and of the nature of a
thing seem basically to be a matter of what claims we make for
the words 'know' and 'thing'. In Hegelian language, we can
never be said to 'know' anything: and since he makes it clear
enough what he does mean by 'know', we have few problems
understanding him. But in the ordinary way we use words, it is
not true to say that we can know nothing. We can 'know' something, as Russell pointed out,[33] without having to claim that we
know everything about it, nor do we have to make the definition
of the nature of a thing synonymous with everything that is
relevant to its 'absolute' nature – its *Ding-an-sich*-ness. A definition of knowing such as Hegel erects is necessary only to itself: it
does not prove that knowing as ordinarily understood doesn't
take place. If the claim made in the idea of 'knowing' and 'nature
of a thing' *were* that we can know or define everything that is
relevant to the constitution and origination of a thing or a fact

(which would indeed entail us knowing everything in the history of the universe), then it would be true in Hegel's sense that we can knownothing that is not fragmentary and self-contradictory. There is, moreover, a chastening sense in which we need to be reminded by Hegel's great vision that we see and know *little*. But this does not mean that we can be said to 'know' nothing, or that the Hegelian definition of knowing rules out the whole of human knowledge, and undermines our attempts to communicate with each other. In fact, we do not *mean* by knowing what Hegel makes us mean; nor do we make the sort of claim he assumes we must make when we talk about a thing, or about its nature. When I say I have a toothache, I don't have to claim to know everything about the cause and course of the physical and mental processes that result in my pain. Similarly, when I name a thing a box, for instance, I don't claim to know all the facts about it and theoretically add up to its total and exhaustive description. One of the problems involved in the theory of descriptions was that it seemed to claim that a name means neither more nor less than the sum of its descriptions (for example, a box is an x which is square, wooden, red, heavy). Do we then have to say that a name is no longer appropriate when we discover another fact about the entity to which it was previously applied? Do two different people (to return to my own earlier example) with different sets of facts about diaphragms *know* different things? Do we, in other words, need a different name for every single sensum?

Obviously not. Yet, absurd as this question seems, it is not so far removed from the theories of language which end in deconstructionism. For these theories in effect say that language must itself make these absolute claims in order to fulfil itself. Let us imagine at the birth of language a group of sophisticated primates. 'Ong!' they agree is that loud noise accompanied by rain, bad light and flashes of fire in the sky. The next week another thunderstorm happens; they understand that time has passed, it *is* another week, the light is slightly different. Is this 'Ong'? They haven't yet got to the stage of being able to say that it is Ong-oid, or Ong-ish. So they say, 'Uck!' But they also realise that one caveman's perception of 'Uck' is different from another's, so we get not only *Ong* and *Uck* (Sunday thunder and next Saturday's thunder), but also *Ock*, *Egf*, *Oudh* and *Allph*! (caveman 1, 2, 3 . . . n's thunder). There are as many words for thunder as there are thunders and perceivers of thunder, and this is as it should be, according to Whitehead. Not surprisingly, this very sophisticated crowd decide that language just isn't on. Who is to say that Neanderthal man, far from being an evolutionary failure, wasn't really the first de-constructionist, who simply dropped out?

My parody is hardly less extreme than some accounts of language fostered by Bergson and Whitehead. Isn't it clear that these 'events' of Whitehead's, 'these emergences into actuality' of something, are only a philosopher's plaything? Isn't the truth that we are perfectly able to describe differences by using the fixed terms we have, and that we do not need a new name for every new appearance of reality or require a numerical superscript for every temporal vision of the 'same' thing (arrow, river, and so on)? But doesn't this in turn oblige us to say that in fact Husserl's, Whitehead's and Bergson's accounts of reality and the apprehension of reality are really strained and forced? That reality is not, in the first place, as fluxy as they maintain? And that, therefore, our apprehension of it is not so warpingly inflected by memory and retention as they suggest?

To these questions we must add a further one. What conditions are necessary for the production of language, and therefore assumed in its functioning? And, then, what do we, and should we, use language to *do*? It is plain that if reality were as fluxy as Whitehead and Bergson supposed, language could never have come into existence: the existence of language presupposes a world of stable and fixed identities. Whether nouns or verbs came into existence first is not important: process and fixity are relative and interdependent concepts, the one determinable in terms of the other. The growth of language was only possible when the processes, events and objects perceived by man were constant and steady enough to be referred to at all. We know of earlier stages of terrestrial evolution when no such stability and continuity existed, where everything was unstable, interchangeable and identity-less. In such a world, language could never have been generated.

This relative stability and fixity, giving rise to persisting identities, might appear to be the first prerequisite of language. It does itself, however, presuppose another, what we might call the logicality of things. We are concerned here with the relations of logic and language. Susanne Langer, for instance, believes that

logic as it were springs from language.[34] The truth is, I think,
that logic is what we mean when we assert, plus the fact that we
mean at all, and aren't just babbling. Logic, in other words, is the
first thing, and language its co-existent. We can have language
because things behave logically, just as we have a sense of time
because the past, as it were, keeps behind the present. We cannot even imagine what a world would be like in which the law of
excluded middle did not hold, in which each thing was *not* what
it was, in which a thing could be both red and green at the same
time, in which a thing could advance towards us and retreat
from us at the same time. Mystics exploit the language of paradox precisely in order to render graspable the ungraspable.

Now this logicality of things cannot itself be said in language.
It is something which shows forth in our language. Many of our
problems in these matters stem from a confusion about what can
be said and what cannot. 'The cardinal problem for philosophy',
Wittgenstein wrote to Bertrand Russell before the publication of
the *Tractatus*, is 'the theory of what can be expressed (*gesagt*) by
propositions, i.e. by language (and, which comes to the same
thing, what can be thought) and what cannot be expressed by
propositions, but can only be shown (*gezeigt*).'[35] What cannot be
said is, precisely, according to Wittgenstein, 'the logical form of
reality'.[36] This can only be shown and 'what *can* be shown *cannot*
be said.'[37]

Thus, the logical form of the world, mirrored in the logical
form of language, cannot itself be established in language. This
is in no way to be seen as a limitation of language, and thence the
reason for head-shaking despair, but as a condition of language
which amounts, on the contrary, to a kind of guarantee: 'Every
proposition *shows* something besides what it says, about the Universe: *for* if it has no sense, it can't be used; and if it has a sense,
it mirrors some logical property of the universe.'[38]

Together with this logicality, another property of language
has to be assumed: its necessary capacity to refer to what *is*. It is
this which I think causes Derrida some confusion in his analysis
of Husserl – his objection to that 'common matrix' of preconcep-
tions about objectivity which Derrida believes compromises the
whole of Western metaphysics with *telos* – unavowed beliefs
about reference. In point of fact, the very existence of language
itself assures us that the world *is*. This, too, cannot be demonstrated in propositions. 'The "experience" that we need in order

to understand logic is not that something or other is the state of things, but that something *is*; that, however, is *not* an experience. Logic is, prior to every experience – that something *is* so.'[39] This, certainly, is part at least of what Wittgenstein meant when he said that 'the sense of the world must lie outside the world.'[40] Far from being despairing or mystical, these statements show Wittgenstein's profound awareness of the frontiers of expression and of the underlying nature of language.

Language, then, shows forth the logical properties of the universe, the logicality of experience and the external existence of things. It is in the very nature of language that, in other words, it refers. We could not have language if we did not feel able to refer to the world. This does not commit us to a naïve mirror-theory of language: we do not have to believe that our language provides us with exact photographs of reality. That in fact is just what it does not try to do. But it does commit us to the view that our language must sustain a certain minimum stability of reference within its signs, just such a stability as the persisting outside world sustains. The world does sustain such a stability: it is, quite simply, less fluxy than Whitehead and others have said it was. Our language, too, sustains a stable correspondence with this state of things – an inner correspondence with the factual structure of the world.

This view is not in conflict with the later theories of Wittgenstein and others that our language is a system of interlocking and interrelated concepts. Language is not a mass of discrete perceptions, each holding iconic relations with bits of experience or phenomena. It is a vast though never complete system of interrelated and cross-referring symbols, receiving meaning and definition from each other. The modish use of Wittgenstein's *Philosophical Investigations* to support a linguistic nihilism is wholly unfounded. Gabriel Josipovici, for instance, believes that the recognition that we see habitually through conceptual frames or spectacles, 'brings with it a kind of freedom, for it stops us from falling into the trap of thinking that meaning inheres in words, objects or events.'[41]

On the contrary, the spectacles theory of the *Investigations is* anchored firmly in the reflective models of the *Tractatus*. Language does not reflect as a camera reflects, and we learn meanings of words by not simply associating vocable with thing (as when we learn the identity of a person) but by learning how to use the word: learning meanings is a complex process of learning rules of association, identification and a general sense of the new word's site in the linguistic and grammatical schemes of the general culture. This expands and enhances the *Tractatus* view of meaning as mirror-like reflection of states of affairs: it certainly doesn't abandon it. Language is a shifting mass of concepts more or less fixed at the centre. When we change our minds, or adjust our picture of things, we do so not by abandoning this conceptual mass but by carrying out certain minor (or major) tailoring operations: we make our conceptual system fit the 'new' facts, and it is an essential part of language that such a coherence holds good. We do not, then, have to choose between a crude realism, in which words have fixed, iconic meanings, and can never be severed from their origination, and a sophisticated conceptualism, dissolving truth and meaning in a mass of discursive relativities. Yet this is precisely what many recent writers – one could mention Foucault as well as Derrida – have in fact insisted.

To these basic properties of language we must add the last, its ineradicable publicity: the very existence of language assumes and rests on the fact of communication – intersubjectivity, in Husserl's term, common sense in empiricism, Objective Mind in Hegel. We do not have to establish the fact of communication: we cannot. It is, like the capacity to refer and the existence of something to refer to, built into language at the outset. Wittgenstein again, in his analysis of the private language problem, has provided the most powerful arguments for this view.[42] Our language is never 'about' our private sensations, always 'about' publicly defined concepts.

These are the basic conditions of language. The next step is to observe that the actual language that has been generated in these conditions has as its *modus operandi* one feature which we might call the truly defining linguistic feature: the ability of being able to refer to phenomena and states of affairs by means of terms which retain their significances in the absence of the phenomena they mirror, and to which they continue to refer. Thus, language is made up of symbols not signs (in Peirce's meaning), and the system built up with them continues to hold its mirror-like relationship to the world, no matter how far removed they are from its actuality. It is this capacity of *abstraction* which the linguistic theorists I have been criticising – Bergson, Whitehead, Husserl and Derrida – largely ignore. This is particularly true of Derrida's critique of 'presence'. Presence, we remember, was defined as a quasi-speechlike thing – the 'hearing-oneself-speak' in the presence of the indicated meaning: it being impossible to establish this (because of the fluxy nature of reality and the interference of memories and protensions and the influence of the code itself), the whole basis of metaphysics was to be undermined. Speech, Derrida argues, is itself writing-like in its distorting and absent qualities.

Yet in fact this is not so. In the first place, the speech-writing distinction is not important. The statement 'London is the capital of England' is true whether spoken or written or merely thought: its logical structure – its *meaning* – remains the same whether spoken or written cynically, absent-mindedly or through a fog of sentimental reminiscences. The whole of Western metaphysics is indeed based upon the assumption that logicality and meaning *are* objective in this sense. Derrida's arguments certainly don't threaten it. There is simply no place here for that sense of presence (whatever it might actually mean) which Derrida finds so important. Logic, language and meaning are so constructed that it does not matter if the speaker-writer-thinker is thinking of an actual lion, musing on lions in general or actually pronouncing the word 'lion' in the presence of a four-legged mammal with a dark mane and a loud roar. Paradoxically, the one case where the statement 'The lion is yellow' doesn't particularly matter is in the presence of the beast itself, where a gesture would do. Wittgenstein had turned his attention to such predicate statements before he wrote the *Tractatus*. He went so far as to doubt that statements like 'This is a lion' were propositions at all: and if they were, they were peculiar: 'Even if there *were* propositions of (the) form "M is red", they would be superfluous (tautologous), because what they tried to say is something which is already *seen* . . . when you see "M".'[43]

Precisely what language may not have, we might say, therefore, is what Derrida somewhat tortuously defines as 'presence': presence is just what metaphysics and logic can do without. The initial mistake, of course, was Husserl's, who had really tried to psychologise meaning. Husserl conceived of meaning as a pure inner state of mind, which compromised itself in the act of indication. He tried to define the conditions in which a successful co-presence of pure inner 'meaning' and outer correspondence would exist. And, of course, he found it impossible. The reason why it was impossible was not that reality and mind are too fluxy and 'ravaged by otherness' or *Verworfenheit*, too overladen with other linguistic traces, but that meaning does not function like that. Husserl remained, I observed above, a psychologiser of meaning: the *Logical Investigations* attempt to prescribe the conditions of an in fact fictitious mental act, 'meaning' – a miraculous coincidence of objective situation and subjective state. This amounts to a seventh variety of *meaning*$_1$: 'I say, I'm meaning', as one might say, 'I say, I'm enjoying this. . .'. Husserl in fact ran foul of what Wittgenstein called 'the old difficulty', the 'illusion that meaning is a special state of mind', for nothing is more wrong-headed than calling meaning a mental activity.[44]

The opposite of a fallacy is a counter-fallacy. And Derrida's fallacious theory of the metaphysics of presence is derived from the inadequacies of Husserl's attempts to analyse meaning. Ernst Cassirer again long ago diagnosed the root of the error: 'The concept must annul "presence" in order to arrive at presentation.'[45] Isn't the error not only of Husserl and Derrida but also of Bergson, Whitehead and Heidegger,[46] precisely to demand of language a kind of poetic thereness which is really alien to its nature? Hegel's theory of the world is a vision of a totality which fairly enough reminds us of the incompleteness of our knowledge. But this cannot provide the basis for a disintegrative attack on the possibilities of language. If knowledge were really impossible, as Hegel sometimes seems to imply, then it would have been impossible for Hegel to frame his critique, which is a critique ultimately of certain possible *claims*. It certainly does not constitute a rebuttal of the capacities of language to refer to and to frame its own world-view. Hegel has become the basis for a number of sceptical theories of language. Bergson's equally poetic error, likewise, was to mistake the claims made by language, and to base upon the manifest impossibility of *these* claims a theory of the inadequacy of language itself. When we describe a thing or an event in intellectual terms, it is our conception of the thing we get clear in propositions mirroring the logical fact: we do not – or at least we should not – imagine that we represent the organic thing. If we claimed that these intellectual transcriptions of ours, these propositions mirroring 'reality' in conceptual terms, did in fact succeed in satisfactorily constituting some kind of experiential equivalent to the organic reality, then Bergson's critique would be apt: it would remind us that we can do nothing of the sort. But if we do not make such claims, if we admit that language simply has other functions, which it is capable of fulfilling quite adequately, then the whole Bergsonian critique itself seems irrelevant.

The question then is, what does language need to do in order that words like 'truth' and 'knowledge' have a viable significance? What should we be using language to do? It is clear that Bergson's error lay in proposing a quite unnecessary function for language. Something of the sort is true also of Whitehead. Language, Whitehead points out, cannot 'characterise . . . the fact of the reality of an event'. True. But why should it try to do so? What is Whitehead expecting language to do? What would be the purpose of an undertaking such as the one Whitehead despairs of our being able to carry out? His assumption is that language should try to provide an account of reality, that such an account will give us 'the truth': since we cannot provide this account without falsifying the facts, we are condemned to despair – the despair of which de-constructionism is one variety. But why should language even attempt the kind of task Whitehead apparently cut our for it? What would be the point? In Whitehead, actual living is replaced by an agonised and exhaustingly lengthy attempt to characterise living: instead of life, we get the constant effort to *say life*. But life cannot be said, nor should we want to characterise living in this way. Saying is only part of living, and it must have a different purpose from the rendition of itself. If we assume that the purpose of language is to try to reproduce reality, replace it, provide a faithful substitute for it, then we shall inevitably be driven to despair when we realise that it is powerless to achieve this end. This powerlessness enters Western art with Romanticism, and is thematised in the researches of Mallarmé and the *Symbolistes*. As such it is a valid part of poetic material, and paradoxically enough receives fully adequate expression in Mallarmé's poetry. If we mistake this rhetoric of Symbolism for the purpose of language and philosophy, we enter the refined cul-de-sac of structuralism and de-constructionism. Once we drop the typically late-Romantic notion that the purpose of language is to replace reality or offer a precise and satisfying substitute for it, we cease to indulge in the gratifying game of deploring the inadequacies of words. Paradoxically, the cult of silence, which is Lévi-Strauss's more dig-

nified equivalent of de-constructionist discourse, stems precisely
from that fallacy of false denotationism it was supposed to supplant. The fallacy dictates its opposite, which is, again, another
fallacy.

If the purpose of language is other than this sterile attempt to
reproduce reality, so Truth has its own rules and knowledge, its
laws of production. The question, what is Truth? really underlies
both the Whiteheadian-Bergsonian philosophies of flux, and the
de-constructionist philosophies of pure discourse. For Whitehead, Truth is a kind of verbalised, conceptualised mirror-world,
identical to the real world in everything except that it is made of
words. Language necessarily failing to provide this ideal and
characterise reality, constantly representing fluxy change in
static images, opennesss with closure, and so on, writers must
resign themselves to renounce forever the concept of Truth, and
hence condemn themselves to a necessary failure. Here again we
see that a naïve denotational theory of meaning (as if meaning
inhered in things like water in a bucket) is merely inverted,
producing a counter-fallacy – that language can have no precise
meaning, and no reference to reality. But in fact such a conception of Truth is as unfounded as the Whiteheadian conception of
the purpose of language as the reproduction of reality.

Truth is not a bag, or a total verbal equivalent to reality
(whatever that could actually be): it is a relationship between
assertion and reality in given situations, under agreed conditions
and with congruent scope in the claims of the statement and the
nature of the facts. Truth has its rules. Truth is, for the doctor,
the patient's description of his pain: this might be brief and
sketchy, 'A stabbing pain here, after I eat, subsiding slowly . . .'.
It would be absurd to say that the patient had failed to tell the
Truth because he hadn't given a total, faithful picture of the pain
or all the events leading up to it. The patient's words *tell of* his
pain – they don't express it or reproduce it. And that is all that is
required.

This is important because it is sometimes said that our words
can only tell of our own private experiences, and therefore that
we can never be said to tell the truth or communicate with each
other. Wittgenstein has given the exhaustive lie to this theory.[47]
Our descriptions of pain do not have to convey its quality, any
more than our references to apples and skies have to specify a
hue identical to that seen by our neighbour. This does not con-

demn us to solipsism. On the contrary, our ability to transmit our common perceptions and sensations rests upon the properties we have agreed on in things. That is where the scope of our language ends: my sensations are mine, yours yours; but our language and concepts are common. It is perhaps the mistaken identification of language with physical sensation which his misled so many theorists. There are as many Truths as there are situations, but out language is capable of expressing them. The father's truth is the boy's admission that *he* took the money from his mother's purse, and the admission is not made more true by the piling on of circumstantial detail. The announcer's report that the result of the 1981 European Cup Final was 'Liverpool 1, Real Madrid 0' is as true as the detailed narration of the spectator who was there, or indeed the exhaustive account of the natural scientist studying flies and mosquitoes who happened to be taking the Parc de Princes Stadium, Paris on the night of 9 May for his field. Truth, like the content of literary texts in our earlier definition, is precisely what *can* be communicated.

Successful linguistic reference is relative to given situations, and has an ordained scope. To say that we cannot *refer* to reality simply because it would be beyond our capacities to give a faithful account of everything that went on at a particular event is as wrong as to say that Truth is beyond our grasp.

11 Neo-Marxism and De-Construction

De-constructionism is less a philosophy than the decadence of a philosophy. It retails the metaphysics of silence and inexpressibility adumbrated by the symbolist poets and Henri Bergson. Like the decadent idealists who trailed along in the wake of Schopenhauer at about the same time as symbolism arose, deconstructionism leaves the world unapproached: the world and its concerns must wait while the logomaniac de-constructionist goes through his mantric rituals, rather as an indulgent grownup might wait dumbly upon the whims of an autistic child. Lacking the grown-up's tenderness, we might simply dismiss the whole thing. Yet it has led to a curious paradox. For de-constructionism has been taken up inside circles which ought, by rights, to be hostile to its spirit. De-constructionism can be interpreted variously as (a) the attempt of an ineffectual bourgeois intelligentsia to reduce the world's action to its own inaction; (b) the attempt of a critical power-group to take over the realm of cultural discourse from the artists traditionally honoured in it; (c) the attempts of this bourgeois intelligentsia to fend off a real Marxism by rendering all discourse ineffectual, and thereby perpetuate the present in which it weaves its fantasies before a credulous audience of the young; or (d) simple sabotage – the genuine efforts of a Marxist intelligentsia to undermine Western discourse as a whole and discredit the 'monuments' of Western culture. It is this last we are concerned with here: the paradox whereby neo-Marxism has sabotaged discourse itself, thus destroying not only bourgeois literature and its 'privileged' discourse, but also the very possibility of a Marxist or feminist or revolutionary literature.

Such a destruction must begin with the destruction of the aesthetic level – the alleged autonomy of art: art must be shown not to be autonomous, with its own value, but to be the product of historico-economic forces. Macherey wants to have it both ways: the text is 'autonomous' but not 'independent.'[1] The literary text is 'determined by its own rules', but is nevertheless not to be considered a 'reality complete in itself, a thing apart.'[2] The aim of this manoeuvre is to eliminate the hated bourgeois 'genius' – the subjectivising demon who produces art-works out of thin air, responsible only to his 'inspiration'. Now such a conception of the artist has been dead in English literary circles since T. S. Eliot's *Tradition and the Individual Talent* (1917), and we must be careful not to get tangled up in unnecessary refutations. We again come up against the fact that there are certain disparities between English and French literary tradition: the preoccupation of recent French criticism with exorcising the ghosts of Châteaubriand and Hugo has caused a certain agitation in France which can have no equivalent in England or America.

Macherey wishes to accomplish not only the elimination of this Romantic Genius, but also the autonomous artefacts (ideolects incomprehensible outside their own terms) he characteristically goes in for. Accordingly, the work is said to be 'produced', and the writer becomes merely *un travailleur*,[3] one who witnesses the production of the work in no more significant a sense than the foreman machinist witnesses the production of today's *Le Monde*. Yet Macherey wishes, like all the new Marxists, to avoid the stigma of the old vulgar Marxism, which 'reduced' works to their ideological contents. The older Marxists had accomplished this task simply by postulating or assuming a certain greatness in art – an inexplicability, associated with Genius and even Inspiration. Marx and Engels, in common with Gorky, Trotsky and Lunacharsky, all accepted such a miraculist view of Art or Literature: Art and Literature, though they will ultimately testify to the class-struggle by affirming Love or Equality, must nevertheless stand outside the determination of forms which afflicts ideology in general. 'A work of art should, in the first place, be judged by its own laws, that is the laws of art,' as Trotsky said.[4] This has remained the (honourably) self-contradictory position of classical Marxism, down to Louis Althusser's conception of 'real art' ('I do not rank real art among the ideologies'),[5] and Lucien Goldmann's concept of the 'valid text'. And it is just this unresolved contradiction of Marxist theory which later critics like Macherey and Terry Eagleton have tried to resolve. Classical Marxist criticism such as Lukács' (which Goldmann follows closely), had early seen that the problem of realism or reflection was closely linked to that of ideology. According to Marx, intellectual behaviour (all forms of 'cultural' or 'spiritual' discourse) ought to be referrable ultimately to the 'base' of the economic production dominant in the society concerned at the given time. Yet Art, we are told, is somehow 'above' this, or exempt from it. Lukács in general assumed simply that the 'great' or 'universal' writer was one to whose work history or the understanding of history lent a third dimension. Hence realism, or 'true realism', is to be defined in terms of the quality of what the 'great' writer (Tolstoy, Shakespeare, Homer are favourite examples) achieves. Thus, the problem of reflection is solved by an appeal to universality or 'greatness'. It was Lukács' assumption, of course, that this greatness as a matter *of empirical fact* was always couched in terms of the writer's implicit understanding of history. Even if he were a high Tory like Scott or a Catholic reactionary like Balzac, his genius would enable him to 'render' or 'realise' the true configuration of historical forces at work in his time. The great writer, therefore, is a great historian; he knows what is going on, even if he holds reactionary views. He might deplore the rise of the capitalist class and the decline of the old aristocracy, but this dislike itself *reflects* the truth, and it is in such relationship of reflection that 'greatness' lies.

This, of course, merely offers a more sophisticated picture of reflection: what is reflected may not appear to the eye. On the contrary, the greatness of the great writer may reside precisely in his ability to deep-read the time, so as to unearth the contours, stress-lines and birth-pangs of the always emergent process of history. Lucien Goldmann in fact did little more than tidy up Lukács' working methods and offer them as a new theory – genetic structuralism. In Goldmann, there is an important new element, that of the function of art as expression of the ambitions, aspirations or paranoias of particular classes or subclasses. Yet fundamentally, Goldmann's notion of the 'homology' repeats Lukács' general sense of the writer as deep-reader or aerial photographer of his time. The literary text, therefore, appears as a mere microcosm of the reality, and there is an ineradicable vagueness in Goldmann's attempts to describe the relations between art-microcosm and world-reality: how does the real appear in art? Does it just emerge there, more or less through the writer's doodlings, transmitted by Time or History?

Or is it the writer's 'greatness' that he can unearth and understand what is going on? If the latter, then we have to assume either an absolute correspondence between the writer's mind and the mind of history or a complete ignorance as to the import of what he is doing. Now in fact this remains another unsolved problem of Marxist criticism. If the art-work 'reduces' to the facts of the historical process, so that a writer can be a great historian without knowing it, what happens when the process has happened, so to speak? Is the art-work then otiose? Macherey skilfully elicits this odd demand from the known fact of Marx's fascination with Balzac's ability to imagine historical types who did not yet exist, but who were later produced by history: 'As anticipation', Macherey observes, 'great art gives the image of an as yet unborn reality . . . but in that case, is not the artistic effect destroyed at the very moment when its success is confirmed?'[6]

Once again the Marxist critic (in this case Marx himself) runs up against the ideological objection: he has, apparently, 'reduced' the art-work to a certain historical process, and so left himself with the paradox that the work retains 'charm' even after the facts have materialised which his 'genius' enabled him to predict. Whence derived this 'charm'? What is the 'value' of the 'form' which apparently is what makes the difference between the merely 'routine' reflection and the 'real' thing? (And how many more key-terms do we have to put inside inverted commas?) It is this problem which Macherey, Eagleton and others have set themselves to solve. It can be re-phrased in these terms: in what consists the art-ness of art, or the literariness of literature? Artness and literariness are certainly unwelcome guests at the Marxian feast, yet they are guests who can produce, upon challenge, invitations issued and signed by Marx himself and counter-signed by a whole string of subsequent commissars, from Trotsky to Althusser. Lukács and Goldmann, as we have seen, implicitly shelve the problem by secretly enlisting the artist on the side of the 'right' historical cause. In their view, great art is great and universal because the artist is deep down a Marxist historian, who knows what's going on and invests his creations with – in fact correct – historical attitudes: he tells the truth without wanting to. Both Macherey and Eagleton are expert at uncovering the anomalies attached to this idea – principal among them the reliance upon an essentially 'bourgeois' conception of 'value' or 'greatness'. They wish to rescue Marxist critic-ism from this limbo of unregenerate bourgeois ideology by articulating a fully 'materialised' criticism. This means describ-ing the function of literature without reference to value or moral-ity. Value and morality are strictly ideological by-products of the historical process and the class-struggle: they are hegemonic, weapons by which the dominant class (the bourgeoisie or the older aristocracy) seeks to ensure its position by dressing up its class aspirations as 'universal' or 'eternal' truth, or as Beauty. What we need (neo-Marxists say) is a criticism which enables us to describe literature effectively without recourse to these invalid categories.

Unfortunately, neither Macherey nor Eagleton succeeds in producing the theoretical definitions required by such a pro-gramme. They carry out their destruction plausibly enough but they are unable to build anything to replace it. Macherey[7] merely stipulates that the literary 'reflection' (that is, the realistic image of the text) must have two properties: it must be 'objec-tive' and it must be 'exact' – that is, measured by 'its degree of correspondence to the reality which determines it.'[8] No one in his right mind would question Macherey's admirable common sense here: that a picture – of whatever kind – should be a picture of *something*, something real, external to itself, on the one hand, and that it should resemble that real thing, on the other, are such obvious requirements as to constitute the thundering truth of banality. What have we been told about literary reflec-tions that we did not know before? Nothing whatever. Macherey has tried (in the preceding pages) to discredit a falsely dualistic structuralism, which differentiates the object from the reflection, such that the literary critic can concern himself with either one (the 'world') or the other (the 'text') but not with both. But he does so only by the vaguest postulation of a material 'relation' between reflection and reality. The reality, we are told, 'deter-mines' the reflection and the reflection 'rests upon' this reality. No insight is given as to the nature of these dual relations of 'determination' and 'resting-upon'. All we are told is that the reflection may not be the obvious one of extreme realism. Some-how the images of a Kafka may be as objective and as exact as those of a Thomas Mann. How? Merely by its being shown that it is 'determined by material reality', 'without necessarily being exact, that is to say identical to that reality . . .'.[9] The nature of these relations is not revealed. We are left with the uncomfortable dogmatism that underlies most Marxist criticism: if the particular piece of 'reflection' exemplifies Marxist doctrine, then it will be claimed as objective (and hence as 'true' in the old-fashioned bourgeois sense). If not, then what we have is not literature but ideology, for it is clear that Marxism, being in possession of the truth about history (dialectical materialism) cannot be called ideological. All ideology is bourgeois.

Terry Eagleton strives to dress up this nude dogmatism in more detail. Literature is to be protected from 'vulgar Marxist' reductionism at all costs: we are not to speak of homologies in the Goldmannian sense of mental structures mysteriously transmitted through texts. Neither, however, are we to elevate art or literature 'above' ideology. What, then, is the relationship between literature and ideology, or between the reflection of reality and the reality itself (for the question is really the same)? In Eagleton also, literature is not determined, but 'produced'. Macherey had first used the term 'production' of literature, but Eagleton interestingly changes the metaphor from the industrial to the theatrical scene: literary texts are produced, exactly as plays are produced. The production is not the same as the text, nor is the literary text the same as the ideological components of which it is composed. Beyond this metaphor, however – which enables Eagleton to escape the charge of vulgar determinism without admitting the unacceptable bourgeois notion of creation or inspiration – Eagleton fails to illuminate the relations of literature and ideology. We are told, for instance, that the Shakespearean drama 'produces, from a specific standpoint within it, the severe contradictions of an ideological formation characterised by a peculiarly high degree of "dissolution" – dissolution produced by a conflict of antagonistic ideologies appropriate to a particular stage of class-struggle'.[10]

Thus, literature is made up out of ideology and nothing but ideology, ideology being the name Eagleton gives to the mass of theoretic, intellectual and artistic categories, ideas and possibilities available at any given time. Now this, in itself, is consistent with the notion of Style as generally accepted in 'bourgeois' art-criticism. Nobody thinks that Schönberg's dodecaphony, for instance, was creatively 'available' at the time of Haydn, though the actual musical and mathematical relations were. Or that, for instance, the emergence of the modern novel was not dependent on the particular market and technological conditions that grew up at the same time. This much is obvious, and no one could take exception to Marxist critics for availing themselves of these standard procedures of 'bourgeois' criticism and art-history. Neither, I imagine, had anyone ever doubted that the historical and other matters treated in Shakespeare's plays were not in some sense *necessary* to the production of those plays as we have them: there is a certain common-sense plausibility about the classical type of Marxist criticism which uncovers the relations between the works of a great writer and the history of his time. Such attitudes and procedures, we must insist, are neither unique to Marxist criticism nor invented by it. All that is unique to Marxism is the particular set of insistences that consistently reduces the art produced to nothing but its relations to the economic forces and processes that precede it and, to some extent certainly, determine it. What is unique to Eagleton's particular brand of Marxism is his refusal to accept the implications of his own reduction, and his claim that – somehow, in some never revealed way – the ideology of the art-work, while never transcending its ideological components, throws light on them.

For although we are forbidden to say that the art-work transcends its ideological components, or that any art-work displays that 'true' realism or greatness beloved of the older Marxists, nevertheless there are differences between works: 'All texts signify', we are told, 'but not all texts are significant'.[11] The basis of this Orwellian difference is nothing less than the text's ability or not to affect us, by a 'more-than-natural flexing and compacting of senses' by which we are 'made to see (and tempted to accept) the versions of historical reality it offers'.[12] The good text obviously is one which 'flexes and compacts its senses'. And how do we know this? By the exercise, clearly, of precisely that value-judgement, that valorisation, which Eagleton has been constantly at pains to unmask as the luxurious delusion of bourgeois elitism.

Eagleton's sabotage of his own methodology, however, goes far beyond this. Not only are some books better (that is, more 'flexuous and sense-compacting') than others; some have 'better' ideology: 'nor does every text's "versions of historical reality" count for much'.[13] You don't have to be exceptionally cynical to hazard the guess that the versions of historical reality that do count for something are those which conform to Marxist ideology. Although Eagleton eschews the classical Lukácsian formula of the great reactionary work which 'shows forth' historical truth in spite of itself, he is still prepared to measure the greatness of the great by the degree of ideological complexity or contradiction they display. Since the field he has chosen to survey in *Criticism and Ideology* is identical to that favoured by F. R. Leavis and other 'bourgeois' critics he affects to despise – the 'great tradition' of bourgeois realism – there are, of course, no ideological winners in this book *Criticism and Ideology*. No writer who does not declare himself an overt enemy of bourgeois society and capitalism can possibly have the 'right' ideology: such an ideology would be overtly revolutionary, and thus would be proleptic. Its types would not as yet exist, and the writer's task would be only to unmask the failure of current bourgeois self-deceivers, or possibly, as Marx said of Balzac, to forecast the future existence of revolutionary enemies of bourgeois ideology.

If there are no winners, the losers are clearly categorised by the degree of complexity of contradiction they show forth in their own ideological configurations. Landor, for instance, is second-rate, and so flees reality by writing 'bizarre epics'. Wordsworth, on the other hand, shows his greatness by the complexity and the contradictions of what Eagleton calls 'the same movement' (away from reality presumably). These, he states, are 'a condition of superior value'.[14] Value, therefore, is ascribed according to degree of complexity, but not just any complexity – complexity with which certain contradictions are shown forth. And this complexity is itself to be evaluated ultimately only by its approximation to a given ideological position – that especially privileged ideological position known as dialectical materialism. If this sounds dogmatic, it must be admitted right away that Eagleton is quite honest about it: throughout the book, dialectical materialism is treated as simply 'the truth' about history and culture, and holding to it enables the critic indeed to stand outside ideology and so to transcend history and put himself beyond criticism.[15]

With such dogmatism there is no arguing: Eagleton himself indeed specifically rejects any proposed open debate as to morality and aesthetics at the end of his book, claiming that the 'material conditions which would make such discourse fully possible do not as yet exist'.[16] This refusal of open debate is ugly and, in a critic engaged in education himself, something of an intellectual scandal. But this is not the important point. What matters is the plain methodological confusion of the moves Eagleton makes towards a 'science of the text': at all points disavowing and scorning the bourgeois critic's reliance upon an elitist value-judgement, he practises that same value-judgement himself at every important juncture. His, too, is a criticism of witness, only the witness is supposed to be working under especially favourable conditions. Not for the first time in Marxist thought, we encounter an elitism among elitisms: self-appointed, the Marxist expert will lead 'the people' away from the captivity of bourgeois expertise into the promised land of dialectical materialism.

How far does Eagleton illuminate the relations he has promised to illuminate – the relation of literature to ideology, on the one hand, and of literature to 'reality' or history, on the other? We know that we are not to grant the 'artist' any particular distinction or privileges: the writer is not an agent so much as 'the insertion of certain specific ideological determinations . . . into a hegemonic ideological formation'[17] – that is to say, merely the representative or symptomatic tool of certain social pressures and interests. Generally, in the capitalist era, he, or in this case she (George Eliot), will 'support', if partly embarrass, the overall hegemony: the ruling power-group. Literature is not, therefore, to be assigned a special place, apart from ideology. As we have seen, classical Marxism was divided on this. In general, the great founding fathers of Marxism were prepared to insist on a special category for art – it was something wonderful, free of ideology, inexplicable and, more important, a source of inspiration to everyone, the underprivileged and the privileged alike. In fact, one of the most moving things about Marx's own writings is his deep conviction that the kind of force and spirituality expressed in great art *in spite of the wishes often of its patrons and sponsors* must surface eventually in a new, rational and free State. The whole point of the critique of the debased culture of the nineteenth century which Marx carried over from Hegel and other Romantic writers, was that it is a decline, the inevitable deterioration of art practised in a 'desolate time' (to use Hölderlin's phrase).

There is, to be sure, a certain inconsistency in this. If man can evade the determinations of the means of production in his art and literature, he can, surely, at other times? We face here the problem of determinism itself and of the relations of base and superstructure. The cornerstone of Marxism is indeed its materialism, the notion that mental and other spiritual structures (religion, journalism, philosophy, education) are dependent on and determined by material ones. Strict materialism has a long history within Marxist thought, and it should be pointed out immediately that Marxists after Marx have alternated more or less consistently between an idealist position – holding that intellectual activity modifies praxis – and materialism, inverting the process, to make means of production the sole source of all human activity, mental or physical. Clearly, a 'common sense' view recommends itself – by and large the determinants of behaviour and thought may be technologico-economic; and we may well be involved (without our really knowing it) in class-struggles that shape our philosophies. The parallel with Sartrean libertarianism is striking. We can supply a general picture of ourselves built up from economic or psychological data ('Petit bourgeois intellectual, afraid of contamination with proletarian forebears, therefore intent on affirming elitist cultural hegemony; also subject to emotional determination from overbearing father, etc., etc.'). But this seems to leave out what counts. It may be useful for some purposes and true up to the limits it imposes upon itself. But there is a yawning sense of absence, and it was just this sense of absence that led Kierkegaard to formulate the first principles of that humanist existentialism which culminates in Sartre.[18] In the field of art, we can equate the general 'account' of personality in terms of economic or psychological determinants with the analysis of art-works into their ideological formations. There is nothing new, as I have already pointed out, in picking out the various cultural and symbolic elements of which an art-work is composed. Nobody really believes that a poem or picture can be purely spontaneous, purely 'personal', purely the invention of the artist. Much recent criticism – Macherey's and Barthes's are examples – has assumed that there was such a critical theory in operation, and so claimed virtue in having knocked it down. But the analysis of the cultural traces and components of art-works is as old as criticism itself, and the Romantics in general assumed that theirs was a mimetic and culture-ridden art.[19] All that is new about this 'new criticism' is its bland assumption that having isolated certain cultural codes and formations in the text, it has done the job of criticism altogether – its belief, in other words, that there is nothing in the text *but* its codes. This fallacy is of particular importance in the present context, since it enables the Marxist critic to 'reduce' the art-work to its isolable ideological components.

Before I go on to criticise the inadequacies of such a view, I must pause to answer an immediate riposte. For Eagleton could claim at once that such a photographic theory is precisely what his book is designed to refute. Again and again he insists that a work cannot be regarded as a mere reproduction of 'reality', nor can it just be reduced to its ideological components: it is, in fact, just to disprove such naïve palaeo-Marxist theories that he wrote his book. Unfortunately, however, Eagleton's practice does not match his protestations. He has two general ways of differentiating between literary texts and 'mere' ideology. One is derived from Macherey (directly) and from Mallarméan symbolism (indirectly); the other from that reverence for complexity common to the English New Criticism. The Machereyan one opposes to an empiricist determination of the text as something we can know merely be enumerating its elements, the symbolist doctrine of silence, absence, the inexpressible: the contradictions of a text are not to be 'grasped as the reflection of real historical contradictions . . .' (what a beginner might think was the goal of Marxist criticism), but because they derive 'precisely from the *absence* of such a reflection – from the contortive effect on the work of the ideology which interposes itself between the work and history'.[22] How does it do this? We aren't told. Macherey had opposed both what he calls 'normative' criticism – criticism which implicitly measures the text up against a norm it ought to fulfil – and what he calls empiricist criticism – criticism which thinks it can account for the text by giving a detailed description of its exteriors – for the same general reason: both seem to posit an ideal work beneath or below the apparent one. No matter how complicated the descriptions of empiricist criticism (New Criticism, structuralism, stylistics, formalism), they will always lack the true 'complexity': Macherey defines this as an awareness of the text's necessary ambiguity: 'Its form, then, is complex; the line of its discourse is thickened by reminiscences, alterations, revivals, absences; and likewise the object of this discourse is multiple, a thousand separate hostile and discontinuous realities'.[21] It is this 'real complexity' rather than the 'mythical depth' which the critic should concern himself to describe. So we arrive at the central symbolist metaphor – that 'absence around which a real complexity is knit' – the serpent, clearly, whose invisible eye transfixes the helpless Adam of criticism, willing him to transgress by naming what he should really simply celebrate (or witness, in our own term). Only the Machereyan critic simply inverts the 'bourgeois' myth: he refuses to name, and so hugs his virtuous silences, to which his interminable discourse is mere prolegomenon.

It is clear, even from so brief an exposition, that this formulation cannot help us explain the critic's role. It merely hides behind a mystique of silence, of absence, of gap and hiatus, hoping that the empiricist critic's forthright blunderings will furnish enough fallacies to nourish indefinitely its own more elegant counter-fallacies. For is it not plain that Macherey's description of 'complexity' in no way differs from those of Richards or Empson, or indeed Leavis and Santayana? All good critics believe that their discourse will lead the reader to the end of language and the beginning of understanding. The only thing new about Macherey is the insistence that the carefully crafted assemblages of formal elements traditionally analysed in rhetoric, and generally held to be the source of a work's significance, be totally disregarded in favour of a certain set of gaps, fractures and contradictions in the work. Yet any such gaps and absences are created *by* the text: *this* anti-structure of hiatuses is different from *that*, those of the 'Ode to a Nightingale' from those of 'Alastor.' So, again, what has been gained? And what permits us to disregard the text's manifestly operative and functional patterns and recurrences? We are left with only an elitist espousal of negation.

In Eagleton, the theoretical consequences of this are manifest. Classical Marxism had at least proffered clear pictures for us to accept or reject: *Hamlet* as the clash of class-interests, the breakdown of mercantilism or whatever. The new Marxism seeks to combine incompatibles. First, it wishes to materialise the aesthetic, so that the literary is seen to be responsive ultimately to the forces of production which drive society and history in general; then, however, it wishes also to destroy (to de-construct) the text as a unity, in order to show that it is inherently contradictory and can only be grasped in spite of itself. Macherey's insistence on complexity or contradictoriness is repeated in Barthes (*S/Z*), Althusser ('Ideological and state apparatuses'), and by a whole generation of younger critics.[22] The identifying characteristic of these various positions in fact might be said to be the notion of complexity: only by its complexity can art overcome ideology. For ideology has now been re-defined: no longer the crude assertion of propaganda, it has become practically identical to the old notion of *Weltanschauung* or Culture. In Gramsci,[23] the old concept of hegemony is sharpened, and at the same time broadened, to be equivalent to whatever a given class believes at any given time. This is what the old *Kulturgeschichte* called *Zeitgeist*, and Gramsci brings to it only an acknowledgement of the importance of factors usually ignored by the 'bourgeois' critics: class-interest, hegemony, history as understood in Marxist thought. Moreover, there is now nothing particularly sinister about ideology: it is necessary – we couldn't be human without it. But it does tend to assume particular formations at particular times, and in an age dominated by the capitalist mode of production, the current ideology (*Weltanschauung, Zeitgeist*) will necessarily reflect the social structure of capitalism. This is where it becomes needful to challenge ideology, of course. Once again, we observe the inevitable dogmatism of Marxist thought: it may seem to be good in itself to challenge ideology, for instance. But it soon becomes clear that challenging ideology is a good thing not just in itself but because capitalism is wrong (exploitative, repressive, unjust); it is tantamount to the proffering of Marxist ideology. Thus, an innocent-sounding formula ('Ask questions', 'Don't accept what you're told', 'Be interrogative, not passive') turns out to be the usual Marxist dogma.

Ideology, that is, is part of our very perceptual apparatus: it is not *what* we see or think, objectively, but also the way we see or think. Can we know anything, then, or can we only reproduce our own ideological categories? Is objective knowledge possible? Marx and Trotsky believed that art yields us 'truth'; the new Marxism relegates it to the level of ideology, leaving it only the escape-hatch of negative complexity. If art cannot transcend its own ideology, it can at least question it and thereby throw it into relief *as* ideology.[24] But again the nature of this transcendence remains obscure: we are left with an advocacy of complexity, interrogativeness, contradictoriness, with the implicit assumption that such things are recognisable by their distinctively Marxist content. Althusser, for instance, postulates the existence of a 'real knowledge' (that is, scientific knowledge, not the endless self-reproduction of ideology), but cannot define its nature:

'while speaking in ideology, and from within ideology we have to outline a discourse which tries to break with ideology, in order to dare to be the beginning of a scientific (that is, subjectless) discourse on ideology.'[25] Unimpeachable; but how? This is merely to cast ideology as an object-language, and so to erect anything we might say into meta-language, and therefore as superior to ideology. Once more, the identifying feature of *real* meta-ideology (for after all, the bourgeois must long since have thought of this pseudo-mastery) is, of course, its Marxist content. This is transcendence by *fiat*.

In Eagleton, the attempt to define the real relations of art (as a kind of prototype meta-ideology) assumes a Laocoon contortedness. The literary text does not reproduce ideology, it 'constructs itself in relation to the ideological signs that encode it'.[26] Alternatively, literature is 'a peculiar mode of linguistic organisation which, by a particular "disturbance" of conventional modes of signification, so foregrounds certain modes of sense-making as to allow us to perceive the ideology in which they inhere'.[27] Or, if that too is felt not to advance matters much (a mish-mash of Mukarovsky and Althusser), we learn that the 'value' of W. B. Yeats's poetry (for, lest we should have been discouraged, Eagleton generously allows that 'Yeats, *nevertheless*, has his value') is a 'function of a specific relation to a concrete ideological formation'. More precisely, 'its value is the function of a particular process of textual production which is itself a sustained relation (overdetermined by the ideological sub-ensemble within which texts are held) to such an ideological formation'.[28]

Such formulations not only do nothing to throw light on the nature of literature or criticism, they confirm us in the suspicion that Eagleton has got his hold on nothing firmer than a metaphor for literary texts: texts are produced, as plays are produced. It is in fact a poor metaphor because while there is an agreed text of the play that is variously produced, there is no agreed, visible and unequivocal set of ideological elements which the literary work produces. Otherwise, we have the concept of literature as ideology capable *at times* of making us see that what they are made up of is indeed ideology, not the God-given truth. And it is the subjective, arbitrary and indeterminable nature of these *times* that is in question: what is Truth to one reader (Tolstoy on Death, Wordsworth on 'something far more deeply interfused') is ideology to another.

How do we know when a text is asking questions, being interrogative, 'flexing and compacting its senses'? Catherine Belsey answers with a distinction drawn from Roland Barthes: there are bullying 'classical' texts on the one hand, and revolutionary 'modernist' texts on the other. Basing herself upon Searle's and Austin's speech-act theory (though she gives her source as Emile Benveniste – a significant fact, perhaps), Belsey discriminates between 'declarative' texts that tell us things, 'imperative' ones that bully us, and 'interrogative' ones that make us ask questions. Following Foucault and Macherey as well as Barthes, she assumes that literature is recognisable by its capacity for disrupting our unity 'by discouraging identification with a unified subject'.[29] This is a classic instance of the pseudo-criterion of course: how do we tell a lying, declarative text from a truth-inspiring, interrogative one? She throws no light on the matter. For according to her Lacanian view of the divided self, bourgeois literature, as part of bourgeois ideology, is characterised by its insistence upon a smooth, unified self, and texts questioning such a view are granted interrogative status. The truth is that the idea of the self as a unified subject is an element of Christian theology – where it figures as the soul – which persists in the aristocratic rationalism of Leibniz as a monad. It is the characteristically 'bourgeois' philosophy of empiricism (Locke, Hume, Berkeley) which challenges this conception. Contrary to Belsey's view of a bullying ideology forcing us to conceive of ourselves as indissoluble subjects (in order that we shall accept authority and yet be able to exercise the amount of initiative and independence to make us productive units of production in the capitalist machine), 'bourgeois' realism is dominated throughout the nineteenth century by a preoccupation precisely with the disintegrative nature of the self. If we wanted a handy defining characteristic of 'realism', in fact, we could do worse than choose this vision of the divided self which, from Poe's *William Wilson* through Dickens's *Edwin Drood* and *A Tale of Two Cities* to Dostoevsky's *Crime and Punishment* and Stevenson's *Dr Jekyll and Mr Hyde*, provides the real core of that classic realism set down by Belsey as concerned to smooth 'over contradiction in the construction of a position for the reader which is unified and knowing'.[30]

These are not maverick instances of covertly revolutionary writers escaping the hegemony of ideology for a moment: such researches characterise the very identity of realism.

This attempt to define bourgeois realism as a vast con trick played upon a semi-literate public, of course, is as old as George Lukács (*Theory of the Novel*) and Q. D. Leavis (*Fiction and the Reading Public*), who define between them the full range of modernist reactions against Victorian positivism and social certitude. Radical criticism followed Lukács in holding that, capitalist society being essentially 'degraded', the novel, as the art-form *par excellence* of the era, is 'essentially critical and oppositional. It is a form of resistance to the developing bourgeois society.'[31] Eventually this view of the novel as essentially ironic and oppositional (it can *affirm* nothing, only suggest the hollowness of what bourgeois ideology itself affirms) led to formulations like Eagleton's and Belsey's. It is important to see how close this way of seeing things is to the primary position of 'bourgeois' modernism, as we see it in I. A. Richards, T. E. Hulme, Ortega y Gasset and Q. D. Leavis. Belsey's notion of the interrogative text amounts to little more than an elaboration of I. A. Richards's definition of the saving balance of ironical poetry, which is characterised by 'extraordinary heterogeneity of the distinguishable impulses'.[32] In both cases, complexity and the presence of discord are regarded as providing evidence of artistic integrity, enabling the writer to transcend mere ideology.

The difference between the two positions, nevertheless, is fundamental. After a brief but intense period of iconoclasm, in which the Victorians were ridiculed for their solemnity and sentimentality, 'bourgeois' criticism began to concentrate more on the density, the semantic richness and the symbolic diversity of writers like Dickens, finding them increasingly 'scriptible', in Barthes' sense, and less and less monolithically deluded by their own 'let's pretend' mechanism. If a realist novel did indeed, as Pierre Macherey suggests, conceal its meanings in order that the coaxed-along reader will be finally enlightened by the final revelation of the truth underlying the goings-on of the narrative, the bourgeois critic discovered that it lost nothing by being re-read in the light of these discoveries: it was constructed with sufficient internal coherence to invest its symbols and metonymies with the weight and suggestiveness of classical myth. This means that the bourgeois critic was prepared to allow the novelist to produce rhetoric, music – and therefore to close his discords and interrogatives with concords, gaining that 'larger unity' of which Richards wrote.

Now it is precisely this larger unity which radical criticism rejects. It is prepared to welcome the text's divergences, discords, discontinuities, hiatuses, but rejects outright its right to resolve them in unity or harmony. Following Lukács (who in turn followed Marx, who followed Hegel), radical criticism denies the writer in the capitalist era the right to harmonise or resolve his dissonances, simply because the society of which it is, however distantly, however distortedly, a reflection is unjust, repressive and self-contradictory. Any attempt to persuade us to accept harmony, or resolution (whether of the 'happy ending' order or of the more sophisticated rhetorical varieties) will be regarded as ideological, somewhere between bullying and brain-washing. What we are left with is a kind of perpetual revolution, an aesthetic based upon Bakunin and Mao.

This leads to anomalies at the theoretical level. Characteristically, the radical critic will happily diagnose internal contradiction as the reason for any 'artistic' failures in the text; but if the writer should not fail artistically, then he is likely to be accused of cheating, of cooking the books. In the case of George Eliot's *Felix Holt*, for instance, Eagleton fairly enough locates certain artistic disparities within the text: some parts are better than others. Now the whole argument provides a classic instance of a radical critic borrowing whole the evaluative structure of a bourgeois critic: in this case F. R. Leavis, whose general reading of the texts Eagleton chooses to discuss in his book is influential on every page. It was Leavis who sorted out the qualitative disparities in George Eliot, and then offered explanations for these disparities. As I have suggested above, Eagleton is generally practising this mode of criticism, although he pretends to be scientific. In *Felix Holt*, Eagleton is happy enough to contrast the excellence of the Mrs Transome episodes with the sense of Felix Holt himself as a 'false centre'. Now this is interesting on many accounts. For the Mrs Transome episodes, Eagleton asserts, protest against the secondary role they are forced to play by the plot (and thereby the historical process) by 'sheer artistry'.[33] Eagleton acknowledges, therefore, that the novelist's *conviction* comes through in quality of texture: she does some things better than others because she believes in them more. Thus, Eagleton assumes (as Leavis does) that the quality of the texture will 'show forth' the confusions or otherwise of the novelist's fundamental commitment to the work.

This implies fairly enough that where we find a novel finally incoherent or unsatisfactory, we are entitled to look beneath the surface for reasons why it is so. The main difference between Eagleton and Leavis in this respect is that Leavis admits that this is what he is doing, whereas Eagleton professes to be acting on other, less 'subjective' principles. But a further difference is, of course, the simple ideological one, that Eagleton invariably looks for politico-societal reasons for disparities in quality, where Leavis looks for others as well – emotional, spiritual, experiential. More important still, Leavis is prepared to let the quality of the work's texture (its aesthetic value, in other words) dictate his rationalisation of its underlying confusions, contradictions or whatever. His is, nominally and intentionally at least, an 'open' criticism (true to its bourgeois liberal provenance). Eagleton, on the other hand, proffers the inevitable dogmatism of the Marxist: the text cannot be allowed to win, as it can in Leavis. Clear disparities in quality Eagleton can handle easily enough as proof of internal contradiction in the writer. But the reader new to Eagleton's mode of criticism will be somewhat distressed to find that a writer's *success* in resolving any internal dissonances or contradictions will immediately be diagnosed as his 'conveniently' resolving his difficulties. The bourgeois novel, according to Eagleton, is either unresolved – and hence the victim of its own internal contradictions, contradictions necessitated by his living in a contradictory and self-divided age – or *spuriously* resolved. When, then, can the text's revelations of ideological conflict assume value? Only when, the answer must be, he says the right things, proffers the right ideology – which is Marxism.

This means that, in fact, there can be no such things as a 'successful' bourgeois novel. It does not matter what the text feels like: if it feels right, this only represents the writer's spellbinding skill, providing him with that spurious 'aesthetic triumph' which is really bourgeois society's greatest ideological weapon. Thus, *Middlemarch* is 'a triumph of aesthetic totalisation deeply suspicious of ideological totalities'.[34] Now George Eliot specifically refused ideology, from something like the Leavisite point of view: she refused to descend from 'picture to diagram'. (Eagleton is contradictory on this point incidentally, seeming to disapprove of this aesthetic decision of George Eliot's, yet elsewhere in his book insisting that art gives us *experience* of ideology, not abstraction – pictures, not diagrams). This is, Eagleton concedes, a 'salutary empiricist check to the tyranny of theoreticism'.[35] Yet it must also represent 'the bleak victory of an entrenched provincial consciousness over rationalist or Romantic drives to transcend it'.[36] This is finally summarised in the judgement that *Middlemarch* 'formally answers the problem it thematically poses'.[37]

The bourgeois novelist, then, cannot win: if the text falls below a required aesthetic standard, this will betray its internal contradictions. If it does not (and Eagleton's treatment of *Middlemarch* testifies at every point to his view that the book sustains itself at the highest level of aesthetic achievement), this will only show that the novelist is glossing over his or her problematic material with spurious aesthetic 'realisation'. Heads I win, tails you lose. This is the essential dogmaticism of the Marxist enterprise. A certain body of conclusions is arrived at *whatever the nature of the evidence involved*. And this means, in the end that the aesthetic level is collapsed into the ideological. The most that aesthetics can claim according to this view is that it enables the reader to experience (to *live*) the fragments of ideology it weaves into its delusive wholes. The literary text dissolves into the ideological assumptions of the critic: there is really no need for literature at all, in fact. We might as well give it up, and contemplate the great gap of existence, sustained by the ineffable rightness of our own ideologies.

To call Marxist criticism dogmatic is more than to say that it is over-assertive. Plenty of bourgeois criticism is that – one things of F. R. Leavis. It is not a matter of letting the other chap have his point of view, of granting that the 'wheel has many spokes and all lead to the hub', and so on. It is a matter of the status the art-work is allowed to have. In Marxist criticism, the art-work is inevitably exemplary, symptomatic, dispensable. In a non-dogmatic criticism (I refuse to call it 'bourgeois' except in the sense of non-Marxist) the art-work is *in*dispensable, the source of experience not otherwise obtainable and, in its success, the touchstone of all our dealings with aesthetic matters. Classical Marxism was non-dogmatic in this way, allowing that the great art of Shakespeare, Michelangelo, Dante, Goethe, afforded us criteria by which not only our experience of other art-works is to be measured, but by which indeed our critical procedures and methodologies are to shape themselves: allowing finally, and most significantly, that 'great art' yields us evidence of the true nature of man, a source of hope in the face of so much squalor and self-seekingness. It is this fundamental sanity in the classical Marxist view of art that has gone by the board in recent varieties, rather as, in the Middle Ages, the great vision of St Thomas faded to give way to the nit-picking and logic-chopping of scholasticism in its decline.

This reveals itself in the narrowness of Eagleton's treatment of 'the great tradition': George Eliot is reduced to the conflict of Romantic individualism and increasingly corporate collectivism. He shows no awareness that this is a fundamental theme of all modern societies, capitalist or state-capitalist, and one which is hardly to be resolved by opting for Marxist or revolutionary orthodoxy. The poetry of Mayakowsky, Esenin and Blok shows that actual Marxism, with its insistence on rigid conformity to the collective, only exacerbates this conflict to the point of hysteria. Nothing is said of the marriage theme, intellectual failure, or of any of the many other strands that make up George Eliot's complex art. It is enough to find evidence of 'organicism' to convict her of self-deception, refusal to accept the logic of history. Nowhere is it allowed that in her treatment of Casaubon and Lydgate, Dorothea and Rosamond, George Eliot has said things which refer to sexual and emotional relations, not just to social history. Neither is it allowed that George Eliot, like Dickens, rejected the revolutionary alternative in good faith simply because it seemed *worse* than that melioristic reformism which Eagleton scorns so much in them. Now, of course, Eagleton would be an odd Marxist if he *did* allow this any respect; and yet it is just at this point that the truly reductive nature of the new Marxism shows itself. In general, the new post-Althusserian Marxists deny the direct reflectiveness of art, or the reduction of art to ideology. Yet it has been unable to define the nature of the relationship of art and ideology. Worse, it has in fact assumed reflection on the grand scale, by insisting that any deviation in bourgeois art from the Marxist reading of history must lead to stultification within the text or, at best, to fruitful self-division. At best they allow that the bourgeois artist can manifest or 'show forth' his internal contradictions: if he is good he will manifest more than if he is second-rate, when he will 'occlude' complexities and strive after bland resolutions. Yet mediaeval society was far more emphatically unjust than capitalist society. This did not prevent it from producing Dante, the Gothic cathedrals and a rich, diversified culture that provides us with many of our criteria of value. Marxism has generally glossed over the oddities of its attitude towards feudal society by saying that the particular conditions of capitalist society – the division of labour, the alienation of classes, above all the accumulation of capital itself – are peculiarly hostile to the creation of great art. Yet its real charge against capitalism is that it exploits the proletariat: and no capitalist ever exploited his work-force so triumphantly as the feudal landlord, or the Greek citizen exploited his. Engels's agonised perception that the glories of Greek culture were peculiarly dependent on the slavery at its economic base is well known. It can be extended generally. The reason why capitalism has been less conducive to the production of great art is not that it is more exploitative and unjust than earlier societies, but that it is *less* so. Of course, much more than the organisation of the means of production and the division of labour is concerned. It is the death of God, the evolution of modern consciousness itself, which we are confronted with here, and of this general process the economic is just one factor among others. Now this, of course, is an explicitly anti-Marxist argument, but the relations of base and superstructure, of economic praxis and cultural consciousness, are not the first matter of interest here. The plain fact is that we do not dismiss feudal art because it was produced within a society unacceptably unjust and hierarchical by our standards: similarly, with whatever qualifications we make with respect to post-Romantic art, we do not have to dismiss the 'closures', resolutions and harmonisations of nineteenth-century art simply because we are aware of the exploitative economics of the society within which it was produced. And that, more or less, is what neo-Marxism has been doing.

No true work of art is without its problematics. No true work of art is 'simple', in the obvious sense of the word. If 'deconstructing the text' means no more than uncovering and witnessing the complexities offered by any true literary text, then we can have no quarrel with it as a critical ideal. If, on the other hand, it means refusing to pay attention to elements within texts which do not support our ideology, simplifying and narrowing the experience *in fact offered* by the great works of the nineteenth century, simply diminishing the human significance to support for a political ideology, then it stands self-condemned as reductive, dogmaticist and small-minded.

What we need to do is to cast our analyses in a more genuine historical framework. The great fault of Marxist criticism of the cruder, more honestly reductive sort, was that it was retroactive: since *we* disapprove of social inequality, for instance, or hierarchy, or women-as-mothers-and-wives, or God, or war, then no art-work of whatever period which assumed or proclaimed these things could have been good. Yet our experience contradicts this at every point. Must not the truth, then, be that the quality of art-works must be related much more carefully to the given conditions in which they were produced, and that this obliges us to grant considerable weight to the simple fact that other ages *did not see these things as we do*? Certainly, we can affirm a number of basic universals. No work of art was ever produced, for instance, which extolled cruelty, persecution or injustice *for its own sake*: it is its basic coherence and consonance with ultimate justice and love which made it possible for Marx and Engels and Trotsky to love and admire the art of the past, even when it conflicted with their own ideology.

There are many such ultimate laws – many of them too obvious to need stating – which derive from and express our common humanity and unite the disparate varieties of art. What we must *not* do is to superimpose our own current political and social and sexual attitudes onto works of earlier ages, and find those works at fault if they do not conform. Milton's attitude towards woman's role in marriage, for instance, is amply stated in *Samson Agonistes*:

> Therefore God's universal Law
> Gave to the man despotic power
> Over his female in due awe,
> Nor from that right to part an hour. (ll. 1053–6).

It is useless 'redeeming' this by trying to find ambiguities, hiatuses or other gaps and absences in Milton's view; it is absurd, on the other hand, to condemn it as illiberal and rampant male chauvinist piggery. Only a 'vulgar feminism', indeed, would do so. What we have to do is to let the poetry itself tell us that the view of women, though it is anomalous to most of us today, is nevertheless *honourably conceived*; it has behind it the authority of the Old Testament and two thousand years of European civilisation. So it is with Shakespeare's 'reactionary' theory of social organisation as it is expressed in *Troilus and Cressida*. No effort of 'placing' the views expressed by Ulysses and reducing them to irony by dramatic structure can reduce the conservatism of Shakespeare's vision. The way to read the play, therefore, is not to make it cohere with our own current ideologies, but to try to understand that it was conceived (or accepted – it is scarcely original) not to repress and deny and exploit, but in order to confirm a society which would be the best for all men. Now, of course, we no longer accept that ruling groups based upon financial or hereditary advantage necessarily know what is best for the rest of us. But *the best minds may have thought so when Shakespeare was alive*.

Now of course Shakespeare was part of the power-elite of his time, and he has often enough been treated as a mouthpiece for Tudor hegemony. All culture is hegemonic. It was the particular distinction of Antonio Gramsci to broaden the traditional Marxist concept of ideology to coincide (or very nearly) with the bourgeois category of *Zeitgeist* or *Weltanschauung*. The nature of the relations between the ideology of a given time and its state apparatus depends upon its general technological and political organisation. In some states – especially extreme totalitarianisms like that of Aztec Mexico – there will be an almost complete coincidence of state ideology and culture. In democratic and capitalist societies, the relationship is far looser: the individualism which is so characteristic of capitalist society and which has caused Marxist criticism so much discomfort is, in fact, directly linked to this looseness. Ideology splits up into smaller and smaller groups: finally we have the group of one, that infinitely repeatable *individuum* whose experience, retailed in 'subjective', 'impressionistic' poetry or realistic narrative, is at once both unique and representative. The artificiality, tortuousness and dogmaticism of the new Marxism derives substantially from its efforts to convert all the disparate elements of bourgeois man's individual yet representative experience into splintered elements of one hegemonic ideology – that of a hypostatical capitalist conspiracy.

Eagleton, for instance, reduces Wordsworth's *The Prelude* to a conflict between the 'organicist' view expressed in the theme of 'the growth of the mind', and the disintegrative effect of the 'spots of time'.[38] In fact, there is no such conflict because there is no contradiction between the two elements. On the contrary, the aptitude for undergoing certain experiences with especial intensity (the 'spots of time') is set forth by Wordsworth as characteristic of the poet, the growth of whose mind the whole poem treats. The poem explores the nature of poetic experience, in the form of an 'autobiography' of the soul: this doesn't oblige Wordsworth to accept the process of growth as bland, continuous and without contradictions. The stages of growth are, of course, interrelated, as they are in Freud: deep experiences and wounds remain in the mind and help form later development. This doesn't oblige us to insist that 'life' is without conflict, irreconcilables or contradiction. Wordsworth's basic vision, on the contrary, shows man as the natural victim of his own powers:

> We poets begin in joy and gladness
> Whereof in the end come despondency and madness.

This is 'the human condition', and it is a condition in which we know less than we don't know, in which the most valuable part of consciousness consists in 'obstinate questionings/Of sense and outward things,/Fallings from us, vanishings,/Blank misgivings of a creature/Moving about in worlds not realized'. Eagleton's ignorance of this essential complexity is just irritating.

In treating of intense 'subjective' experiences, Wordsworth showed his originality: the epics of Landor were bad not because they were bizarre but because they used dead structures, dead themes and concerns. In speaking of his own predicament, in knowing what was important, Wordsworth spoke for all men. It is the peculiar feature of Marxist criticism that it must try to show that this predicament, this 'condition', was created and constituted purely by materialistic forces. Hence, Wordsworth's sense of 'organic' life in things, a 'motion and a spirit that impels/All thinking things, all objects of all thought', must be a pleasing illusion, a way of preventing him from seeing the real Truth of his condition, which is sordidly economic. If we do not accept this Marxist myth, we are left with the fact that the peculiarities of modern development, in the broadest sense of philosophical, cultural, spiritual, religious and political culture, have left man in a certain predicament. The great art of the nineteenth century, from Wordsworth to Tolstoy, expresses this predicament, in all its complex contradictoriness. But this complex contradictoriness is not unique to capitalist societies. Neither is the treatment of it by writers in the capitalist era without joy and transcendence. Life had to go on, consciousness to persist, even under capitalism. The Marxist treatment of the high art of the nineteenth century assumes that all its products had to be vitiated from the outset, poisoned at the root. But this is to make the retroactive mistake with a vengeance: all art takes its origination in a double reaction of exultation and retrieval, and it is a naïve delusion to imagine that men of good faith in the nineteenth century need constantly to be labouring under a sense of guilt and corruption. Even a desolate time had its springs and loves.

This erroneously puritanical view of nineteenth-century art is really repeated, with less rigorous disapprobation, in the neo-Marxist view of all art. The symbolism and organicism of Romantic poetry, like the realistic symbolism of the later fiction and drama, reflect the adaptation by the alive writers of the time to changing historical and spiritual circumstances: they cannot be regarded as delusion, refusal to admit the truth of a historical condition. Our disagreement here is, of course, fundamental: it is a question about what sort of thing human existence can and ought to be, not just about a particular historical period. To wish to restore the level of the aesthetic, and to insist that in the words and music of actual texts, as we encounter them, reside the power and significance of art, is to make a particular set of assumptions about life and art. But this power itself assumes the common potentiality of writer and reader, poet and student, to respond to certain experiences in the world. In the new Marxism, this capacity, these experiences, go by the board, reducing literature to the arid interplay of ideology. But what is ideology? And what isn't? What fills the void of our humanity once we accept the Marxist view of culture as ideology? The theory, finally, measures the theorist. To the ideologue, all *is* ideology.

12 A Literature for a Criticism without Contents

(i) INTRODUCTION

It has been possible (and necessary) to distinguish at least three broad theories within the loose congeries of methodologies and practices generally known as critical modernism. First, and most ambitiously destructive, there is the theory of language latterly associated with Derrida and others, but in fact deriving from Bergson, Heidegger and Whitehead, that language is powerless to 'express' truth or reality adequately. (In Foucault this is wedded to a dissociation-of-sensibility thesis, dating a particular divorce of language and meaning at around the beginning of the seventeenth century.)[1] Secondly, there is the theory of *literary* language, again associated with Bergson, but more familiar to English and American readers in the formulations of I. A. Richards and Susanne Langer, that literary language is different from ordinary language in consisting not of real statements, which assert feelings and truths, but of pseudostatements, which amount to a kind of linguistic play. Lastly, there is the soft-core, or historicist version of *this* theory, that modern texts in particular (dating from the middle of the nineteenth or the end of the eighteenth century) differ from earlier literature in being incapable of 'holding' truth or reality of emotion or whatever, and so are non-referential or self-referring.

Neo-Marxist criticism is a more hard-minded variety of this last position. But it is as well to remember that the basic position of the neo-Marxist critic is, in this respect, not different from that of the 'bourgeois' aesthete or intellectual. Both sorts of critic believe that we live in a particularly debased society incapable of any belief that is not either bitterly ironical or abjectly self-deceiving. In Lukács, the novelist is either a fool who propagates the ideology of an entrenched capitalist elite, or a disabused critic who expresses in bitter ironies the contradictions of a debased society. The general view here derives from Hegel, who in turn merely represented the Romantic feeling that we live in a 'desolate time': Blake, Wordsworth, Coleridge, Schiller and Hölderlin had already given expression to this sense of cultural alienation before Hegel worked it into a philosophy. In the twentieth century, there is no essential difference between the savage critiques of T. S. Eliot, D. H. Lawrence and Ezra Pound on the one hand, and Brecht and Lukács on the other.

There is a profound difference, however, between this set of 'critiques' and that theoretical development, associated with Bergson and Richards, which converts this sense of creative alienation into a general doctrine of linguistic powerlessness. There is an unbridgeable gulf between the view that the alive modern artist testifies to the desolateness of the time, on the one hand, and the theory, on the other, that literature characteristically and by definition fails to refer to our common human experience and therefore can have no 'content'. As I have repeatedly stressed, this theory has two forms, and critics often fail to keep them separate. If, after all, we hold that all literature is play, fictive, pseudo-statement, there is no particular problem raised in the non-realistic forms of much modernist art: they are the same as older art-forms. Our theory doesn't make much difference to anything, but we have no problems. If, on the other hand, we hold that there is something about modern art that sets it apart from earlier literature, we have to be sure that we stick to the lines of our historicist thesis; we also have to make sure that we can explain the oddities of modern art satisfactorily.

Generally speaking, critics have not worked hard enough to keep these two theories clearly separate. Neither have they satisfactorily explained modern art – its power, and its persisting relevance to us as human beings. What has happened is that 'realist' literature has slid into a kind of vague disrepute (because it is so obviously concerned with 'saying things'), while a modern*ist* literature – as distinct from merely modern – has been celebrated principally on account of a number of marginal properties. Modernist criticism, I submit, has neutered modern literature by concentrating attention more or less exclusively on its fracturing of illusion, realism, empathy and organicism. What to the artists themselves were ways of saying new things forced upon them by new circumstances, have become, in modernist criticism, simply testimonies to the bankruptcy of illusion. By this means, we have had foisted upon us what we can only call academic modernism, in which the only 'theme' is the difference between illusion and reality and the only technique to find ways of reminding reader or listener that he is not enjoying real life, but an artifice. I shall be concerned in this chapter to redeem modern art from this limbo of critical academicism. This means, in effect, showing that modernist texts are no more self-referring than classical ones, and that they have contents, which our criticism has been unable to define. We shall provide a literature for the criticism without contents.

(ii) SCRIPTIBLE AND LISIBLE

Perhaps the most striking statement of the modernist attitude with its characteristic vacillation between hard- and soft-core positions, is contained in the distinction Roland Barthes drew between the classical 'work' and the modern 'text'. Works are Newtonian, authoritarian and closed, and de-limit their meanings, restricting the reader's interpretation and dictating his response; 'texts' are Einsteinian, libertarian, open, and allow the reader to make his own meaning and thereby, in effect, the text itself. Barthes disclaimed the intention of making a crude historical distinction between, for instance, pre-Flaubertian and post-Flaubertian writing, 'declaring certain literary productions to be "in" and others "out" on the basis of their chronological situation'.[2] Barthes's disclaimers were infallible guides to his own self-doubts: seeing the scornful tone he later adopted towards the 'classique' in *S/Z*, we can hardly refrain from thinking that this is exactly what he is doing; the solid 'works' beloved of the bourgeois, with their complete imaginary worlds and definite meanings, are being downgraded at the expense of the open-ended modernist 'texts'. Certainly, his distinction is little more than a pseudo-criterion: 'text'-ness is obviously identified with certain richnesses and excellences (usually called 'multivalent'): 'A very ancient work can contain "some text", while many products of contemporary literature are not texts at all'.[3] Not only is his distinction circular, moreover, like all such pseudo-criteria (what is excellent is what is excellent), it is also clearly not an objective property of literature at all, but rather a suggestion as to how we should read literature. 'Text is a methodological field', Barthes says: but this is not a property, it is a theory of reading; there are in fact no works, no texts to be contradistinguished, only good and bad ways of discussing them.

This profound uncertainty attends also Barthes's attempt to distinguish between 'lisible' and 'scriptible' works in *S/Z*. Like the fuzzy pseudo-scientific metaphors of 'From work to text' ('Newtonian', 'methodological field'), and the meaningless terminology ('stereographic plurality', 'irreducible plurality', 'integrally symbolic nature', 'network'), this so-called distinction is also interesting more for what it tells us of Barthes's attitudes towards literature than for any referential content it might have. Barthes's essay is no more than an expression of a determination not to acknowledge the old 'bourgeois' literature, and we should waste our time chasing shadows if we tried to assign his phrases any concrete meaning. Post-structuralist criticism in general is better viewed as the expression of a socio-political attitude than as either a new science of reading or a new theory of literature.

What serious meaning does attach to Barthes's concept of the *scriptible* text is plainly historicistic. It derives from Sartre's *Qu'est-ce que la littérature?* in which the honest transparency of prose is contrasted to the evasive opacity of poetry: for the modernist writer, defeat becomes success, and success defeat; the authentic writer admits the role of literature as the unveiling of significant content. What Barthes does is to turn Sartre on his head, so that the transparency of prose becomes bad faith, in that it presumes preoccupation with content and message to the exclusion of the *écriture*. Good prose, in other words, takes on the very quality Sartre defined as poetic, and bad faith becomes good. A case of S/B. Obviously the inauthentic *lisible* text is one into which the reader is encouraged, nay forced, to identify and project. As such, Barthes's schema is orthodox enough: it is a soft-core theory basically concerned to differentiate the contents of good modernist 'fiction' from those of bad bourgeois 'realism'. This is a problem which bedevilled English criticism for several decades in this century: modernist criticism took its stand by James Joyce and generally espoused the *scriptible* 'art-novel', derived from Flaubert and Turgenev and represented in our century by Ford Madox Ford, which could appear precisely to have the self-interested opacity of Sartrean poetry. 'Great Tradition-

ists' took their stand in Lawrentian message and *lisible* meaning.
Now Dickens, as representative Victorian reformist, was ignored
by both schools until critics of the fifties and sixties began to
analyse his novels as literary texts instead of as reformist tracts of
which the principal interest was their social message and the
principal disadvantage, their gross sentimentality. Here, as in
S/Z, the question was primarily one of the definition of content
or contents. It was necessary for critics to show that Dickens's
very elaborate rhetoric of symbol, image and gesture itself constituted a content hitherto hidden from readers principally
attracted or repelled by more obvious manifest contents – pov-
erty, love, injustice. The history of the new Dickens criticism in
itself constitutes a fascinating example of the way texts once seen
as primarily or exclusively *lisible* could be revealed as adamantly
scriptible ones.

Such a shift is of the greatest relevance to the present argument. For it can be carried out in the reverse direction. If *lisible*
texts are *scriptible*, it is no less true that *scriptible* texts are *lisible*.
Modernism has done no worse disservice to the study of literature than to reduce the rich, subtle and hierarchically layered
contents of eminently *lisible* texts such as Joyce's *Ulysses* and even
A la recherche du temps perdu, to arid critical abstractions. According to much modernist criticism the only function of modernist
writing (in Josipovici this encompasses Homer and Dante as
well as Joyce and Proust) is to inform us of the difference between illusion and reality by reminding us of the fact that when
we read a fiction we are not observing reality. What becomes of
all the imaginative diversity of the different material realised
within the text? Is the only purpose of the fragmentations and
discontinuities, the discords and stammers of modernist texts, to
jerk us awake? Do they proffer nothing but themselves? Does
their juxtaposition and alignment, their counterpoint and
rhythm, amount to no more than the clacking of a spiritual
alarm-clock?

This is a question of the greatest importance: until it is answered successfully we shall be left with the academicised modernism that turns *Ulysses* into bodiless signifiers[4] and, conversely,
is incapable of making serious contact with the *lisible* text. The
real benefit to accrue, therefore, is twofold: by re-stating the
problem of modernist form, we redeem modernist texts like *Ulysses* and *The Waste Land* from the limbo of self-referring semiosis,

and we bring ourselves face to face with that *scriptible* creativity that informs the conjured worlds of realism. Modernism can only properly be understood when its realism is grasped, realism when its 'style' is appreciated. For the significance of the shift in Dickens criticism was not that Dickens's novels were better when their themes and contents were ignored, but simply that these contents were richer than had been thought. We cannot analyse Dickens without taking into account all the elements they contain, and this includes social, psychological and political matters as well as the recurrence of certain figures, tropes and rhythms.

One possible objection can be disposed of fairly easily. This is the contention that the theme or content of a text is a mere peg to hang something else on (signifiers, discourse, rhetoric, style). Some works favour this theory more than others: we don't feel that an interest in whaling is essential to an understanding of *Moby Dick*, or sailing to 'get' *The Ancient Mariner*. Certain writers, too, seem less conscious of what they are doing, so that the theme doesn't seem important. Now in fact the works which appear to sustain such an approach – as we see as well from the Poe story analysed by Lacan – are usually allegorical, and in allegory theme and meaning are related analogically. Yet, it is obviously absurd to say that the theme (manifest plot or action) of an allegory is irrelevant if the meaning shadowed forth in that allegory could not be revealed without its particular lineaments. What is true of the allegory (and, in spite of what some critics have said, there are many excellent and important allegories in the modern period, from *Bleak House* to *Waiting for Godot*) is true with interest of other types of narrative: it is a naïve delusion to believe that the theme of a novel, play or poem can ever be irrelevant, a mere peg to hang something else on. In the work of art, the main subject or theme can never be irrelevant to the work's total meaning. The surface could never be apprehended as what it isn't, if the underlying structure were not important for what it is. Peg and garment are part of the same material – the final work: there is no *res materialis*, no underlying somewhat (peg or theme) within the shroud of language. The shroud is the peg, the form is the content. For the literary work is not a garment hanging on a peg, or even *like* a garment hanging on a peg; it is a hierarchy, each of whose levels holds structural relations with the others, those above with those below, those within with those without. When this is not true, then we have bad art: the Victorian verse-tragedy in which the theme or action holds no real relationship to the gorgeous imagery and stylish prosody which is its real *raison d'être*. Or the twentieth-century symphony, with its scherzo and slow movement flanked by 'probing' opening allegory and 'rousing' rondo finale, none of which has real functional meaning for the composer, whose true interest is probably betrayed in a delicate pastoral quality in the instrumentation here and there, or a suggestive harmonic nucleus embedded in the irrelevant symphonic paraphernalia.

If the work of art (I assume in the phrase that it is a real or good one) is a hierarchy, of which the levels hold true structural relations to each other, the peg or theme can be seen to be of the utmost importance. The poet will show his seriousness or his intelligence in his choice of theme as much as in his verbal skill. The difference between the merely good and the great poet may well emerge in the wisdom with which they respectively choose their themes.

(iii) THEME AS *TELOS*

But what is theme, exactly? Modernism, we have seen, characteristically ignores theme, or relegates it to the realm of the absent signifieds, not the true concern of the critic. 'Subject', Roland Barthes said, 'is an illusory category, a level in the hierarchy of interpretation.' Yet it is surely simply odd, or evasive, to deny that we can talk about the theme of *Macbeth* or *Phèdre*. The need to destroy the category of theme is sometimes painfully important to modernism, as important as the correlative need to discredit the idea of content. Against this modernistic objection to talking of theme as an impoverishment of the text, Y. K. Scheglov and A. K. Zholkovskii assert that talking about theme is just a way of handling the meta-language:

> What we propose to call the Theme of the work of literature corresponds approximately to the statement of the meaning of a sentence in the meta-linguistic notation of structural semantics. Hence it is meaningless to talk of the theme (the meta-linguistic formula) as an impoverishment of the artistic text.[5]

As well say, they point out, that an architect's plans are an impoverishment of the house. The problem is perhaps a little more complicated than this suggests: you can't build a house without a plan, but it wouldn't be easy to show that an isolable theme is in the same functional way necessary to the production of a literary text. Moreover, the content of theme is not always easy to isolate or define in the case of a literary text. Unless we reduce the problem to a merely terminological one – as Barthes in effect does – so that content is identified with everything that is the case, and thus is simply a shorthand way of pointing to the work itself – we must admit to difficulties in isolating the real theme or purpose of a work. A poem, for instance, can have several thematic layers of which the named one may not be the most important: it may be consciously a springboard for a medi-tation: 'Ode to a Nightingale', for instance, does not prepare us for a disquisition on ornithology. What is Keats's poem *about?* Suffering? Time? Love? The human condition? It is only com-mon sense, as Scheglov and Zholkovskii point out, to allow that 'the theme of Racine's tragedies is a conflict between higher duty and passion',[6] and it is merely peculiar to deny that this is poss-ible. But as the Keats example shows, it isn't always possible to isolate theme so easily. In part, this problem can be answered in the terms I have proposed for the hermeneutical problem: a poem can be *read at* different levels, and so long as the readings keep to their levels and are coherent, the multiplicity of readings needn't be a problem. Keats's Ode, for example, is about suffer-ing and such a theme is structurally compatible with the broader or more fundamental 'theme' of time; this in turn can be *read as* 'the human condition'. At a higher, or at any rate different, level, the poem could be read as a disquisition on language: nightin-gales have the advantage among others of having no words or concepts to retard the mind, and therefore become an inverted mirror-image of our own concept-ridden sluggishness. Thus, our suffering, we could say, derives from our language. This sort of reading can in fact be applied to most poems, and might well be sliced off with Ockham's razor. At any rate, there is clearly no structural incompatibility in speaking of all or any of these vari-ous (thematic) levels as providing the theme of the work. At first sight, it seems simply easier to talk about long plays and novels, where we have to have characters and situations, and plots which in themselves seem to dictate theme: the story of the Moor who murders his young bride specifies jealousy as its theme in its very series of incidents. Yet we must remember that here too we face, in the end, the problem of deciding what is the *real* theme. When Othello says

> Here is my journey's end, here is the very butt
> And sea-mark of my utmost sail . . .

it is difficult to think that his words *derive* from the theme of jealousy, or that jealousy is a part of the emotion we feel when we hear these words spoken or see them written. In the end, theme itself leads us to the edge of discourse where discourse ceases. If this is what Barthes meant, he was right. Certainly, it is not possible to derive the poetry from the theme, in the mechanical ways suggested by Scheglov and Zholkovskii, who want to show that everything in the work is *generated by* the theme, much as a living body is generated by the interaction of ribo-nuclear acids and certain proteins or – to use a crueller simile, which seems closer to what they attempt – as a cup of hot soup is generated by pouring boiling water on dried essence. We have had cause to note more than once the thundering banality of theoreticians' attempts to characterise the ultimate meanings of works of art: Jakobson's so-called interpretation of 'Th' expense of spirit in a waste of shame' would not have passed muster in an O-level examination; Lacan's final reduction of 'The Purloined Letter' to 'Every letter finds its true home' seems a joke in poor taste, the sort of thing brilliantly parodied by Thomas Rymer when he said that the moral of *Othello* is that ladies should look after their linen.

All these attempts simply miss the point of literature, and the forthright efforts of Scheglov and Zholkovskii often seem sadly wide of the mark. In their case, a new error is added to the old heap. In their conviction that everything in a text can be 'accounted for' (which is the real flaw here), they posit a relationship between isolable theme and generated text that cannot hold. The DNA chains generate bodies because they are of the same substance as the bodies they generate: though they are said to pass on information, and have been given letters as if they were in fact codes, the strings of the double helix do not stand in relation to the flesh and blood they produce as the abstractable theme stands in relation to the final play or poem. In the first place, the theme itself is stated, as Scheglov and Zholkovskii observe, in the meta-language: to speak of theme, as of content, must ultimately be seen as merely a convenience. It is a convenience that only a lunatic would refuse to avail himself of: as, for instance, only a lunatic would refuse to step out of the way of a railway train because of a belief in pre-destination, or refuse to get up in the morning because he didn't believe in free will. To deny that we can talk about Love and Death and Freedom as themes of poetry is not lunacy, it is at worst affectation, at best double-think: *qua* theoretician the critic refuses to acknowledge theme or content or subject; *qua* practising critic or sane reader, he implicitly assumes it.

Nevertheless, to accept the convenience shouldn't be taken as a licence for believing in a substantival entity – theme – which can be isolated and studied as the DNA molecule can be studied in the laboratory. Theme is a convenience of the meta-language; text is not. There is no way of guaranteeing passage from one to the other. Let us return to the analogy of the architect's plans: the architect's plans are structurally analogical with the actual house; they will allow us to expect a window here, a long wall there. But they 'are' paper and ink, marks and signs. They aren't bricks and boards and glass. Thus to speak of the critic's theme as a blueprint for the actual poem is to confuse theoretical planes, unless it is taken as merely a set of analogies in the meta-language. Scheglov and Zholkovskii admit that isolating the theme is an exercise in the meta-language, then they proceed to 'derive' the work's texture from it like living matter from DNA. But there is no bridge from critical blueprints to textual bricks and mortar, only more and more closely approximating transcriptions of structure in the meta-language, which can be continued until the meta-language is abandoned and the work reproduced, according to the law of formal differentiation outlined above.

I submit that there is no way of formally defining theme so as to relate it to structure. Theme can only be made sense of as a response to what the poem tells us *matters*. Fundamentally, theme denotes a direction of attention, a postulation of *telos*. This in turn denotes the writer's susceptibility to certain feelings and thoughts alive in his time. Theme denotes the writer's sensitivity to what is important to him. And it is this teleological commitment represented in theme which scares the modernist, for whom all such commitment is extra-textual, impure, irrelevant. We must now try to give some account of this hierarchy which we have noted in literary texts so as to bridge the gap between classical and modern texts, showing that one set is *scriptible*, the other *lisible*.

(iv) THE PYRAMID OF CONTENTS

At the bottom of the hierarchy of contents which makes up a literary text is, first, the fact of our being human. This rests upon a prior animality: humanness must be understood to comprise the animal and chemical grounding of the species. We aren't concerned with that abstract *humanitas* outlawed by empiricism and existentialism, but with the simple fact that to speak of being human supposes spiritual and intellectual capacities without which the word human cannot be applied. Thus, a certain human *Grundwerk* may be described as the content of language. It is a mistake to regard man's language itself as being the first defining human quality: it is the capacities for wonderment as well as for abstraction and remembering which make language possible, not vice versa. At the bottom of the hierarchy, then, is simply our humanness, our being-as-man, that upon which all human culture is variation. Language itself is the next layer, that enabling thing that has the dangerous capacity to enable, and thus to appear autonomous. It is not, it is instrumental, and it presupposes, as I have argued above, logicality, the existence of an external reality and the wish to communicate. Logicality and the wish to communicate are essential to the language enterprise: a sense of purpose or meaninglikeness in behaviour must also be counted as a content of language.

Already, therefore, before we even approach the area of the literary, we have amassed a cluster of informing contents in the literary text. The next layer of content in the text concerns the articulation of these informing contents through the cultural differentiations of myth. These cultural differentiations are, initially, responses to environmental conditions: climate, food-scarcity, national temperament and so on. Now the degree to which the underlying *humanitas* persists through different historical circumstances has been illustrated by Northrop Frye: the various forms, myths, modes and archetypes of literature are, indeed, as Frye asserts, its content. The myths and modes themselves imitate what I shall call the logicality of nature: spring following winter, youth becoming age, hunger requiring nourishment. The modes and archetypes documented by Frye as constituting the content of literature themselves form a diagram of the 'human condition'. Frye's insistence on forms (or structures) which can be inherited and passed on from century to century lends itself to a structuralist line. Yet such an alignment is subject to the kind of caveat mentioned above: if Frye's contents are structures, his structures are contents. There is no brief here for dispensing with the notion of content. On the contrary, Frye's is like Barthes's an essentially content-oriented criticism: its underlying presupposition is that works of art affect us because of the structures and archetypes of art-traditions; and these in turn endure because of the ways in which human beings habitually tend to think and feel.

Yet Frye's structures and archetypes do not tell even half the story of literary contents. No literary work is as purely archetypal as Frye suggests; nor indeed is it as purely 'literary'. *Anatomy of Criticism* is a refusal to take the description of contents beyond the stage of the skeletal and archetypal, a failure to acknowledge that a more immediate social and political concern, for instance, to say nothing of more 'personal' factors, is as much a content as the more distant and skeletal forms and inherited structures also there. Ibsen's critique of contemporary society, Shakespeare's analysis of power – these are simply absent from Frye's analyses.

What is true of Frye's reduction of literature to its myths and modes applies equally to all those attempts to explain literary texts away purely in terms of their unconscious or half-conscious ideologies, their discursive formations – all those forms in fact into which recent critics have attempted to dissolve the literary work of art. Such attempts frequently seek to discredit the myth of the creative genius, changing what he inherits: 'Working at his text, the writer, in particular', says Pierre Macherey, 'does not make the materials with which he works. Nor does he find them spontaneously laid out before him, stray pieces, free to help with the construction of any kind of scaffolding: they are not transparent, neutral elements which will obligingly abolish themselves, disappear in the structure which they help to constitute, providing it with material adopting its form or forms.'[7] We are not to ask how the given poem, then, materialises out of these materials: the materials, the ideologies somehow dictate the poem, as in the wildest dreams of Romanticism. There is nothing in the poem's particular arrangement of particles but the ideological components which lay around before the poet started. This kind of account is just as mysterious as Frye's: no suggestion of how the poem came into existence is put forward. More, no attempt is made to account for all those elements in poems and plays which elude the ideological or formational reduction – those expressions, phrases, shapes and tones which are what confront us when we read or hear the work. Again, as in Frye, the critic ignores the 'text' for the structures given in his own theory. If Frye's refusal to ignore the more local and political elements in literary texts amounts to one sort of failure of articulation – a refusal to extend the description of the contents beyond the stage of the skeletal – Macherey's reduction of the text to the external quasi-autonomous forms of ideology with 'specific weight of their own' is surely another. If in Frye we cannot recognise the plight of the hero who is not a mere instance of an archetypal pattern but a king caught in the transition from one societal order to another, so, in Pierre Macherey, we are unable to find the lost human being for whom life is a tale told by an idiot, full of sound and fury, signifying nothing. Neither critic takes us to the level of the text itself, neither allows for the fact that meaning and significance may be governed in these upper reaches of the text – those that relate to current situations and personal reactions. Both sorts, equally, cancel the reality of the work of art, much as French historians and ethnologists under the influence of structuralism were driven to expel the concept of the 'event'.[8] Foucault, who had contributed much (so an outsider would have thought) to this evacuation of real content from the human sciences by concentrating too much attention on the languages and discourses with which events were tabulated and too little on the events themselves, was driven later to object this semiotic structuralisation of history and to insist that history was made up of 'Relations of power, not relations of sense'.[9] We might similarly protest that the actuality of literary texts has been demolished by the preoccupation with structures, laws, forms and ideologies, much as history has been reasoned out of existence by the down-grading of the *'evènemen-tial'*. But to get back the work of art we must not retreat from

structuralisation, and return to some mystical essence of literature. On the contrary, we must simply take structuralisation
further, to the point where we see that not only the underlying
myths and the more local political situations and ideological
formations, but also the individual predicaments and expressions of the text surface, are part of the work's structure. If we
take the structuralisation of art as far as we consistently should,
we shall see that not only these transmittable 'contents', but also
the 'form' – the image-patterns, tones and contextual inflections
of the verbal text – belong to structure. We end up with the
unique, finally differentiated work, in which we can no longer
speak of structure as existing apart from content, or of content as
anything other than what the words that make up the work
actually say. Imagine an account of *Macbeth* that related elements in the play to certain underlying patterns – the sacrifice of
the winter god, or the May king – but which failed to mention
speeches such as 'She should have died hereafter . . .'. The
enraged reader could be forgiven for saying that such speeches
were the play, and that this was exactly what the archetypal
analyst had failed to illuminate. The structure of the text is the
text, and nothing which contributes to the effect it has on us can
be left out of an account of its structure. There is no line to be
drawn in the text which parts structure from content.

It is just such a conception of the structure of works of art
which the present book has been designed to articulate. The
various accounts of Frye, Macherey and others have left out of
account too much that is important to do more than supply
material for interpretations. As such, Frye's is, of course, of great
value: he threw light on many of the shared anatomical properties of literary works. If he claimed to do no more than this, then
he can indeed claim to have 'misled no one'.[10] But in fact Frye
consistently claims more than this in the *Anatomy*. Like
Macherey, he implies fairly unequivocally that what he is doing
is real literary criticism, and that this has nothing to do with
expression and individuality. It is at this point that a specific
historical factor, the interpretation of Romanticism, becomes
difficult and treacherous. It is really Romantic 'genius' that
Macherey dislikes. Frye himself, who assumes throughout the
Anatomy a godlike catholicity, shows himself distinctly human in
the presence of nineteenth-century writing. He can handle the
Romantics when they are peddling the myths and structures of
the 'tradition', but to the newly evolved idioms of realist fiction

he remains blind, and with the no less significant 'subjectivity' of Carlyle, positively tetchy.[11] This is an issue of the greatest importance, because we have here once again the uncertainty of modernist criticism in dealing with Romanticism. Comfortable with the easily isolated and identified structures and archetypes, Frye has nothing to say of the 'personal' meaning of the work. The whole difficulty of Romanticism lies in its alleged subjectivism, and it is with the relations of subjectivity and objectivity that we must now be concerned. The objective contents or formations of literature – one can accept – are its public or inherited themes, structures, myths and symbols. As we shall see, not only these literary elements but the actual language itself is public: the language does not belong to the man who uses it. Neither, so the argument often runs, does the poem he makes out of it. The contents of literature, as I have described them above, are given by the social and historical facts surrounding the provenance of the individual work. To this extent, we must grant that the work does not belong to the writer: not only his language, but his emotions, his very personality were generated out of interaction with his fellow human beings.

This has led to the anomalous views of these various critical schools: Frye's reduction of literature to its shared anatomical properties, the radical sociologist's reduction of the work to its ideology. The truth is surely that literature can never be explained purely as mere excretion, either psychic, cultural or societal. No true work was ever produced as the surrealist tablet was supposed to have been, with no intervention from the 'author'. Yet neither was it ever made simply by history, the race-memory, the tradition, contemporary consciousness, *Zeitgeist* or 'discourse'. Too much of the writer's thematic material is given him by his being-as-a-man, by social tradition, and historical circumstances, for him to be able to claim that the work he offers is all his own. But if no work is purely the invention of the author, neither is it the invention of anyone or anything else. The work of art is not simply given, or picked up off the street; there is something spurious in the attempt to derive a work wholly from its cultural or social provenance. Macherey's idea of the poem as a 'product, at the point where several lines of necessity converge'[12] is paralleled by Foucault's exteriorities of discourse, which reduces utterance to an impersonal 'Anyone-who-speaks'.

Sartre over-stated the freedom of consciousness, but surely he was right about the nature of our actual decisions, our actual awareness of consciousness: we can accept a deterministic theory of every act we ourselves have ever performed, but not of the one we are about to make. Similarly, we can successfully enough ground any work of art in its surrounding and preceding formations – cultural influences, productive forces, ideologies, iconographies, personal complexes or whatever. But we cannot dematerialise the actual work itself – its difference, its power over us, its uniqueness. We have seen what happens when we try to arrive at the rules for establishing this identity: they vanish before our eyes, until we are confronted by nothing but the work itself, which we can only point at. So it is with Foucault's enunciative functions: the enunciative function is a perfectly reasonable account of verbal community, or rather, since it is proffered only in the most general terms, a reasonable suggestion for the way an account of verbal community in social history might be made. It might said to add nothing to what we already knew, but it cannot be dismissed: it is clarificatory. Yet it really fails to dispose of the subject – the *cogito* – which Foucault confidently disparages. To say that 'certain intersections indicate the unique place of a speaking subject and may be given the name of author'[13] is merely to rephrase, with peculiar cumbersomeness, the subject whose mediation is required for the work of art to come into being. This does not matter for Foucault's own purposes: he has already defined his own relativising position clearly in saying that his concern is not with the phenomena retailed in, say, medicine or economics, grammar or psychiatry, but with the interrelations of the statements making up those studies. This need not be quarrelled with. What must be opposed is the tendency for this kind of study to insert itself into literary criticism.

Foucault's analysis of discourse and cognition, and sociological theories of literature like Macherey's, alike leave out of account the all-important fact that literary works require the mediation and participation of a writer: his choice and decisions exercise such a decisive influence upon the performance of the work that we may be excused for believing that if the language, plots and themes belong to society, the work resulting from the writer's performance – its rhythm, tone and atmosphere – is 'unique': only he could have done it, and the value the work has derived from the mediation of what used to be called the writer's genius.

(v) OBJECTIVITY, SUBJECTIVITY

The literary work comes into existence at a point where the individual consciousness and the greater contents of language and general experience meet and fuse. I find that I have fallen into one of the most common of Coleridgean metaphors to describe the process by which works of art are made. Yet how is it to be otherwise? For it was the great Romantic critics and poets (in the English tradition, this means Coleridge) who shaped our awareness of the new situation in which the development of modern civilisation had placed writer and reader alike. The Romantic emphasis upon individual genius became, over the course of the nineteenth century, an over-emphasis, giving rise to the minor novelists' predilection for Promethean geniuses creating great art out of nothing but their imaginations. This in turn has produced the reaction of which Pierre Macherey's book *Pour une théorie de la production littéraire* is a late but interesting example, attempting to deny the inventive or productive capacity of the writer altogether, and placing the onus of 'creation' of literature entirely upon the shoulders of a complex societal process, geared *au fond* to the 'means of production'. Yet the truth is that, in the English tradition at least, it has never been the case that the artist has been regarded as a Promethean creator *ex nihilo*, responsible to nobody and nothing outside himself. The image for the creative process was early set in the brilliant crystallisations of Coleridge, with his conception of the 'secondary imagination' as that which 'dissolves, diffuses and dissipates, in order to re-create'. This sentence is one of the best known in English critical history. It should, of itself, have served to ward off Macherey's simplistic assumptions. It is plain that Coleridge conceived of the poetic imagination as essentially co-operating with 'nature' – and indeed with received literature – in its dissolving and diffusing operations. All that we need add to this account of things is the obvious fact that the organ which carried out this dissolving and diffusing and creating is the subjectivity of the writer, his 'mind' not somebody else's, certainly not History or the Means of Production.

It is for this reason also that Langer's account of poetry as the creation of 'virtual experience' seems unsatisfactory. The symbological school in general – in which category we must include the American New Critics as a group – found no way to account for the objectivity of poetry while at the same time admitting the self-expressive habits of the mind. Langer failed to understand that the poet subjectivises everything – even those so-called objective contents or formations into which French critics wished to dissolve literature – and that this is precisely his abstractive capacity. Until the received, inherited and shared contents of literature have been subjectivised, which is to say *experienced as being personally important to the poet*, they will be unable to function as part of a work of art. We shall have, then, the dead work, the lifeless formalistic reproduction of other works or public 'current' themes – that other kind of bad work which, in any comprehensive account of criticism, must complement the self-expressive badness which Langer could handle so subtly. It is a pity that this is the case, because there was a certain appealing purity about the symbological case, as there was in Frye's archetypalism. Frye too could handle the self-expressive badness, but not the opposite sort: the bad work which failed to subjectivise the public or mythic could easily be absorbed into the Frye system. With his lordly disdain for the mere value-judgement, Frye could accept by ignoring the numerous stereotyped reproductions of mythic archetypes, and treat them as poor but valid members of the club. Yet this procedure ignores all the questions that matter. It is precisely the effort of trying to understand the nature of the badness and the goodness, and the consequent understanding of the subjectivising process of all art, that brings us to the realisation of that *literaturnost'* which is the proper concern of criticism.

What is required is a theory which respects the role of the inherited and 'objective' themes and formations of art but at the same time allows that these have to be material for the artist. Such a theory is provided by the art historian Erwin Panofsky.[14] Panofsky distinguishes three levels in the work of art – iconology, iconography and intrinsic meaning. Iconology deals with the primary identification of images – shoes, boxes, trees, women, suns – without which we cannot be said to have 'seen' or 'read' a painting. Iconography deals with particular hierarchies of significance among these icons: it enables us to tell that a particular picture is of St Bartholomew or of St Jerome. Iconology establishes that the pigment before us is a woman with a child; iconography that it is a picture of the Virgin and the Infant Christ. 'If the knife that enables us to identify a St Bartholomew is not a knife but a corkscrew, the figure is not a St Bartholomew.'[15]

If we equate Panofsky's iconographic analysis with the codes, formations and ideologies beloved of modern literary criticism, we can see that critics like Foucault, Frye, Macherey and Eagleton fail to take analysis beyond Panofsky's second level. His third level of interpretation takes us beyond the mere identification of codes and icons to the 'intrinsic meaning or content' of the particular work. This is nothing less than the use a particular artist makes of his iconographic resources, and it is the level most significantly absent from so much contemporary literary criticism. It is here that we encounter the 'problem' of expression, personality and subjectivity. Panofsky is dealing with Renaissance art, an art rich in conventional iconographic resources. But he goes beyond it to see into our contemporary situation: 'the correct analysis of images, stories and allegories', he observes, is 'the prerequisite of their correct iconological interpretation, unless we deal with works of art in which the whole sphere of secondary or conventional subject matter is eliminated and a direct transition from motifs to content is effected, as is the case with European landscape painting, still life and genre, not to mention "non-objective" art'.[16] It needs little calibration of terminology to bring Panofsky's conception into line with the basic contentions of the present book. By 'motifs' here, Panofsky means the icons (trees, shoes, women) of painting without their conventional significances; this is our 'content'. By 'content' he means his third level of art – the 'intrinsic meaning' of the particular work; this is our 'meaning'. With this adjustment, we can see that Panofsky has expertly defined the condition not merely of landscape painting – the Turner or Constable scene with little or no iconographic significances – but of all Romantic and post-Romantic art, up to and including the 'non-objective' painting and poetry of our own age. It is the elimination, through historical development, of so many of the traditional iconographic and conventional resources of literature and art which resulted in the characteristic 'realism' of European literature of the nineteenth century, on the one hand, and the 'subjectivism' of its lyric poetry, on the other.

Where modernist criticism errs is in looking from the apparent 'objectivity' of pre-Romantic art and literature to the apparent 'subjectivity' of Romanticism, and deducing from the contrast a painful and humiliating dereliction from true art to a kind of therapeutic substitute – the self-expressiveness and pseudo-photographic realism of the nineteenth century. From this contrast it moves on, with relief, to the 'experimental' arts of the twentieth century, and infers from the fractures and discords of the modern *avant garde* some return to sanity – to something like the objectivity of pre-Romantic art, when men could tell illusion from reality and representation from fact. Panofsky's account gives us a way of circumnavigating these twin errors. We have defined the inherited themes, myths and formations of culture as the 'objective' elements of art, such that no work can really be said to be wholly the invention of the author. Similarly, we have defined the process of mediation through which these objective contents of the culture are turned into actual art-works as the necessary subjectivity of all art. Given Panofsky's interpretative structure, we can see that classical or pre-Romantic art was no more objective and no less subjective than Romantic and realist art. This means that what we are confronted by in the development of Romantic and realist art is not a progressive personalisation of art, a deterioration from the external and the concrete to the inner and the inchoate, but simply a catastrophic dereliction of the iconographic resources available to the artist. The themes and subjects, the myths and allegories of the Renaissance artist reflected beliefs and preoccupations important enough to society and artist to be realisable in art. We cannot make a live art out of a dead iconography. The alleged subjectivism of the Romantic artist, therefore, is nothing more than his recognition that those motifs and themes important enough to serve as material for the classical artist – political, religious, philosophical – were no longer available for artistic treatment. We have already given above the example of Landor and Wordsworth. Eagleton preferred Wordsworth's 'poem about a poem' (*The Prelude*) to Landor's 'bizarre epics' on account of its greater ideological complexity. The real difference surely is that Wordsworth was too honest and intelligent to manufacture poetry out of myths and tales that had no real significance to him; Landor was not, he was content to flee reality into legend. Thus, Wordsworth's recognition of the new content of poetry – his own spiritual and perceptual processes, his own role and situation as a poet – constitutes a new objectivity: the difference between Landor and Wordsworth is not, as Pound thought, the difference between a rugged 'objective' poet on the one hand and a self-preoccupied subjective narcissist on the other, but between a poet who recognised that to be 'objective' the poet had now to be subjective: to take the facts of his own subjective experience as the material of his poetry. But, to say it again, if this means that Romantic poetry is no more subjective than classical art, it means also that classical poetry, for all its apparent objectivity, is no less subjective than Romantic poetry. All that has changed is the ground and frontier of the objective. Art-forms change because the attitude and capacity (which is to say the reaction to the world-situation) which is invested in the power of perception have themselves changed.

By the same token, if Romantic and realist art can be seen as the artist's adaptation to a changed cultural and societal situation, so can modernist *avant garde* be understood as a further mutation of the power of perception. The modernist *avant garde* not only continues the thrust of Romantic art, it does so with predominantly Romantic instruments. There is no question of a 'return to objectivity', a waking-up from the Romantic and realist dream. On the contrary, an inspection of the art of Joyce and Picasso, Eliot and Schönberg, together with their statements about their aims, makes it abundantly clear that they regarded their eschewal of 'realism' not as a retreat to the high grounds of objectivity, but as a more real realism. Joyce's stream-of-consciousness, Lawrence's vacillating characters, the Cubists' breaking-up of the traditional Gestalten of perception, Schönberg's disintegration of the common chord and diatonic harmony, all these characteristic manoeuvres of the *avant garde*, were conceived not in the spirit of neo-modernism, but to secure greater and greater truth. This truth cannot, any more than the Will of God, in Jaspers's phrase, be made into a possession. The prisms need to be re-set, our frontiers with 'reality' constantly to be re-drawn. The purpose of artistic form is precisely to chart this process of re-setting, re-drawing.

A theory such as the one I have tried to outline restores to modern art its contemporaneity. For we can see its products as registering the shock of contact as 'the reality of experience' in Joyce's phrase, is encountered and re-encountered for the millionth, and the million-and-first time. And this requires the artist to be 'fully alive in his own time', as Leavis said of T. S. Eliot. The trouble is that the themes which appear imperative to the critic and theoretician do not always seem so to the creative writer. The artist has an excellent nose for dead ideas. To study the changing relations between the themes and forms of contemporary art – that is the task for a counter-modernism.

Notes

1 A CRITICISM FOR A LITERATURE WITHOUT CONTENTS

1. Robert Scholes, *Structuralism and Literature* (Yale, 1974) p.5.
2. S. K. Langer, *Feeling and Form* (London, 1953) p.5.
3. Ibid., p.256.
4. Ortega y Gasset, *The Dehumanisation of Art*, tr. H. Weyl, (Princeton, N.J., 1968) p.25.
5. Ibid., p.25.
6. Susan Sontag, *Against Interpretation* (London, 1967) p.30.
7. Ortega, op. cit., p.27.
8. Roland Barthes, 'Style and Its Image', in S. Chatman, ed., *Literary Style: a Symposium* (Oxford, 1971) p.10.
9. Ibid., p. 11.
10. Ibid., p.11.
11. Roland Barthes, *S/Z*, tr. R. Miller (London, 1975) p.4.

2 THE PROBLEM OF ART-LANGUAGES

1. G. Frege, 'On Concept and Object', tr. P. T. Geach, *MIND*, vol. XV, no. 238 (Apr. 1951) pp.174–5.
2. Wolfgang Iser, *The Act of Reading* (London, 1977) p.12.
3. Pierre Macherey, *A Theory of Literary Production*, tr. G. Wall, (London, 1978) pp.41–2.
4. Barthes, *S/Z*, tr. R. Miller, p.8.
5. Ibid., pp.8–9.
6. Jean-Paul Sartre, *Qu'est-ce que la Litterature?* (Paris, 1948) p.52.
7. Iser, op. cit., p.27.
8. Quoted in ibid., p.27.
9. See Chapter 7 below.
10. Roman Ingarden, *The Literary Work of Art*, tr. C. G. Grabowicz (Evanston, 1973).
11. Ludwig Wittgenstein, *Tractatus Logico-Philosophicus*, tr. D. F. Pears (London, 1960) p.150.
12. Moritz Schlick, 'Form and Content', *Philosophical Papers*, vol. II, ed. H. L. Mulder *et al.*, (London, 1979) pp. 285–369.
13. Erwin Panofsky, *Meaning in the Visual Arts* (Harmondsworth, 1970) ch. 2.
14. Claude Lévi-Strauss, *Triste tropiques* (New York, 1974) p.58.
15. Ibid., p.58.

16. Ibid., p.58.
17. J. V. Harari, 'Critical Factions/Critical Fictions', in Harari, ed., *Textual Strategies* (Ithaca, 1979) p.22.
18. A. C. Danto, *What Is Philosophy?* (New York, 1968) p.100.
19. C. Levi-Strauss, *Structural Anthropology*, tr. C. Jacobson (New York, 1963) p.131.
20. Harari, op. cit., p.22.
21. Rudolf Arnheim, *Art and Visual Perception* (London, 1953) p.27.
22. Martin Heidegger, 'The Origins of the Work of Art', *Poetry, Language and Thought*, tr. A. Hofstadter (New York, 1975).
23. Nelson Goodman, *Languages of Art* (London, 1969) p.262.
24. Ibid., p.262.

3 STYLISTICS AND STRUCTURAL POETICS

1. Iser, op. cit., p.15, 'New Criticism has changed the direction of literary perception in so far as it has turned attention away from representative meanings and onto the function operating within the work.'
2. William Empson, 'A Masterly Synthesis', *Poetry*, vol. LV (Chicago, 1939) no. III, p.164.
3. Harari, op. cit., p.23.
4. *Communications*, vol. 8 (Paris, 1968).
5. D. Freeman, 'Linguistic Approaches to Literature', Freeman, ed., *Linguistics and Literary Style* (New York, 1970) p.4.
6. Stanley Fish, 'What Is Stylistics and Why Are They Saying Such Terrible Things About It?' in M. S. Chatman, *Approaches to Tactics* (Columbia, 1973) p.118.
7. Ibid, p.112.
8. Ibid., p.109.
9. Ibid., p.144.
10. Michael Riffaterre, 'Describing Poetic Structure', J. Ehrmann, ed., *Structuralism* (New York, 1970) pp.201–2.
11. Ibid., p.203.
13. Riffaterre's notion of a 'super-reader' shelves the question of judgement by suggesting a statistical survey of reader-reactions: the 'correct' reading is the one that gets most votes (when? In the long run? . . .).
14. Tzvetan Todorov, *Poétiques de la Prose* (Paris, 1971) p.246.
15. Roman Jakobson and L. R. Jones, *Shakespeare's Verbal Art in 'Th'expense of Spirit in a Waste of Shame'* (The Hague, 1970) p.14.
16. F. W. Bateson, *Essays in Criticism*, no. XVII (1967) p.337; Roger Fowler, ibid., p.339.
17. F. W. Bateson, op. cit. p.337.
18. Ibid., p.337.
19. Roger Fowler, op. cit., p.339.
20. Ibid., p.339
21. See Stanley Fish, *Is There a Text in This Class?* (London 1980) p.351, for a view of this unconscious interest of the New Criticism.

4 THE ANALYSIS OF VALUE-JUDGMENTS

1. William Elton, ed., *Aesthetics and Language* (Oxford, 1954).
2. Helen Knight, 'The Use of "Good" in Aesthetic Judgements', in Elton, op. cit., p.151.
3. Ibid., p.148 ff.
4. Ibid., p.157.
5. It is of course a member of the class of classes of human artefacts.
6. Arnold Isenberg, 'Critical Communications', in Elton, op. cit., p.137.
7. Samuel Taylor Coleridge, *Biographia Literaria* (London, 1906) p.160.
8. Catherine Belsey, *Critical Practice*, (London, 1980).
9. Ibid., p.91.
10. Terry Eagleton, *Criticism and Ideology* (London, 1975) p.185.

5 CRITICAL WITNESS AND THE EVOLUTION OF CULTURE

1. Northrop Frye, 'Reflections in a Mirror', M. Krieger, ed., *Northrop Frye in Modern Criticism* (New York, 1966).
2. Vladimir Propp, tr. L. Scott, *Morphology of the Folk-Tale*, (Texas, 1970).
3. Mircea Eliade, tr. W. R. Trask, *Shamanism* (New York, 1964) ch. 1.
4. G. W. Leibniz, ed P. P. Weiner, *Selections from the Works of Leibniz* (New York, 1951) pp.29–30.
5. Ludwig Wittgenstein, *Remarks on Frazer's 'Golden Bough'*, (Brynmil, 1979) p.4e.
6. See J. E. Spingarn, *A History of Literary Criticism in the Renaissance* (New York, 1954) esp. part first, I.
7. Samuel Johnson, 'John Milton', *The Six Chief Lives from Lives of the Poets*, ed., Matthew Arnold (London, 1879) pp.96–7.
8. Coleridge, op. cit., p.165.
9. Edgar Allen Poe, 'The Philosophy of Composition', in R. Brimley Johnson, ed., *Complete Poetical Works* (London, 1909) p.246.
10. See Enid Starkie, *Arthur Rimbaud* (London, 1938) pp.123–4.
11. John Stuart Mill, *Early Essays* (London, 1897) p.242.

6 MEANING

1. Leo Tolstoy, *What Is Art?*, tr. A. Maude (London, 1904) p.54.
2. Barthes, *S/Z*, p.8.
3. Willard van Orman Quine, *From a Logical Point of View* (Cambridge, Mass., 1954) pp.42–6.
4. Iser, op. cit., p.13.
5. G. W. F. Hegel, *Selections*, tr. J. Loewenberg (London, 1929) p.325.
6. Iser, op. cit., p.10.
7. Ibid., p.11.
8. Barthes, 'From Work to Text', in Harari, *Textual Strategies*.
9. Anton Ehrenzweig, *The Hidden Order of Art* (London, 1967) pp.7–8.

10. E. H. Gombrich, *Art and Illusion* (London, 1960) ch. 1, 'Psychology and the Riddle of Style'.
11. Edith Sitwell, 'Some Notes on My Own Poetry', *Edith Sitwell: a Selection By the Author* (Harmondsworth, 1952) p.xxxi.
12. Iser, op. cit., p.12.
13. Sontag, op. cit., p.10.
14. C. S. Peirce, *The Collected Papers*, (vol. 2, pp.227–8), eds. C. Harsthorne, P. Weiss and A. Banks, 8 vols (Cambridge, Mass., 1931–58).
15. John Locke, *An Essay Concerning Human Understanding* (London, 1947) pp.201–2.
16. S. K. Langer, *Philosophy in a New Key* (Cambridge, Mass., 1951).

7 INTENTIONS/INTENSIONS

1. See *On Literary Intention*, ed. D. Newton de Molina (Edinburgh, 1974).
2. Umberto Eco, *L'opera aperta; forma e indeterminazione nella poetica contemporanea* (Milan, 1962).
3. Macherey, op. cit., p.80.
4. Barbara Herrnstein-Smith, 'Poetry as Fiction', *New Literary History*, vol. 2 (1970–1) pp.259–81.
5. Iser, op. cit., p.61.
6. Sartre, op. cit., p.35.
7. V. I. Voloshinov, *Marxism and the Philosophy of Language* (New York, 1975).
8. Michael Riffaterre, 'The Self-Sufficient Text' *Diacritica 3*, (Fall 1973).
9. Roland Barthes, *Mythologies*, tr. A. Laver (London, 1972).
10. Ibid., p.116.
11. See for instance Hugh Kenner, *Joyce's Voices* (London, 1979) p.83.
12. Jan Mukarovsky, 'Standard Language and Poetic Language', in Freeman, p.46.
13. Arnheim, op. cit., p.165.
14. Barthes, *S/Z*, pp.11–12.
15. Ibid., p.12.
16. See Sigmund Freud, *The Interpretation of Dreams*, tr. J. Strachey (London, 1954) pp.530–1.
17. Fish, op. cit., p.355.
18. F. R. Leavis, 'Anna Karenina', *The Cambridge Quarterly*, vol. 1, no. 1, p.16.
19. Michel Foucault, 'What Is an Author?', in Harari, op. cit., p.159.
20. Fish, 'What Makes an Interpretation Acceptable?', *Is There a Text in This Class?*
21. See M. H. Abrams, 'How To Do Things With Texts', *Partisan Review*, no. 4 (1974); 'The Deconstructive Angel', *Critical Inquiry*, vol. 3, no. 3 (spring, 1976); Hirsch's *Validity in Interpretation* is also relevant (New Haven, Conn., 1967).

8 INTERPRETATION

1. Macherey, op. cit., p. 7.
2. Ibid., p. 6.

3. Ibid., p. 6.
4. Ibid., p. 6.
5. Ibid., p. 7.
6. Ibid., p. 2.
7. Ibid., p. 11.
8. Ibid., p. 6.
9. Ibid., p. 13.
10. See for instance W. J. Bate, *The Burden of the Past* (Cambridge, Mass., 1970); and Harold Bloom, *The Anxiety of Influence* (New York, 1973).
11. Jonathan Culler, *Structural Poetics* (London 1975) p. 178.
12. Ibid., p. 178.
13. Ibid., p. 178.
14. Harold Bloom, 'The Breaking of Form', Bloom, ed., *De-construction and Literature* (New Haven, Conn., 1980) p. 7.
15. Ibid., pp. 7–8.
16. Harold Bloom, *A Map of Mis-reading* (New York, 1975) pp. 33–4. Bloom dismisses Eliot's concept of tradition as a 'fiction . . . a noble idealisation', though since his own mis-readings are avowed fictions it is hard to see the force of his sneer.
17. Ibid., p. 32.
18. Bloom, 'The Breaking of Form', p. 9.
19. Foucault, *The Order of Things*, tr. A. Sheridan (London, 1970) p. 43.
20. Geoffrey Hartman, preface, Hartman, ed. *Psychoanalysis and the Question of the Text* (Baltimore, 1978) p. xv.
21. Hartman, 'Psychoanalysis: the French Connection', *Psychoanalysis and The Question of the Text*, p. 101.
22. Sigmund Freud, *The Interpretation of Dreams*, tr. J. Strachey, (London, 1953) p. 160n.
23. Ibid., p. 396.
24. Ibid., p. 236.
25. Ibid., p. 372.
26. Ibid., p. 161.
27. Ibid., p. 553.
28. Jacques Lacan, 'The Agency of the Letter in the Unconscious', *Ecrits*, tr. A. Sheridan (London, 1977) p. 14.
29. Hartman, preface, *Psychoanalysis and the Question of the Text*, p. xi.
30. See Chapter 9 below.
31. Jacques Lacan, 'Seminar on *The Purloined Letter*', *Ecrits*, Jacques Derrida, 'The Purveyor of Truth', *Yale French Studies*, no. 52 (1975) pp. 31–113.
    See also Barbara Johnson, 'The Frame of Reference; Poe, Lacan, Derrida, in Hartman, *Psychoanalysis and the question of the Text*.
32. Johnson, op. cit., p. 153.
33. Ibid., p. 161.
34. Ibid., p. 159.
35. Macherey, op. cit., p. 20.
36. Hartman is undecided about this and admits the meat of the empiricist contention: 'every literary narrative contains another narrative' (p. 102) and offers perception after the destruction, 'perception similar to that offered by myths and positive interpretation' (p. 102). This is

characteristic paper-tiger de-constructionism, unable to follow Derrida into the wilderness of mirrors, yet uncomfortable in the presence of honest empiricism.

37. See M. A. Mugge, *Friedrich Nietzsche, His Life and Work* (London, 1908) pp. 43–7.
38. Bloom, 'The Breaking of Form', p. 13.
39. Ibid., pp. 13–14.
40. R. S. Crane, *The Language of Criticism and the Structure of Poetry* (Toronto, 1953) p. 123.
41. Ibid., p. 124.
42. Ibid., p. 124.
43. Ibid., p. 124.
44. Ibid., p. 144.
45. Maud Bodkin, *Archetypal Patterns in Poetry* (London, 1934) p. 4.
46. Michel Foucault, *The Archaeology of Knowledge*, tr. A. Sheridan-Smith (London, 1972).

9 THE ROOTS OF DE-CONSTRUCTION

1. See, for instance, Paul de Man, 'Semiology and Rhetoric', in Harari.
2. Monroe Beardsley and W. K. Wimsatt, *'The Intentional Fallacy'*, *The Verbal Icon*, (Kentucky, 1954) p. 334.
3. Ibid., p. 335.
4. Gerald Graff, *Poetic Statement and Critical Dogmas* (Chicago, 1970) and *Literature Against Itself* (London, 1980).
5. Herrnstein-Smith, op. cit.
6. J. L. Austin, *How To Do Things With Words*, ed. J. O. Urmson, (Cambridge, Mass., 1962) p. 22.
7. Iser, op. cit., pp. 59–62.
8. Barthes, *S/Z*, pp. 54–6. Barthes also writes: 'the novelistic real is not operable' and 'in the most realistic novel, the referent has no reality', ibid., p. 80. Barthes' cart as usual pulls his horse. The novelistic 'real' doesn't have to be 'operable', whatever that might in fact mean; nor need its referent have more or less reality than in any other type of sentence. If I say aloud 'The cat sat on the mat', the referents of 'cat' and 'mat' are neither more nor less 'operable' than in novels; nor have they more or less 'reality'.
9. F. R. Leavis, 'Eliot's Classical Standing', F. R. and Q. D. Leavis, *Lectures in America* (London, 1969) p. 33.
10. Roland Barthes, 'Changer l'objet lui-même', *Esprit*, 4, (Paris 1971) pp. 614–15.
11. Roland Barthes, *Critical Essays*, tr. R. Howard (Evanston, 1972) p. 218.
12. Claude Lévi-Strauss, *Structural anthropology*, vol. II, tr. M. Layton (London, 1977) p. 131.
13. Jean Piaget, *Structuralism*, tr. C. Maschler (New York, 1970) p. 41.
14. Ibid., p. 41.
15. Ferdinand de Saussure, *Course in General Linguistics*, tr. W. Baskin (New York, 1966).

16. Locke, op. cit., book III, 1, p. 201.
17. Roland Barthes, *Elements of Semiology*, tr. A. Lavers and C. Smith (London, 1967) p. 39.
18. Dan Sperber, 'Claude Lévi-Strauss', J. Sturrock, *Structuralism and since* (Oxford, 1979).
19. Erik Schwimmer, 'Semiotics in Anthropology' in Sebeok, *A Perfusion of Signs* (Indiana, 1970) p. 160.
20. Umberto Eco, *Struttura Assente* (Milan, 1968).
21. de Man, op. cit., p. 123.
22. Ibid., p. 124.

10 LOGOCENTRICITY AND LOGOMANIA

1. Jacques Derrida, *Positions* (Paris, 1972).
2. Jacques Derrida, *La voix et le phénomène* (Paris, 1967), tr. D. B. Allison (*Speech and phenomena*, Yale, 1970).
3. Jacques Derrida, *De la grammatologie* (Paris, 1967), tr. G. Chaksavorty Spivak (*Of grammatology*, Baltimore, 1974).
4. Edmond Husserl, *Logical Investigations*, tr. J. N. Findlay (London, 1970).
5. See Chapter 2, note 1, above.
6. Edmond Husserl, *Die Philosophie der Arithmetik* (Halle, 1891).
7. Bertrand Russell, 'On denoting', *MIND*, 1905.
8. Husserl, *Logical investigations*, pp. 321–2.
9. Ibid., pp. 321–2.
10. Derrida, *Speech and phenomena*, p. 99.
11. Ibid., p. 99.
12. Ibid., p. 99.
13. A note on this so-called logic of the supplement seems called for here. Webster's Dictionary can have a 'supplement' because a dictionary cannot, in the nature of things, be regarded as complete. Masturbation, similarly, is another string to the sexual bow, and might therefore be called a supplement to sexuality. But it is not therefore a supplement to sexual coition *itself*. It is simply that the sexual life of men and women cannot have the kind of formal completeness to which nothing can be added. It is not like a box with just so many compartments, or an argument with so many elements, to which we might then discover a lack or flaw. The existence of various sorts of supplement does not of itself amount to anything important. The fact that masturbation can be enjoyed does not mean that sexual coition is not complete when it is enjoyed: it is not the sexual act that is supplemented in masturbation (if that is also later enjoyed by one of the participants), but the shapeless agglomeration of acts which makes up sexual life in particular and life itself in general. Thus to observe that masturbation in some sense supplements sexual coition is not to have discovered a huge flaw in nature or sexuality: it is not like suddenly finding that a supplement to oxygen is needed. The things supplemented by Derrida are so amorphous or aggregative that they can be neither supplemented or complemented. You might as well say that the present

moment is a supplement to the past, or that a new symphony exposes a lack in all the previously existing symphonies, and base upon this fanciful assertion a theoretical de-construction of all the events or symphonies already existing. If there is no question of a possible completeness, there is no particular significance in the additions we can make. What Derrida does is to erect an Aunt Sally – the supposed plenitude or completeness of language and then erect a quasi-revolutionary philosophy upon its destruction. It is worth noting that such procedures are common in French philosophy, where metaphors assume the status of facts, and words in their usage are not subjected to the kind of analysis habitual to Anglo-American empiricism.

14. Derrida, op. cit., p. 116.
15. Bertrand Russell, 'The Philosophy of Logical Atomism', in *Logic and Knowledge* (London, 1956).
16. Ludwig Wittgenstein, *Tractatus Logico-philosophicus*, 2. d271.
17. Husserl, op. cit., pp. 321–2.
18. See for instance G. Vlastos, 'Zeno', in W. Kauffmann, *Philosophical Classics: Thales to St. Thomas* (New Jersey, 1961).
19. Henri Bergson, *Matiere et memoire* (Paris, 1896), ch. 2, 'De la reconnaissance des images'.
20. Alfred North Whitehead, *Science and the Modern World* (Cambridge, 1953) p. 116.
21. Ibid., p. 116.
22. Ibid., p. 116.
23. Ibid., p. 116.
24. Joseph Riddel, 'De-Centering the Image', in Harari op. cit., p. 326.
25. Ibid., p. 325
26. Ibid., p. 325.
27. Ibid., p. 326.
28. T. E. Hulme, *Speculations: Essays on Humanism and the Philosophy of Art* (London, 1924).
29. F. I. Tyutchev, 'Silentium', *Polnoye sobranniye sotchineniya* (Petersburg, 1890) p. 92. [My translation].
30. Eugenio Donato, 'The Two Languages of Criticism' in R. Macksey and E. Donato, eds, *The Structuralist Controversy* (Baltimore, 1970) p. 96.
31. Ernst Cassirer, *Language and Myth*, tr. S. K. Langer (London, 1952) p. 7.
32. Ibid., p. 7.
33. Bertrand Russell, *The Problems of Philosophy* (Oxford, 1948) p. 143. See also Wittgenstein, *Tractatus Logico-Philosophicus*, 2.01231 ff.
34. S. K. Langer, *Philosophy in a New Key* (New York, 1950) p. 68.
35. Ludwig Wittgenstein, Letter 18, Cassino, 19.8.19.
36. Wittgenstein, *Tractatus*, 4.121,a.
37. Wittgenstein, 4.1212.
38. Ludwig Wittgenstein, *Notes Dictated to G. E. Moore*, 107–26–28.
39. Wittgenstein, *Tractatus*, S.552. tr. D. Pears, N. C. Guinness (Oxford, 1961).
40. Wittgenstein, 6.41: 'Der Sinn der Welt muss ausserhalb ihrer liegen.'
41. Gabriel Josipovici, *The World and the Book* (London, 1970) p. 296.
42. Wittgenstein, *Philosophical Investigations*, tr. E. Anscombe, p. 196e.

43. Wittgenstein, quoted in J. Griffin, *Wittgenstein's Logical Atomism* (Oxford, 1964) p. 43.
44. Wittgenstein, *Philosophical Investigations*, p. 177e.
45. Ernst Cassirer, *The Philosophy of Symbolic Forms*, tr. R. Mannheim, vol. III (New Haven, Conn., 1953) p. 307.
46. Martin Heidegger, *Being and Time*, tr. J. Macquarrie and E. Robinson (Oxford, 1973).
47. Wittgenstein, *Phil. Invests*, 81e–138e. ff.

11 NEO-MARXISM AND DE-CONSTRUCTION

1. Macherey, op. cit., pp. 51–4.
2. Ibid., p. 53.
3. Ibid., p. 41.
4. Leon Trotsky, *Literature and Revolution* (New York, 1957) p. 178. [no translator given.]
5. Louis Althusser, *Lenin and Philosophy*, tr. B. Brewster (London, 1971) p. 203.
6. Macherey, op. cit., p. 44.
7. Pierre Macherey, 'Problems of Reflection', tr. J. Coombes, in F. Barker, ed., *Literature, Society and Sociology of Literature* (Essex, 1976).
8. Macherey, op. cit., p. 44.
9. Ibid., p. 50.
10. Terry Eagleton, *Criticism and Ideology* (London, 1979), p. 96. I take this work as best representing Eagleton's contribution to Marxist theory of literature. Obviously, other of his works, notably *Marxism and Literary Criticism* (London, 1976) might have been chosen, though with less satisfying results.
11. Ibid., p. 185.
12. Ibid., p. 185.
13. Ibid., p. 185.
14. Ibid., pp. 186–7.
15. Ibid., p. 24.
16. Ibid., p. 187.
17. Ibid., p. 113.
18. Jean-Paul Sartre, *Being and Nothingness*, tr. H. Baines, (New York, 1956) part 4.
19. See for instance, P. B. Shelley, 'Preface to *Prometheus Unbound*', *Poetical Works*, T. Hutchinson ed., (Oxford, 1935) p. 202.
20. Eagleton, op. cit., p. 95.
21. Macherey, *Theory of Literary Production*, p. 99.
22. See for instance Catherine Belsey, op. cit., p. 119.
23. Antonio Gramsci, *Selection from Prison Notebooks*, eds and trs. Q. Hoare and G. Nowell-Smith (London, 1971).
24. Barry Hindes and Paul Hirst, *Mode of Production and Social Formation* (London, 1977), maintain a strictly ideological theory, with more consistency than plausibility denying the capacity of ideology to transcend itself or of discourse to transcend ideology. Here as elsewhere the problem

is largely a philosophical one: what Hirst and Hindes do basically is to re-define all discourse as ideology, leaving us with the problem of differentiating different sorts of language-use: even if all discourse is called ideology, some types still seem more 'noble', distinterested, than others.

25. Louis Althusser, *For Marx*, tr. B. Brewster (Harmondsworth, 1969) p. 162.
26. Eagleton, op. cit., p. 186.
27. Ibid., p. 185.
28. Ibid., pp. 184–5.
29. Belsey, op. cit., p. 91.
30. Ibid., p. 90.
31. Lucien Goldmann, *Towards a sociology of the Novel*, tr. A. Sheridan (London, 1964) p. 13.
32. I. A. Richards, *Principles of Literary Criticism* (London, 1923) p. 250.
33. Eagleton, op. cit., p. 112.
34. Ibid., p. 119.
35. Ibid., p. 119.
36. Ibid., p. 119.
37. Ibid., p. 120.
38. Ibid., p. 94.

12 A LITERATURE FOR A CRITICISM WITHOUT CONTENTS

1. See Foucault, 'The Prose of the World', in *The Order of Things*, p. 43.
2. Barthes, 'From Work to Text', in Harari, op. cit., p. 74.
3. Ibid., p. 74.
4. Colin MacCabe, *James Joyce and the Revolution of the Word* (London, 1980).
5. Y. K. Scheglov and A. K. Zholkovski, *Russian Poetics in Translation*, tr. L. M. O"Toole and A. Shukman (Essex, 1975) p. 6.
6. Ibid., pp. 6–7.
7. Macherey, op. cit., p. 54.
8. See F. Brandel, 'History and the Social Sciences: the *longue duree'*, in *On History*, tr. S. Matthews (London, 1981).
9. Foucault, 'Truth and Power', Interview with A. Fontano and P. Pasquino in *Power/Knowledge*, ed. and tr. C. Gordon (Brighton, 1980) p. 33.
10. Frye, op. cit.
11. Frye, *Anatomy of criticism*, p. 328.
12. Macherey, op. cit., p. 47.
13. Foucault, *Archaeology of Knowledge*, tr. A. Sheridan-Smith (London, 1972) p. 122.
14. Panofsky, op. cit.
15. Ibid., p. 55.
16. Ibid., p. 58.

Index